Pluriform Love

AN OPEN AND RELATIONAL
THEOLOGY OF WELL-BEING

THOMAS JAY OORD

SacraSage Press
SacraSagePress.com

© 2022 SacraSage Press and Thomas Jay Oord

Editorial Consultation: Rebecca Adams
Interior Design: Nicole Sturk
Cover Design: Thomas Jay Oord

Print (Hardback): 978-1-948609-58-6
Print (Paperback): 978-1-948609-57-9
Electronic: 978-1-948609-56-2

Printed in the United States of America

Library of Congress Cataloguing-in-Publication Data

Pluriform Love: An Open and Relational Theology of Well-Being / Thomas Jay Oord

Table of Contents

Preface

I've been writing this book since birth.

 Books that explore love should probably start with a mother's love…experienced in the womb, through infancy, in childhood, and thereafter. I'm grateful my mother loved me in a plurality of ways. I'm also thankful for the love shown by my fathers, wife, children, siblings, extended family, friends, and so on. But I dedicate this book to the one I call "momma."

I experienced love growing up in Othello, Washington, and I've witnessed love in many communities since. Pastors, mentors, teachers, and elders have modeled love. The global heroes of love — people like Martin Luther King, Jr., Ghandi, Mother Teresa, and Mr. Rogers — influenced me too, albeit indirectly. It's hard to measure the influence of loving exemplars and communities. We learn through experience.

The rock-n-roll of my youth and today proffers lyrics of love. What songwriters mean by "love" varies, as much as it varies in everyday conversation, literature, philosophy, and even scripture. Shakespeare is right: "Love is a many splendored thing." But the lyrics and poetry of love move me immensely.

What the Bible says about love captured my attention as a young man, and scripture guides my reflection today. I cannot account fully for the Bible's influence on how I think, both my direct interpretations of the text and the indirect ways it shaped those who loved me.

But what scripture says about love is not as straightforward as many think. Biblical writers use love words in many ways, and we have good reason to be confused. I explore these ways in this book.

My thoughts here have taken a long time to gestate and have gone through many stages. While an undergraduate, I began to imagine love as theology's guiding principle. As an avid evangelist, I preached the gospel as I understood it. After encountering sophisticated arguments against faith, I admitted my reasons for believing were weak. I became an atheist/agnostic for a time.

Love was crucial to my return to faith. The existence and activity of a loving God made sense of my intuition that I ought to love, others ought to love, and love was the purpose of existence. The ultimacy of love, I believe, provides plausible answers to my biggest questions. Love matters most.

While a student at Nazarene Theological Seminary, I became convinced love could function as *the* locus for theology. I began to understand John Wesley's ideas of holiness and sanctification in light of love. A book I co-wrote with Michael Lodahl, *Relational Holiness: Responding to the Call of Love*, expressed this conviction. I learned from Professor Rob Staples about Wesley's focus on love, and Mildred Bangs Wynkoop's classic book on Wesley, *A Theology of Love*, underscored this point.

My first course at Claremont Graduate University was on the religious significance of Alfred North Whitehead. The promise of process thought had lured me to Claremont.[1] David Ray Griffin taught that course, and he would become my doctoral advisor. My course paper explored love in Whitehead's thought — especially persuasive love — and sparked many original ideas.

My doctoral thesis was the first written articulation of this book. I addressed major theologies of love and, to a greater or lesser degree, found each wanting. I argued that putting love first could transform both the Evangelical theology of my upbringing and the process

---

[1] I explore the promise of process theology in Al Truesdale, ed., *God Reconsidered: The Promise and Peril of Process Theology* (Kansas City, Mo.: Beacon Hill, 2010).

theology I had discovered in the academy. Years later, I rewrote and published the dissertation as *The Nature of Love: A Theology* (Chalice Press, 2010).

As my thinking about love has continued to deepen and expand, I've had some "aha" moments, developed new theories, and strengthened earlier convictions. This deepening and expanding prompts me to write the book you now hold.

Of the 25+ books I've written or edited since graduate school, most have "love" in their title or subtitle. With each publication, my wife teases me, "*Another* love book? Haven't you said all you can say?"

I shrug and reply, "Apparently not."

To me, pondering love is like pondering God: my interest never tires. Words never capture love or God fully, but I hope to make progress. I want "to grasp how wide and long and high and deep is the love of Christ, and to know this love that surpasses knowledge" (Eph. 3:18b-19a). A winsome vision of a loving God is central and motivates me to love God, others, myself, and all creation.

To say love is "pluriform," as this book's title does, is to say love has multiple dimensions and expressions. Love cannot be understood well nor experienced fully if confined to only one or a few forms. A holistic account of love includes, but goes beyond, the typical categories of sacrifice, sex, desire, friendship, generosity, compassion, and more. Pluriform love points to the diversity of this term.

Not only do creatures express pluriform love, but God does too. Divine love is not just sacrificial. Nor is love simply desire for what's valuable; it's not just communal relationship, and it's not primarily aimed at God's own glory. To put it positively, divine love is compassionate, involves forgiveness, repays evil with good, delights in beauty, rejoices in the good, and enjoys a good joke. God's love is pluriform.

God's love is not altogether different from ours, as some theologians have suggested. It's not an exception to the fundamental principles of love that apply to all. In fact, the basic meaning of love — although having multifarious expressions — applies to both creatures and Creator. While a good definition of love should apply uniformly to God and others, the expressions of love are pluriform.

Conventional theologies cannot account well for love. Ours *or* God's. Some theologians embrace *agape*, for instance, but reject *eros* and *philia*. In those theologies, God gives but can't respond to, delight in, or befriend us. Others think of love as desire rather than acting to promote well-being. In some theologies, God only loves Godself.

In my book, *Defining Love*, I addressed in detail how we best define love. In it and *The Science of Love*, I explore the contributions science and philosophy make to understanding love. Theology takes center stage in the present book. I build from Christian scripture, because the Bible provides crucial resources for a Christian theology of love. But good theology requires more than scripture. This book also appeals to reason, experience, and aspects of the Christian tradition. Along the way, I will criticize theologians and biblical scholars who fail to follow the logic of love. I also criticize philosophical assumptions and biblical interpretations that undermine love's supremacy.

When understood well, love illuminates. It answers our biggest questions about God and life. Perhaps the biggest questions for theists and atheists alike revolve around evil. If a loving and powerful God exists, why doesn't this deity prevent unnecessary suffering, pointless pain, and genuine evils? I've answered that question in previous books, including *The Uncontrolling Love of God* and *God Can't*. In this book, I point to what I call "essential kenosis" as crucial to solving the problem of evil.

If the Apostle John is correct that God *is* love, we need to ask about God's nature. Can God choose *not* to love? I'll answer this by claiming God is *essentially* loving. The essence-experience binate means God unchangingly loves but changingly experiences and expresses love moment by moment.

If God always loves creatures, we might wonder if there ever was a time God did not relate to creation. I argue that God's steadfast love literally endures forever, and I call this "essential hesed." In covenant with them, God everlastingly relates with and loves creatures and creation.

This book argues that for life to flourish, we need the light of love. We need it to blaze in all directions, not just one or a few. We should celebrate the diversity of love both God and creatures can express.

Creatures can imitate the Creator whose love is pluriform.

1

Love Neglected

THE PRIMACY OF LOVE

It's not hard to make a scriptural case for the primacy of love.

"And the greatest of these is love" (1 Cor. 13:13),[1] says the Apostle Paul in what many call the New Testament's "love chapter." Love never ends, says Paul, and without love, we are nothing (13:2, 8). Even a person who gave away everything and chose death but did not love would gain nothing (13:3). Above all, we should "pursue love" (1 Cor. 14:1), because it is "the more excellent way" (1 Cor. 12:31).

The one whom Christians believe loved best — Jesus — says that the greatest commandments orient around love. We should love God and neighbor as ourselves (Mt. 22:34-40; Mk. 12:28-34; Lk. 10:25-28). His commands were not new; we find them in the Old Testament.[2] The law and prophets rest on them.

Our salvation is oriented around love. In a passage many Christians memorize, Jesus says, "For God so loved the world that he gave his only Son, so that everyone who believes in him may not

---

[1] Unless noted, I use the New Revised Standard Version for biblical references. I assume the Protestant canon throughout much of this book.

[2] I will refer to the writings in the first part of the Christian canon as the "Old Testament," while realizing this label carries some negative connotations. In doing so, I do not mean to imply supersessionism or that the latter parts of the Christian Bible are authoritative while the earlier parts are not.

perish but may have eternal life" (Jn. 3:16). And "By this will all know
that you are my disciples," he tells his followers, "if you love one another" (Jn. 13:35). Even obedience is ultimately about love, says Jesus
(Jn. 14:15).

The New Testament doctor of love, the Apostle John, puts the relationship between God and love simply: "God is love" (1 Jn. 4:8,16).
For millennia, scholars have debated the meaning of this three-word
sentence. At a minimum, it positions love as central to who God is
and what God does. On a spectrum between literal and symbolic,
"God is love" rests closer to literally true than perhaps any other biblical statement.[3] The person who doesn't love, says John, doesn't understand God (1 Jn. 4:8).

Because God loves, we ought to love. Paul tells Ephesian readers
to "imitate God, as dearly beloved children, and live in love, as Christ
loves us..." (Eph. 5:1). We can love like God loves, and Jesus is our example of what this looks like. An adequate theology will make sense
of divine love as a model to emulate.

Even before the special incarnation of God in Jesus, biblical
authors considered love *a*, if not *the*, primary divine attribute. The
phrase "steadfast love" is the most common Old Testament description of divine activities. The Psalmist often says, "the earth is full of
the steadfast love of God" (Ps. 33:5). Such love is relentlessly loyal:
Jeremiah records God declaring, "I loved you with an everlasting
love" (31:3). The Chronicler says God loves the chosen people (2 Chr.
2:11) and the Deuteronomist says God loves aliens (Deut. 10:18). God
loves all creation (Ps. 117:1).[4] Old Testament writers witness powerfully to divine love.

A recurring description appears in full form like this: God is
"The Lord, the Lord, a God merciful and gracious, slow to anger,
and abounding in steadfast love and faithfulness, keeping steadfast
love for thousands, forgiving iniquity and transgression and sin..."

---

[3] On this claim, see Gustavo Gutierrez, *The God of Life* (Maryknoll, NY: Orbis, 1996).

[4] On loving nonhuman creatures, see William Greenway, *Agape Ethics: Moral Realism and Love for All Life* (Eugene, Or.: Cascade, 2016).

(Exod. 34:6-7). No description of God occurs more often in the Old Testament, although it takes various forms and abbreviations.[5] Old Testament writers clearly describe God as loving. The major themes of the Old and New Testaments promote love's primacy.

Not every biblical passage portrays God as loving, however. Scripture does not provide a consistent voice on love, creaturely or divine. Sometimes God is also portrayed as wanting or causing harm. God threatens to abandon or bring pain. I'll address this issue later because it's so important. For the moment, I simply say love is the main theme of scripture...even though contrary themes are also present.

LOVE IS OFTEN NOT CENTRAL IN CONTEMPORARY THEOLOGY AND BIBLICAL STUDIES

Given that love is central to Jesus and arguably the focus of scripture, one might assume this theme would be central in all biblical studies and constructive theology. But leading theologians and Bible scholars often neglect love, relegate it to secondary status, or adopt theological beliefs that undermine love's primacy.[6] Christian intellectuals have often failed to recognize or promote love's preeminence. To illustrate, I'll identify two 21st century examples of this kind of theology. These thinkers are among many influential Christians who fail to make love a priority in theology.

---

[5] I first encountered this claim in the work of Terence Fretheim, *The Suffering of God: An Old Testament Perspective* (Philadelphia: Fortress, 1984), 25. It's developed in various of Fretheim's writings, many of which are compiled in *What Kind of God? Collected Essays of Terence E. Fretheim*, Michael J. Chan and Brent A. Strawn, eds. (Winona Lake, Ind.: Eisenbrauns, 2015). For other occurrences of this phrase, see Exod. 20:6; Num. 14:18; Deut. 5:9-10; 7:9; 1 Kings 3:6; 2 Chron. 30:9; Neh. 9:17, 31 Ps. 86:15; 103:8, 17; 106:45; 111:4; 112:4; 145:8; Jer. 30:11; 32:18-19; Lam. 3:32; Dan. 9:4; Joel 2:13; Jon. 4:2; Nah. 1:3.

[6] George Newlands makes this argument forcefully in *Theology of the Love of God* (London: Collins, 1980). Kevin J. Vanhoozer does as well in "Introduction: The Love of God — Its Place, Meaning, and Function in Systematic Theology," *Nothing Greater, Nothing Better, Theological Essays on the Love of God*, Kevin J. Vanhoozer, ed. (Grand Rapids, Mich.: Eerdmans, 2001). Two exceptions to this general truth are Gary Chartier, *The Analogy of Love: Divine and Human Love at the Center of Christian Theology* (Charlottesville, VA: Imprint Academic, 2007); and Daniel Day Williams, *The Spirit and the Forms of Love* (New York: Harper and Row, 1968).

BIBLICAL SCHOLAR RICHARD HAYS

In his influential book, *The Moral Vision of the New Testament*, biblical scholar Richard Hays does not regard love as the focus of Jesus or the New Testament.[7] His relegation of love to the margins is explicit. Instead, Hays considers community, cross, and new creation as focal themes. According to him, they encapsulate the crucial elements of the New Testament narrative and focus our attention on the common ground shared by the various biblical witnesses.

Community, cross, and new creation are important. But why not make love the focus for understanding who God is and how we ought to live? And isn't love central to these themes?

Hays expects these questions. "Some readers will be surprised to find that I have not proposed love as a unifying theme for New Testament ethics," he says. "The letters of Paul, the Gospel of John, and the Johannine Epistle explicitly highlight love as a (or the) distinctive element of Christian life," he admits. "It is the 'more excellent way' (1 Cor. 12:31- 13:13), the fulfillment of the Law (Rom. 13:8), the new commandment of Jesus (John 13:34-35), and the revelation of the character of God that is to be reflected in the relationships within the community of believers (1 John 4:7-8)."[8]

Hays then offers three reasons he does not consider love central, and I list each below. Because I find each reason inadequate, I will offer responses.

1. Hays says not all New Testament books emphasize love.

"Jesus' promulgation of the double love commandment [in Mark 12:28-34] stands as an isolated element [in Mark's gospel]," says Hays. In Hebrews and Revelation, "we encounter only scattered incidental references to love, mostly with regard to God's love of human

---

[7] Richard Hays, *The Moral Vision of the New Testament: A Contemporary Introduction to New Testament Ethics* (San Francisco: Harper and Row, 1996).

[8] Ibid., 200.

beings." Furthermore, he says, "where love is mentioned, it is closely identified with good works...." And "nowhere in [the Acts of the Apostles] does the word 'Love' appear, either as a noun or a verb."[9] Because not all New Testament books include or emphasize love, Hays chooses not to.

My response: Hays seems to use a brute word count approach to decide which themes should be central to New Testament ethics. A few biblical books do not mention love, he says, and a few only mention love occasionally. Let frequency of use determine one's focal themes, he argues.

This reason to emphasize themes other than love simply does not withstand scrutiny. The word "love" appears more often in the New Testament than Hays's preferred words "cross," "community," or "new creation." It appears in more books overall than his preferred themes. If word counts are the criteria for choosing focal themes, we should choose love over the themes Hays picks.

Love is the focus of Jesus' commands in all four gospels. Why not embrace this? Love is also the Apostle Paul's focus for many New Testament arguments. Examples of love are present in other New Testament writings, even when the word is not used. Take the book of Acts as an example; surely acts of healing are expressions of love, despite the absence of Greek love words in these pages.

2. Hays says love is not an image; it's an interpretation of an image.

The second reason Hays gives for not making the love central to New Testament ethics pertains to his theological method. We cannot observe love, he says, we only see it when expressed in actions.

"What the New Testament means by 'love' is embodied concretely in the *cross*," says Hays. "The content of the word 'love' is given fully and exclusively in the death of Jesus on the cross; apart

---

[9] Ibid., 200-201.

from this specific narrative image, the term has no meaning. Thus to add love as a fourth focal image would not only be superfluous, it would also move in the direction of conceptual abstraction, away from the specific image of the cross."[10]

My response: Here Hays seems to have chosen a method — images as focal themes — and neglected love because it isn't an image. Love, as he sees it, might "move us in the direction of conceptual abstraction."

My first response is to note that words like "community" and "new creation" are just as abstract. Like love, they make sense only when expressed concretely. So why not make love the central focus and then point to concrete expressions of it in the biblical witness?

Second, while we should emphasize Jesus' death, it is not true, as Hays alleges, that the cross gives love's meaning "fully and exclusively." The New Testament writers speak of love in various ways, and many forms do not involve self-sacrifice or death. We find biblical writers identifying love with friendship, mutual giving and receiving, desire, family affection, self-love, passion, compassion, and so on.

The cross is one expression of love. It cannot be its exclusive meaning.

3. Hays says popular discourse has debased love.

The third reason Hays gives for why he does not consider love a focal theme may be his most important. The term love "has lost its power of discrimination," he says, "having become a cover for all manner of vapid self-indulgence."

Hays develops this claim. "One often hears voices in the church urging that the radical demands of Christian discipleship should not be pressed upon church members because the 'loving' thing to do is to include everyone without imposing harsh demands," he says. Instead, "the biblical story teaches us that God's love cannot be

---

[10] Ibid., 202.

reduced to 'inclusiveness:' authentic love calls us to repentance, discipline, sacrifice, and transformation (see, e.g., Luke 14:25-35; Heb. 12:5-13)."

Hays concludes, "In combination with the [first two] considerations, [popular discourse] suggests that love as a focal image might produce more distortion than clarity in our construal of the New Testament's ethical witness."[11] Putting love first, he argues, perverts rather than elucidates Christian ethics.

My response: Hays is correct that love has been misunderstood and abused in popular discourse. I'd add that scholars have a poor history of using this term too! Some Christians appeal to love to shirk responsibility or avoid accountability. Some believe love justifies self-centeredness and extreme tolerance. I agree with Hays that love, at least sometimes, calls for repentance, discipline, and sacrifice.

But love remains the central word New Testament writers used to talk about ethics, God, and other issues of faith. Love is the heart of the New Testament, if not the entire canon. Christians should be concerned with how the language of love has been misused, but there are better ways to address problematic language than to neglect the word Jesus, Paul, and other New Testament writers considered central.

There are no perfect words. Hays's choices — "cross," "community," "new creation" — are also misunderstood and abused. The word "community," for instance, has been used in ways that oppose the concept of *koinonia* described in scripture. Crosses are more often fashion symbols in contemporary culture than references to self-sacrifice. Even the phrase "new creation" is problematic; just ask an advocate of total depravity. Words are slippery and multi-meaningful.

So I believe theologians and biblical scholars would be wise to address the misuses of love language. And they should offer clear definitions that align with the broad biblical witness. Their claims about love should also make sense of common experience. And scholars

---

[11] Ibid., 202.

should account for the diverse forms of love we find in scripture and everyday life.[12]

But Hays's work is helpful in at least one respect. It prompts us to clarify what we mean by love and what it means to say love should be our primary theme. If the language of love is essential to the biblical witness, biblical scholars and theologians must make sense of love.

Systematic Theologian Millard Erickson

Millard Erickson is a Reformed theologian whose work coincides with ideas common in the tradition of John Calvin. He calls his theology a "mild" or "moderate" form of Calvinism.[13] The connection with this tradition becomes evident when Erickson speaks about love. Unfortunately, his ideas about God's omnipotence, independence, and predestination are at odds with the meaning of love in most scripture and everyday experience.

In his magnum opus, *Christian Theology*, Erickson chooses the magnificence of God, instead of love, as his overarching theme. By magnificence, he understands "the greatness of God in terms of his power, knowledge and other traditional natural attributes, as well as the excellence and splendor of his moral nature."[14] Power comes first in Erickson's list and in the way he thinks.

Erickson affirms divine mercy, grace, and benevolence. He says we ought to love. But as the quotations below will show, Erickson's views of divine power and independence make his love claims difficult to square with central themes in the Bible and the logic of love in everyday life. Consider these quotations:

---

[12] New Testament scholars that emphasize the priority of love include Richard A. Burridge, *Imitating Jesus: An Inclusive Approach to New Testament Ethics* (Grand Rapids, Mich. Eerdmans, 2007); Paul Victor Furnish, *The Love Command in the New Testament* (Nashville: Abingdon, 1972); Scot McKnight, *The Jesus Creed: Loving God, Loving Others* (Brewster, Mass.: Paraclete, 2007); Russell Pregeant, *Knowing Truth, Doing Good* (Minneapolis: Fortress, 2008).

[13] Millard J. Erickson, *Christian Theology*, 2nd ed. (Grand Rapids, Mich.: Baker, 1998), 448.

[14] Ibid., 82.

God controls all. "God's power is evident in his control of the course of history," says Erickson. "God's will is never frustrated…God's decisions and actions are not determined by consideration of factors outside himself, but are simply a matter of his own free choice."[15] God "is in control of all that happens as history moves to the fulfillment of his purpose."[16] Erickson puts it simply: "God is in control of all that occurs."[17]

All that happens is God's plan. "We may define the plan of God as his eternal decision rendering certain all things that will come to pass,"[18] argues Erickson. "From all eternity, [God] has determined what he's now doing. Thus, his actions are not reactions to unforeseen developments."[19] "God foreknows what…individuals will freely do, for he in effect made that decision by choosing them in particular to bring into existence."[20]

Humans are free but not free. "God has created in such a way," says Erickson, "that the good of his world may be perverted into evil when we misuse it or something goes awry with the creation."[21] And yet, he says, "the evil actions of humans, contrary to God's law and moral intentions, are…part of God's plan, foreordained by him."[22] Erickson puts it this way: "human freedom exists and is compatible with God's having rendered our decisions and actions certain."[23] In other words, humans freely sin and yet have been predestined to do so. We are free but not free. It is difficult to make sense of this claim.

---

[15] Ibid., 303-304.

[16] Ibid., 57.

[17] Ibid., 437.

[18] Ibid., 372.

[19] Ibid., 301.

[20] Ibid., 387.

[21] Ibid., 449.

[22] Ibid., 380.

[23] Ibid.

God wills sin. "God never says, 'Commit this sin!'" says Erickson. "But by his permitting the conditions that lead a person to commit a sin and by his not preventing the sin, God in effect wills the sin."[24] This means that "even the sinful actions of humans are part of God's providential working."[25] God can predetermine sin and even will sin, and yet, according to Erickson, humans sin freely.

God loves himself. "God must choose his own glory ahead of all else," says Erickson. "To do anything else would in fact be a case of idolatry."[26] "When we think of God's love, a dilemma arises," he admits. "Does he love us for his own sake, apparently jeopardizing the unselfish, giving character of his love; or does he love us for our sake, thus apparently jeopardizing his status as the highest value? The former would seem to compromise the love of God, the latter his glory." There is, however, a third possibility for Erickson. "God loves us on the basis of that of himself which he placed within us, in creating. He therefore in effect loves himself in us."[27] This means God's love "for us and for his other creatures is completely disinterested." It "is *agape*, not *eros*."[28]

God can't forgive without payment. "God's justice requires that there be payment of the penalty for sin," says Erickson. "God's love, however, desires humans to be restored in fellowship with him. The offer of Jesus Christ as the atonement for sin means that both the justice and the love of God have been maintained…There is tension between these two things only if one's view of love requires that God forgive sin without any payment being made." This means "the offer of Christ as atonement shows a greater love on God's part than would simply indulgently releasing people from the consequences of sin."[29]

---

[24] Ibid. 388.

[25] Ibid., 423.

[26] Ibid., 314.

[27] Ibid., 320.

[28] Ibid., 319.

[29] Ibid., 324-25.

God predestines some for hell. Erickson says that "God decided that he would create humans; that they would fall, and then that among this group who will be brought into existence, all of whom would come under the curse of sin, some individuals would, acting as he intends, freely choose to respond to him."[30] This means that "not only is the future judgment of unbelievers irreversible, but their punishment is eternal."[31] "Sometimes the justice of God is impugned on the grounds that some receive this grace of God and others do not," he admits. "That any are saved at all is, however, the amazing thing, for if God gave to all what they deserve, none would be saved."[32]

My Response to Erickson

These quotes and other statements in *Christian Theology* indicate that Erickson endorses ideas inconsistent with love, at least love as typically understood. These inconsistencies begin with his view of divine power. But they also pertain to Erickson's strong view of God's independence, in the sense of God not being affected by creatures. And they come from a particular way of understanding love as desire.

Erickson thinks God controls all of history, having predestined all things. God controls you, me, everyone, and everything. God even wills sin. This means God planned and predestined the evil we encounter. These notions, however, oppose our commonsense view that love is uncontrolling of others. They oppose our intuitions that love involves a measure of freedom. Love does not control.

Erickson wants to say we freely sin. But we are not free if we must do what we have been predetermined to do. Besides, a loving person would not predetermine that we harm others or ourselves. Love does not predestine evil. And we don't hold morally responsible someone who cannot do other than what they're predetermined to do.

---

[30] Ibid., 387.

[31] Ibid., 1244.

[32] Ibid., 322.

Erickson believes God loves what is most desirable. Because God is most desirable, God loves himself. Erickson tries to avoid the self-centered implications of this view by saying God loves creatures insofar as God loves the divine image in them. But this argument fails to convince, because this is still self-love, not love which is also other-directed. In his schema, God loves himself in others, not others in themselves.

The payment view of atonement has long been criticized by Christians who believe God expresses unconditional love. The penal theory of atonement accepted by Calvinism and other theologies assumes God's forgiveness is conditional, in the sense of needing compensation. Rather than offering indulgent release from punishment, God won't forgive unless he receives a brutal payment: his son's death. But this makes little sense. Would we consider a father to be loving who, instead of forgiving those who offended him, required the death of his daughter?

According to Erickson, God creates and predetermines some for everlasting joy and others for eternal punishment. But is it loving to send people to eternal torment? Especially if they have been predestined to do what they do? Loving parents would not have a child and predetermine it to everlasting pain. Erickson says he's amazed God would save anyone. But how much more amazing, we should respond, to think God wants to save *everyone*. A truly magnificent God is unconditionally loving!

The work of Millard Erickson and Richard Hays illustrate my claim that love is often neglected or badly misunderstood in contemporary biblical studies and theology.[33] Of course, there are exceptions. Some aim to make love a priority. But Hays and Erickson represent what seems to me the majority.

Countless Christians fail to put love first.

---

[33] Gerald Bray's theology suffers from many of the problems we find in Erickson's, albeit Bray's views are more confusing, and he appeals to mystery more frequently. Bray lays this out in *God is Love: A Biblical and Systematic Theology* (Wheaton, Ill.: Crossway, 2012).

OBSTACLES TO PUTTING LOVE FIRST

Why have biblical scholars and theologians failed to affirm the priority of love?

I don't know every reason. Nor can I ascertain well the motives of those who fail to put love first. But I can identify some key obstacles that likely keep many Christians — scholars and otherwise — from making love their conceptual priority. In some cases, scholars even admit that these obstacles impede them.

1. Love is sometimes identified with sex/romance, self-indulgence, sentimentality, or extreme tolerance.

In everyday language, "love" has many meanings. We all know this. This variety contributes to the tendency among scholars to relegate love to secondary status or neglect it. Why focus on a word that lacks clarity?

In common parlance, "love" sometimes refers to romance or sex. To be attracted romantically or be sexually involved is to be "in love" or in a "love relationship." This language has its place and is even used occasionally in the Bible. But Christians usually mean something different when they speak of God's love for us, loving strangers, loving oneself, or about love for enemies.

Sex and romance *can* be expressions of love, but not always. Rapists and stalkers are not models of love, and yet their actions are sexually oriented or involve romantic infatuation. Thinking love is only or even primarily about sex and romance restricts love's meaning too much. Following Jesus' call to "love one another" often does *not* involve sexual or romantic activity.

Other people think of love primarily, if not exclusively, as oriented toward oneself. Richard Hays rejects the primacy of love, in part, because he believes love has "become a cover for all manner of vapid self-indulgence." But self-gratification and love are not identical. In fact, they are more often thought to be opposites. Most of us know this.

There is a place for self-love. Love is not always self-sacrificial or oriented toward strangers. But, to quote Jesus, "No one has greater love than this, to lay down one's life for one's friends" (John 13:15). An adequate view says love sometimes requires self-denial and sometimes acting for one's own good. Acting for the common good often also benefits oneself.

Others think of love primarily as sentimentality, in the sense of warm feelings or affection. Understood this way, love pertains entirely to warm emotions. Some researchers in contemporary psychology think of love in this way and point to chemicals in the brain as love's source.[34]

It's better to think love *may* involve warm affections. But it also sometimes requires helping others without having warm feelings. Jesus says we ought to love enemies (Mt. 5:44), people for whom we are *not* likely to feel any warm fuzzies.

Emotions often, if not always, play a role in love. They sometimes spur us to love, and there are good reasons to cultivate positive emotions.[35] But love sometimes acts for good *despite* not feeling emotionally inclined to do so. So love is more than emotion.

Some think of love as extreme tolerance. To love someone is to accept and condone any idea, belief, or activity a person proposes. While tolerance has its place, the biblical witness condemns sinful activity that undermines well-being. God does not tolerate evil, so this cannot be an adequate definition. "All things are lawful, but not all things are beneficial," says the Apostle Paul (1 Cor. 10:23). Love wants to benefit, so it does not embrace extreme relativism.

To counter inadequate views, some Christians attach adjectives to "love." A popular addition is *agape*, one of the Greek words for love often associated with God's action. A Christian might appeal to "*agape* love" to distinguish what she has in mind from lesser or

---

[34] Helen Fisher makes this argument in *Anatomy of Love: A Natural History of Mating, Marriage, and Why We Stray* (New York: Fawcett, 1992).

[35] On the relation between feeling and thinking, see Anastasia Philippa Scrutton, *Thinking Through Feeling: God, Emotion and Possibility* (New York: Continuum, 2011).

inappropriate loves. "Secular love has its place," she might say, "but God's love is *agape*."

This approach presents a host of problems. Chief among them is the assumption we know what makes *agape* different from other loves. Few who assume this also define their terms. Even the scholarly literature reveals a wide variety of definitions for *agape*. This variety confuses.[36] I'll address *agape* in later chapters and argue that, when carefully defined, it is one form of love among others. But those who appeal to *agape* should clarify what they mean.

Other theologians add the adjective "holy" to love. God expresses holy love, they say, and we should do the same. Kenneth Collins advocates this addition, because he thinks love is "soft, naively wishful, and likely self-indulgent."[37] The Church of the Nazarene considers "holy love" an attribute of God, apparently to distinguish divine love from other loves.

But the strategy of adding "holy" fails. If love comes from God (1 Jn. 4:8) and if God is holy, *all* love is holy. Adding "holy" to love is redundant, like saying a circle is round or a bachelor is male. Besides, the phrase "holy love" does not appear in scripture and rarely in Christian tradition. Instead of adding "holy," we're better off to define love well.

Given the diversity of meanings, reclaiming the centrality of love requires defining it from a biblically oriented perspective. A strong definition will draw from other disciplines and sources, of course. But central claims about love in scripture help to overcome these many misunderstandings common today.

---

[36] See my discussion of this in *Defining Love: Philosophical, Scientific, and Theological Investigations* (Grand Rapids, Mich.: Brazos, 2010), ch. 2.

[37] Kenneth J. Collins, *The Theology of John Wesley: Holy Love and the Shape of Grace* (Nashville: Abingdon, 2007), 9.

2. Biblical writers are sometimes unclear about love's meaning.

I have criticized theologians and biblical scholars for not taking seriously the biblical witness to love's primacy. I opened by citing scripture passages that champion love, and I said Christians should attend to the biblical witness to love's prominence. But I must acknowledge a reason some overlook love:

The Bible does not provide a uniform view of love.

Biblical writers refer to different expressions of love, and they seem to assume love has various meanings. In many cases, we can encompass these differences under a larger and inclusive definition of love. In some cases, however, this encompassing isn't possible. Genuine tensions remain. Without clarity, a persuasive theology of love is unlikely.

Here are a few examples of how biblical writers sometimes talk about love in conflicting ways:

God "so loved the world," we read in John's gospel, God gave Jesus so we might have eternal life (Jn. 3:16). Paul tells readers to imitate God by loving as Jesus loved (Eph. 5:1). The Good Samaritan showed love to a half-dead victim, and New Testament writers often tell readers to love one another. The meaning of love in these cases and in most scripture pertains to helping the world, people, or ourselves. Love so understood promotes what is beneficial and life-giving. Love does good.

Elsewhere, love has a different meaning. John says, "the love of the Father is not in those who love the world," for instance (1 Jn. 2:15). Paul regrets Demas loves the world (2 Tim. 4:10). Jesus says hypocrites "love" attention (Mt. 6:5) and "love the places of distinction" (Mt. 23:6). These passages imply humans should *not* love in the "wrong" way. Incidentally, these passages use the words *agape* and *philia*. Rather than love as doing good, love in these instances pertains to desire and commitments.

Consider another example. The Apostle Paul criticizes people who "will be lovers of themselves" (2 Tim. 3:2). And he says love does not seek its own interest (1 Cor. 13:5). Drawing upon these passages, influential theologians say self-love is sinful. According to them, we shouldn't love ourselves.

But other biblical passages encourage self-love. Jesus implies self-love is necessary when he says the second greatest commandment involves loving neighbors "as oneself" (Mk. 12:31). Paul says self-love plays a positive role in knowing what it means to love one's spouse (Eph. 5:28). If God calls us to love all people, Christians who fail to love themselves would not follow this call. So, we *should* love ourselves.

Lack of clarity sometimes arises from the words biblical writers use. New Testament writers most often use noun, verb, and other forms of *agape*. But they also use *philia* (commonly understood as "friendship") to talk about love. The meanings of these two words are sometimes interchangeable but other times unique. In addition, if we understand *eros* to mean love for what is valuable, its meaning appears in scripture too, even though the word itself is absent. Old Testament writers use a variety of words rendered "love" by English translators. The most used and best known are *hesed* and *ahavah*, but they have various meanings too.

Biblical writers use many words translated "love," and those words have diverse meanings.

Given this variety, it's understandable that many theologians fail to place love — understood biblically — at the center of their theological construction. An adequate theology of love, therefore, must acknowledge this diversity, and offer a way forward. That project is central to this book.

The diverse meanings for love in scripture should prompt Christians to pursue at least two paths. The first examines the Bible to determine if one meaning of love predominates. If biblical writers use words we translate "love" in one sense more than others, a theologian justifiably builds from this prevailing meaning. This predominant meaning can be the core of an adequate love definition and theology.

The many meanings of love in the Bible should also prompt theologians to pursue a second path. They should define love clearly. Because so few scholars define love, confusion reigns.

A good definition will correspond with the principal meaning of love in the biblical witness. It will be consistent with the broad biblical description of God's love and the love God calls creatures to express.[38] This definition will help Christians identify specific forms of love and it will clarify these forms in ways that complement rather than contradict love's general definition.

Without an encompassing definition and complementary conceptual scheme, it's unlikely love can play the leading role in biblically oriented Christian theology.

3. Biblical writers sometimes portray God as unloving.

Although the Bible points to a God of love and writers urge their readers to live lives of love, some passages depict God as causing harm and evil. Others glorify or justify violent human action. Unfortunately, the "Good Book" doesn't always portray God as good.

"I form light and create darkness, I make weal and create woe; I the LORD do all these things," we find God saying (Is. 45:7). In a passage that sounds like God endorses killing babies, the Psalmist says, "Happy shall they be who take your little ones and dash them against the rock!" (137:9). Upon entering the promised land, the Israelites are told, "when the LORD your God gives them over to you and you defeat them, then you must utterly destroy them…show them no mercy" (Deut. 7:2). "I will send my terror in front of you," the Lord says, "and will throw into confusion all the people against whom you shall come" (Exod. 23:27). The Lord commands Saul to "go and attack Amalek, and utterly destroy all that they have; do not spare them, but kill both man and woman, child and infant, ox and sheep, camel and donkey" (1 Sam. 15:1-3). In a flood story known even by children, an angry God destroys nearly every human and creature (Gen. 6-9).

---

[38] Much of my book, *Defining Love: Philosophical, Scientific, and Theological Engagements*, explores the role of science for understanding love (Grand Rapids, Mich.: Brazos, 2010). See also *Research on Altruism and Love: An Annotated Bibliography of Major Studies in Psychology, Sociology, Evolutionary Biology, and Theology*, Stephen G. Post, et. al., eds. (Philadelphia: Templeton Press, 2003).

These are just a few biblical passages that say God does or wants harm.

Fortunately, there are helpful ways to deal with these problematic passages.[39] One of the best ways privileges Jesus as the clearest revelation of divine love. In light of the revelation of love in Jesus, we should consider some biblical passages misguided portrayals of God's actions or wishes. To put it bluntly: Sometimes biblical writers get God wrong.

Another helpful response takes a broad view of the biblical witness. Looking at the whole, one discovers that love plays a more pronounced role than evil. Biblical writers portray God more often as loving than unloving, as forgiving than vengeful, as kind than cruel. This approach says we should privilege the major themes of love over the minor themes that oppose it.

A third approach makes the case that as humans increased in understanding, they grew to see God as consistently loving rather than the cause of death and destruction.[40] We witness this development in the Bible itself. Jesus contradicts the plain reading of Leviticus (24:19-21) and Exodus (21:23-27), for instance, when he says, "You have heard that it was said, 'An eye for an eye and tooth for a tooth.' But I say to you, if anyone strikes you on the right cheek, turn the other also" (Matt 5:38-39). Changes in how biblical writers portray God also occur in the Old Testament itself.[41]

Christians should critique biblical passages that portray God as wanting or causing violence. They should 1) Look for internal critiques of violence within the text. Some passages *seem* or *appear* to endorse divine violence but actually criticize it. 2) Use nonviolent voices to undermine violent ones. This approach uses the Bible

---

[39] For instance, see Eric A. Seibert, *The Violence of Scripture: Overcoming the Old Testament's Troubling Legacy* (Philadelphia: Fortress, 2012); Matthew Curtis Fleischer, *The Old Testament Case for Nonviolence* (Oklahoma City, Ok.: Epic Octavius, 2017).

[40] On progressive or developmental revelation, see Gregory Boyd, *Cross Vision: How the Crucifixion of Jesus Makes Sense of Old Testament Violence* (Philadelphia: Fortress, 2018); Bernard Ramm, *Protestant Biblical Revelation* 3rd ed. (Grand Rapids, Baker, 1980).

[41] I address change within the Old Testament in my discussion of *hesed* later in this book.

against the Bible by privileging nonviolent readings. 3) Read from the perspective of victims and the marginalized. When Christians read scripture from the perspective of the harmed and hurting, they are more likely to identify problematic aspects in the Bible. Putting themselves in the shoes of the disenfranchised and outsiders can reveal to Christians how mainstream interpretations minimize biblical passages that endorse violence. 4) Appeal to commonly accepted standards of morality. Appealing to common decency and morality means rejecting biblical passages that condone violence.[42]

I find these critiques convincing.[43] As I see it, we should admit biblical writers sometimes portray God as unloving. The Bible is not an entirely consistent witness to love.[44] Sometimes the Bible gets God wrong.

Some who see this inconsistency appeal to mystery: "God's ways are not our ways." They claim the Bible *is* perfectly consistent, but in a way we cannot fathom. This approach does not support a coherent theology of love. I believe it is better to admit biblical inconsistencies and seek a way to account for them. Better to be honest about the problematic ways biblical writers sometimes portray God than pretend they don't exist.[45]

We best address the problematic biblical passages by privileging the persistent and dominant portrayals of love. When seen in the broader context of and predominant witness to God's unwavering

---

[42] Find these suggestions in Seibert, *The Violence of Scripture*, ch. 6.

[43] On what it means for love to guide interpretation, see Alan Jacobs, *A Theology of Reading: A Hermeneutics of Love* (New York: Routledge, 2018); Edward F. Mooney, "Love, This Lenient Interpreter: On the Complexity of a Life," in *Transforming Philosophy and Religion*, Norman Wirzba and Bruce Ellis Benson, eds. (Bloomington, Ind.: University of Indiana Press, 2008); Norman Wirzba, "The Primacy of Love," in *Transforming Philosophy and Religion*, Norman Wirzba and Bruce Ellis Benson, eds. (Bloomington, Ind.: University of Indiana Press, 2008).

[44] In his assessment of open theism, Manuel Schmid argues that some open theists fail to account well for passages that oppose their views of God. See *God in Motion: A Critical Exploration of the Open Theism Debate* (Waco, Tex.: Baylor University Press, 2021).

[45] David Fergusson recommends a similar tack to interpreting problematic biblical passages. See *Faith and Its Critics: A Conversation* (Oxford: Oxford University Press, 2009).

love, we rightly pass judgement on and reject passages that depict God as unloving.

4. The Bible has no precise definition of love.

In their quest to understand love, most Christians look to the Bible as their main guide. Scripture is not their only source, of course, and everyone comes to the Bible already influenced by culture, philosophy, science, and more. But the Bible provides an authoritative witness Christians consider when thinking theologically.

Scripture offers key insights into who God is and how God acts. I've offered biblical evidence to support the claim that those insights center on love, although I've acknowledged the Bible isn't always consistent. But many Christians believe Jesus is the lens through which they best understand the nature of love. Jesus points to love's primacy. So we can say that the Bible provides necessary information for formulating an adequate Christian understanding of love.

But…the Bible does not provide a precise definition of love.

Although in Jesus "the love of God was revealed" (1 Jn. 4:9), Jesus himself did not offer a definition. Instead, Jesus lived a life of love. He healed the sick, helped the poor, cast out demons, forgave sinners, offered hope, and ministered in many ways. His life, message, ministry, suffering, death, and resurrection show love in action. But Jesus does not give a definition that unifies the various forms and expressions of love.

Jesus also told stories to illustrate love. The Good Samaritan story, for instance, expresses well what love of neighbor might entail (Luke 10:25-37). He tells the story of a steadfastly loving Father who welcomes home a prodigal son (Lk. 15:11ff). Jesus tells stories about how the owner of a vineyard pays all workers well, even though some came late to the job and worked less (Mt. 20). He says laying down our lives can be a significant expression of love (Jn. 15:13), but so can simple friendship (Jn. 15:15). And more.

We find profound passages about love throughout scripture. In 1 Corinthians 13, the apostle Paul says powers, abilities, and resources are worthless without love. He identifies many forms: "Love is patient; love is kind; love is not envious or boastful or arrogant or rude. It does not insist on its own way; it is not irritable or resentful; it does not rejoice in wrongdoing, but rejoices in the truth. It bears all things, believes all things, hopes all things, endures all things" (1 Cor. 13:4-7).[46]

This great love chapter tells us what love looks like, some of its common characteristics, and promotes its priority. But the Apostle Paul offers no definition of love. And he does not mention every form of love. For instance, love sometimes gives to the needy, encourages the discouraged, feeds the hungry, fellowships, seeks justice, thinks on good and lovely things, and so on. Despite the profundity of this chapter, Paul neither gives a love definition nor tells us all we need to know about love.

We might respond to the absence of a definition by thinking one is unnecessary.[47] We might catalog love's forms and expressions and then assume cataloging is all theology requires.[48] Why worry about defining love if Jesus (apparently) did not? Why not leave it undefined and simply go about loving God, others, all creation, and ourselves?

The most obvious reasons we should define love may be the most important. If we don't know what love is, how do we know what it means that God loves us? Without a definition, how will we know if we are loving one another? How will we know what it means to love God, ourselves, and all creation?

How can we catalog the forms of love if we don't know the catalog's parameters? Without a definition, how would we know if helping a friend or forgiving an enemy are expressions of love? Or why

---

[46] On the ways of love, see Norman Wirzba, *Way of Love: Recovering the Heart of Christianity* (New York: HarperOne, 2016).

[47] Werner Jeanrond argues similarly, saying the "Bible does not contain any pure or original passage on love to which we could return for any timeless and unambiguous understanding of love" (*A Theology of Love* [London: T & T Clark, 2010], 40).

[48] For instance, bell hooks writes eloquently about love but never defines it succinctly. See *All About Love: New Visions* (New York: HarperCollins, 2001).

should we say nonconsensual intercourse is unloving if we have no definition of love? How will we know what distinguishes *agape, eros,* and *philia* or *hesed* and *ahavah*? And so on.

An adequate theology of love needs an adequate definition of love.

5. Theologians often fail to define love well.

Most theologians do *not* define love.[49] Even those who focus on love rarely clarify what they mean. This practice is especially odd, because most theologians know love has diverse and often confusing meanings. There's a dearth of explicit definitions.

The few theologians who define love often fail to use their definitions consistently. They'll say we ought to love the world, for instance, which sounds like we should treat creation well. In the next breath, they'll say we shouldn't love the world but should love God instead. Others say God causes or permits evil but also claim God loves everyone. The harmed and hurting doubt this. Theologians will say suffering is a necessary part of love, but they'll claim heaven is a loving place without suffering. Others say God loves everyone, but God does *not* love the wicked. Some say God loves us like a friend and then say friendship with God is impossible. Or theologians will say love isn't about feelings, but then urge us to feel compassion for the needy. Some claim humans are incapable of love but criticize them for being unloving.

Theological claims about love often make no sense!

So...theologians need to define love well.[50] And then employ their definitions consistently. Of course, definitions cannot capture

---

[49] Edward Collins Vacek also complains that scholars fail to define love well. See *Love, Human and Divine: The Heart of Christian Ethics* (Washington, D.C.: Georgetown University Press, 1994), 34.

[50] In his influential book, *The Four Loves,* C. S. Lewis explores several types of love but never defines love. Martin D'Arcy notes this omission ("These Things Called Love," A review of C. S. Lewis's The Four Loves. *The New York Times* [July 31, 1960]) as does Lewis scholar Jason Lepojarvi (*God Is Love but Love Is Not God: Studies on C.S. Lewis's Theology of Love* [PhD thesis University of Helsinki, 2015], 68).

everything that's true. Just as we will probably never grasp the full meaning of God, we will never grasp the full meaning of love. Words cannot provide all-encompassing explanations.

Despite imprecision and failure to be comprehensive, however, words *are* meaningful. They can partially describe reality. Words also move us to act, feel, think, and live in particular ways. We often need them to, as the Apostle Peter put it, "make a defense to anyone who demands from you an accounting for the hope that is in [us]" (1 Pet. 3:15). If we thought words useless, we would stop using them altogether. And yet we persist.[51]

Because I think theologies of love should offer clear definitions of love, I devote the next chapter to doing so. Later chapters explore the details and implications of my definition in light of key theologians, doctrines, and intuitions.

CONCLUSION

The Bible provides crucial resources for constructing a theology of love. The primacy of love in its pages should incline Christians also to make love primary. But many Christians — including professional scholars — fail to put love first. Sometimes, this involves a conscious decision to relegate love to secondary status. Other times, views of God are actually antithetical to a coherent theology of love.

Failure to make love primary is, in some ways, understandable. Real obstacles present themselves, both within and beyond the

---

[51] For accessible accounts of the primacy of love, see Jim Burklo, *Tenderly Calling* (Haworth, N.J.: St. Johann, 2021); Jared Byas, *Love Matters More* (Grand Rapids, Mich.: Zondervan, 2020); Jason Clark, *Prone to Love* (Shippensburg, Penn.: Destiny Image, 2014); Jonathan Foster, *Reconstructionist* (Glen Oak, Ca.: Quoir, 2021); Daniel K. Held, *Love's Resurrection* (Springfield, Oh.: Higher Ground, 2013); Jacqui Lewis, *Fierce Love* (London: Harmony, 2021); Andrew Lightbown and Nick Fane, *ReDiscovering Charity* (Buckingham: UBP, 2009); Brian McLaren, *A New Kind of Christianity* (New York: HarperOne, 2010); Chuck Queen, *A Faith Worth Living* (Eugene, Or.: Wipf and Stock, 2011); Niq Ruud, *Only Love* (Glen Oak, Ca.: Quoir, 2021).

biblical witness. Overcoming those obstacles requires careful theological reflection, attention to the biblical text, and a coherent definition of love.

The following chapter provides a definition of love consistent with the primary ways scripture writers understand love.

2

Love Defined

*I*n this chapter, I will do what I criticize others for not doing. I define love.

This exercise may strike some as pedantic. But as I have argued, failing to define love leads to a host of problems. Although words cannot capture all that love entails, they help us make progress in understanding what love means.[1] A clear definition can also help fulfill the Christian aim to love.

Defining love is essential to an adequate theology of love.

WHAT IS LOVE?

I intend for the definition of love I propose to arise from and be coherent with the broad biblical witness, especially the love Jesus expresses. My definition also accounts for what we know about love in human experience as studied by various sciences.[2] I intend this defi-

---

[1] For an example of one who fails to define love and denies it has an essence, see John Armstrong, *Conditions of Love: The Philosophy of Intimacy* (New York: W.W. Norton, 2002).

[2] I have offered a sustained defense of my definition of love in *Defining Love: A Philosophical, Scientific, and Theological Engagement* (Grand Rapids, Mich.: Brazos, 2010). I explore scientific dimensions of love in *The Science of Love: The Wisdom of Well-Being* (Philadelphia: Templeton, 2005) and *The Altruism Reader: Selections of Writings on Love, Religion, and Science* (Philadelphia: Templeton, 2012). On the science of love, see Beverley Fehr, et. al., *The Science of Compassionate Love* (London: Blackwell, 2009); Stephen Post, et. al., *Altruism and Altruistic Love* (Oxford: Oxford University Press, 2001).

nition to account for the core features of God's love too. As I see it, an adequate definition of love is appropriately broad without being so broad as to include every action, desire, or relationship.

I define love this way:

To love is to act intentionally, in relational response to God and others, to promote overall well-being.

Actors and factors that include God, others, creation, and one-self influence what we rightly call an act of love. We love when we respond by purposely doing something good, beautiful, or valuable. Well-being is love's aim, and love always occurs in relationships.

To explain my definition, I explore its key phrases, beginning with the last.

To Promote Overall Well-Being

Although biblical writers use the term in many ways, they mostly identify love with doing what is beneficial, positive, or helpful. Saying love aims to promote well-being is crucial for avoiding problems I identified earlier and others I will address. Love is value-positive.

To put it succinctly, love aims to do good.

Jesus understood love this way. "Love your enemies," says Jesus, by "doing good" to them (Lk. 6:35). His followers should love, Jesus said, by doing good even to those who hate them (Mt. 5:44). When doing so, they imitate the God who does good by sending rain for the righteous and unrighteous (Mt. 5:45). God gave Jesus so we might have eternal life (Jn. 3:16; 1 Jn. 4:9), which involves enjoying well-being.

Jesus explains the first and second greatest commandments as doing good to friends and strangers. Matthew's account has Jesus saying the law and prophets — two broad categories whose chief concerns are ethical — "hang" on love (22:35-40). Luke explains what love means by telling the story of a Samaritan who does good to an injured stranger (10:25-37).

Understanding love as promoting well-being prevails in the Old Testament. "The Lord is good to all, and his compassion is over all that he has made," says the Psalmist (Ps. 145:9). "I have loved you with an everlasting love," says the Lord, "I have drawn you with unfailing kindness" (Jer. 31:3). We should "give thanks to the Lord, for he is good, and his love endures forever" (Ps. 136:1). "You shall not take vengeance or bear a grudge against the sons of your own people, but you shall love your neighbor as yourself," says the writer of Leviticus (19:8).

The most frequent description of divine love in the Old Testament portrays it as doing good. It describes God as "The Lord, the Lord, a God merciful and gracious, slow to anger, and abounding in steadfast love and faithfulness, keeping steadfast love for thousands, forgiving iniquity and transgression and sin…" (Exod. 34:6-7).[3]

The Apostle Paul emphasizes the essential relationship between love and goodness when he says love "repays evil with good" (Rm. 12:21). Paul prays, "may our Lord Jesus Christ himself, and God our Father, who loved us and gave us eternal comfort and good hope through grace, comfort your hearts and establish them in every good work and word" (2 Thess. 2:16-17). Love builds up rather than destroying (1 Cor. 8:1b), he says, and we should love by hating evil and clinging to good (Rm. 13:9). Paul mostly understands love as actions attempting to promote well-being, blessedness, or the common good.

The Apostle John wrote often and well of love, and he identifies it with promoting well-being. John says Jesus' love benefits us: "We know love by this, that [Jesus] laid down his life for us — and we ought to lay down our lives for one another" (1 Jn. 3:16). "How does God's love abide in anyone who has the world's goods and sees a brother or sister in need," John asks rhetorically, "and yet refuses to help?" (1 Jn. 3:17) Love that promotes well-being — salvation — motivated God's

---

[3] See also Exod. 20:6; Num. 14:18; Deut. 5:9-10; 7:9; 1 Kings 3:6; 2 Chron. 30:9; Neh. 9:17, 31 Ps. 86:15; 103:8, 17; 106:45; 111:4; 112:4; 145:8; Jer. 30:11; 32:18-19; Lam. 3:32; Dan. 9:4; Joel 2:13; Jon. 4:2; Nah. 1:3.

sending Jesus "so that we might live through him" (1 John 4:9). All these passages point to love as an action that seeks to benefit.

Peter identifies love with acting to promote well-being. In his instructions on love, he says Christians should "not repay evil for evil or abuse for abuse; but, on the contrary, repay with a blessing" (1 Pt. 3:9). People should "maintain constant love for one another, for love covers a multitude of sins" (1 Pt. 4:8).

Biblical authors use several synonyms for "good" when describing love's aim. The word "blessing" points to the well-being love promotes, for instance. Others use the word "peace," in the sense of *shalom*, the Hebrew word for desiring the flourishing and wellbeing of every creature and creation. Jesus uses the phrase "abundant life" to describe well-being (Jn. 10:10). Perhaps the most common reference to love's purpose is "salvation," a therapeutic word pertaining to health, healing, happiness, and wholeness.[4]

I've chosen "well-being" instead of "good" for my love definition because well-being encompasses various biblical words and phrases pertaining to benefiting, helping, flourishing, or doing positive things. It has the added benefit of being a common phrase in contemporary studies in health, ethics, and philosophy.[5]

Love wants flourishing to flourish.

Promoting overall well-being involves a variety of activities.[6] It might mean providing basic needs, like food, water, air, and suitable living conditions. It can involve enhancing physical and mental dimensions of life. Promoting well-being may mean caring for others or establishing a sense of community. It can involve conserving diverse life forms, opportunities, and cultural expressions. To do good by promoting well-being may mean securing feelings of self-worth, providing medical soundness and physical fitness, fostering deep

---

[4] See John B. Cobb, Jr., *Salvation* (Anoka, Mn.: Process Century, 2020).

[5] For essays on the theology and science of love, see Matthew T. Lee and Amos Yong, eds., *The Science and Theology of Godly Love* (DeKalb, Ill.: Northern Illinois University Press, 2012).

[6] Randy Woodley explores well-being from an Indigenous perspective in *Shalom and the Community of Creation: An Indigenous Vision* (Grand Rapids, Mic.: Eerdmans, 2012).

personal relationships, or cultivating social and political harmony. Promoting well-being encourages the development of virtues and positive practices.[7] According to scripture, loving God promotes well-being.

Love promotes overall well-being in one but often in many ways.

Overall, Justice

"Overall" is an important word in my definition. It reminds us that while we often act for the good of one or a few, love does not violate the good of the whole. It does not heap benefits upon one or a few to the obvious harm of the many. Lovers consider how localized actions affect wider well-being.

God gives the Spirit "for the common good," says Paul (1 Cor. 12:7), and countless biblical passages rebuke those who seek individual pleasure but neglect the poor and hurting. Jesus said promoting the overall good includes promoting the well-being of enemies and strangers. If God loves the entire world, all creatures are potential recipients of love. The word "overall" in my definition accounts for this.

"Overall" also indicates the role justice plays in love.[8] By justice, I don't mean punishment or exacting revenge in the retributive sense of the word. I mean acting for the good of all in a restorative sense, especially the neglected or mistreated. When doing good to one or a few leads to the detriment of the many, love's justice demands repentance.

Rather than standing in opposition to love, justice is a dimension of it. To act justly is to act fairly by seeking to promote *overall*

---

[7] For strategies and research in promoting well-being in humans, see Matthew T. Lee, Laura D. Kubazansky, and Tyler J. VanderWeele, *Measuring Well-Being: Interdisciplinary Perspectives from the Social Sciences and Humanities* (Oxford: Oxford University Press, 2021); Margaret Schneider Jamner and Daniel Stokols, eds., *Promoting Human Well-Being: New Frontiers for Research, Practice, and Policy* (Berkeley, Ca.: University of California Press, 2000).

[8] Nicholas Wolterstorff offers a powerful argument for the role of justice in *Justice in Love* (Grand Rapids, Mich.: William B. Eerdmans, 2011), ch. 9.

well-being. This is what Cornel West means when he says, "justice is what love looks like in public."[9] Justice looks like love in private too, because love considers how private actions affect the public good.

We typically direct our love toward those near and dear, as we help those we know. This is appropriate, because we have special obligations to family, friends, and local communities. But we must also think broadly about how to love those we know less well or not at all. Loving the foreigner, the outcast, and the disenfranchised means promoting the common good so that "justice rolls down like waters, and righteousness like an ever flowing stream" (Amos 5:24). Our actions to help those close at hand often, but not always, benefit those at a distance.

Jesus begins his ministry by proclaiming the possibility of God's loving reign: "The time is fulfilled," he says, "and the kingdom of God has come near; repent and believe in the good news" (Mk. 1:15). Those who want the good life must seek the "kingdom of God" (Mt. 19:16, 17, 24). Seeking the kingdom of God is another way to talk about acting to promote overall well-being. The Greek phrases *basilea theou* and *basilea ouranos* — or what I call God's "loving reign" — conjures what is multidimensional, multifaceted, and multitudinous.[10] Those who take part in this reign of love live "in a manner worthy of the gospel of Christ" (Phil. 1:27). The reign of love is possible when we "strive first for the kingdom of God and his righteousness" (Mt. 6:33).

Love isn't *entirely* about good consequences, however. For instance, a person obviously does not love who wants to injure or harm but accidentally helps or does good. Motives matter. We should not

---

[9] Cornel West, *The American Evasion of Philosophy* (Madison, Wis.: University of Wisconsin Press, 1989), 271.

[10] On how *kenosis* can be a framework for politics and civilization, see Roger Haydon Mitchell and Julie Tomlin Arran, eds., *Discovering Kenarchy: Contemporary Resources* (Eugene, OR: Cascade, 2014). See also Thomas Jay Oord, "A Loving Civilization: A Political Ecology that Promotes Overall Well-Being," *The Kenarchy Journal* Vol. 2 (2021).

call an act "loving" when done with evil intentions, even though it may generate positive outcomes.

Take the biblical story of Joseph as an example. Joseph's brothers at first intended to kill him but decided instead to sell him into slavery. Their actions were not loving; their motives were not good. Joseph consistently cooperated with God despite his difficult circumstances. He eventually moved into a position to help his brothers. "What you intended for evil," Joseph tells his brothers, "God used for good" (Gen. 50:20). While Joseph promoted his brothers' well-being, he did so despite their failure to love.

We cannot, from results alone, determine if someone has loved.

In Relational Response to God and Others

The second phrase in my definition addresses the relational aspect of love. It speaks to the role a relational God plays in making creaturely love possible. Love is inherently relational.

Love takes at least two. Entirely isolated individuals — if such even existed — could not love. An act of love in one moment presupposes past relations and influences from others in previous moments. In fact, relational bonds partly determine each person and creature. Love also assumes possible futures, which involves a vision for how our actions might promote well-being.

A relational God acts in each moment to call, inspire, and empower creatures to love. "We love," says John, "because [God] first loved us" (1 Jn. 4:19). We rely upon divine action, because in God "we live and move and have our being," as Paul puts it (Acts 17:28). Without God's loving providence, we can do nothing (John 15:5). To put it another way, Christ who strengthens us makes possible every loving expression (Phil. 4:13).

By "relational," I mean more than logical relation. More than saying, for instance, the number 3 is logically related to 4 because it comes prior. The relational aspect of love involves degrees of causal influence, often empathy. This causal influence often includes affective and emotional tones.[11] The number 3 doesn't influence or empathize with the number 4.

It's common for Christian theologians to say creatures rely upon God. But many also say God relies in no sense upon creation. According to this view, God is impassible, unmoved, and unaffected. This way of thinking fails to take seriously the relationality inherent in love. Just as creaturely love requires relations between self and the other, the God who loves by nature requires relations with others. God can both love by nature and experience moment-by-moment relations with creation. I address this issue often in later chapters.

Love is more than relations, however. Reacting to views that ignore relationality, some define love as simply as mutual relatedness. Vincent Brummer, for instance, defines love as "a reciprocal relation."[12] "We should look on love as a relationship," says Brummer, "which involves partners adopting a complex set of attitudes towards each other."[13] Charles Hartshorne says, "love means realization in oneself of the desires and experiences of others, so that one who loves can insofar inflict suffering only by undergoing this suffering himself."[14] By "suffering," Hartshorne means relating.

Brummer, Hartshorne, and others rightly say relations are essential for love, even divine love. But they wrongly imply *all* relationships are loving. To define love *only* as relational response would

---

[11] Philosophers like Charles Hartshorne, George Herbert Mead, Herbert Spencer, and Alfred North Whitehead use the word "sympathy" to identify this "feels with" others. Psychologists often use the word "empathy" for the same activity. See, for instance, Pearl M. Oliner's argument on this in *Toward a Caring Society: Ideas in Action* (Westport, Conn.: Praeger, 1995), 32. L. G. Wispe also offers a fine article on the issue of the uses of sympathy and empathy, "The Distinction between Sympathy and Empathy," *Journal of Personality and Social Psychology*, 50 (1986).

[12] Vincent Brummer, *The Model of Love* (Cambridge: Cambridge University Press, 1993), 162-161.

[13] Ibid., 156.

[14] Charles Hartshorne, *Man's Vision of God* (Chicago: Willit, Clark, and Company, 1941), 31. Elsewhere, Hartshorne uses the phrase "life sharing" to define love as mutual relations (Charles Hartshorne, *Wisdom as Moderation: A Philosophy of the Middle Way* [Albany, N.Y.: State University of New York Press, 1987], 119). Like many, Hartshorne is inconsistent in his use of "love." Sometimes, he uses the word to speak of mere mutuality; other times he uses it to speak of acting for the good.

mean unhealthy, abusive, and vengeful relationships express love. Defining love as relationality alone ignores the truth that sometimes, for everyone's overall well-being, we should sever an unhealthy relationship, as we "flee evil" and "cling" instead to what is good (2 Tim. 2:22).

In some circles, love is defined primarily as seeking union. Theologian Paul Tillich, for instance, defines love as "the drive towards the unity of the separated."[15] This definition is problematic. Love defined simply as seeking relational union fails to account for well-being as love's goal. We can unite with others but do so intending harm. Thieves can seek union in their mutual goals of theft; mafia may unite to have a prostitution monopoly.

"Union" as love's aim is also easily interpreted as losing individuality. Two or more become one, it's implied, and lose independent distinctiveness. Better to emphasize the essential relatedness of persons-in-community or community-created-persons. While marriage is a "blessed union," healthy partners retain individuality. Lovers do not disappear entirely in relationships of love.[16]

Love includes relationality *and* the intentional aim to promote well-being.

Affection and Social Relations

"Love" is sometimes used in everyday speech and occasionally in the Bible to describe fondness for an object, person, or group. We "love" a cooing baby, for instance, or favorite restaurant. I often love my wife, children, and grandchildren in actions inspired or accompanied by warm feelings. Feelings of warm affection may spur us to promote well-being, and when we act on them, we "love one another with mutual affection" (Rom. 12:10).

---

[15] Paul Tillich, *Love, Power, and Justice: Ontological Analyses and Ethical Applications* (Oxford: Oxford University Press, 1960), 25.

[16] Erich Fromm makes the point that "mature love is union under the condition of preserving one's integrity, one's individuality," *The Art of Loving* (New York: Harper, 1956), 19.

We should not define love *simply* as affections or emotions, how-ever.[17] Fondness is not always loving. Motivated by fondness, parents can "pamper," "smother," or "coddle" children. This does not promote their well-being. Families may intentionally confine themselves to the affection of familial relations — isolated from outsiders — and fail to promote the common good. We should not define love *simply* as fondness or affection.[18]

My phrase "in relational response to God and others" speaks to the possibility of love in larger groups and social arrangements. Christians may naturally think of the church as a relational network in which love can be expressed. As the church "called in one body," says Paul, Christians might clothe themselves "with love, which binds everything together in perfect harmony" (Col. 3:14-15). At its best, the church aims to show love in profound ways.

Christian communities do not *always* love, of course. Sometimes, the damage groups do to others, themselves, or creation reveals a profound lack of love. Their love "has grown cold" (Mt. 24:12). In fact, those outside Christian communities sometimes respond bet-ter to God. Non-Christians sometimes love in profound and consis-tent ways.

No matter the person or group, the phrase "in relational response to God and others" points to the relational requirement of love. And it points to the necessary role of God in making creaturely love pos-sible. While love is more than relationality, it requires relations with God and others.

---

[17] Some psychologists define love as one emotion among others. For an example see Barbara L. Fredrickson, *Love 2.0: Creating Happiness and Health In Moments of Connection* (New York: Plume, 2013; Susan Hendrick and Clyde Hendrick, "Love," in *Handbook of Positive Psychology*, C. R. Snyder and Shane J. Lopez, eds. (Oxford: Oxford University Press, 2002). I explore theology and love as well-being in "Love, Wesleyan Theology, and the Psychological Dimensions of Both." *Journal of Psychology and Christianity* 31:2 (Summer 2012): 157-166.

[18] On how familial love can become idolatrous, See Janet Fishburn, *Confronting the Idolatry of Family* (Nashville: Abingdon, 1991).

To Act Intentionally

I began explaining my definition of love with the last phrase: "to promote overall well-being." I then focused on the relationality love requires, relation to God and others. I conclude with the first phrase of my definition: "to act intentionally." This phrase refers to several ideas.

Scripture emphasizes the importance of intentional decisions to do good. In the first and second greatest commandments, Jesus commands intentional action: "Love the Lord…and love your neighbor as yourself" (Mk. 12:29–31). The Apostle Paul urges his readers to act intentionally to promote well-being when he says they should "love one another" (Rom. 13:8). "Choose this day whom you will serve," says Joshua (24:15), and many other biblical passages refer to intentional decisions.

The word "intentional" has three facets: deliberation, motive, and freedom. While they overlap, each offers something distinctive for understanding the intentionality love requires.

The deliberation facet of love pertains to decision-making. We decide to love. Decisions do not always involve long and drawn-out reflection. We often make split-second, spur-of-the-moment decisions to love. We deliberate on the few options of which we are aware. We do not need to know everything, focus deeply, or reflect at great length when loving.

The motive facet of intention says love *purposely* does good. We should not call an act "loving" when the person meant to harm. Ill will is incompatible with actions we should deem as loving.

Consequences alone do not determine what is loving. Sometimes actions with good motives result in terrible consequences; sometimes actions with bad motives result in good consequences. Aims and aspirations are crucial, however, because love assesses prospectively among potential outcomes. To determine whether an action is loving, we should not simply assess retrospectively whether it yielded the greatest good.[19]

---

[19] I discuss in detail love's motives and consequentialism in *Defining Love*, chs. 1-2.

The freedom facet of acting intentionally refers to what philosophers call "self-determination" or "libertarian freewill." Love is meaningless if we are not free to some degree.[20] Love's freedom, however, does not mean the ability to do *anything*. Freedom is always limited, because concrete circumstances limit what is genuinely possible.[21] Our bodies, histories, environment, and more constrain, but do not entirely determine, what we might freely do in any moment.

To say love requires intentional action does not mean love must impose, interfere, intrude, or intervene in the affairs of others. Sometimes "letting be" is a profound act of love. Our five senses may not even perceive the action of love. Silent prayer can be an act of love, for instance, and listening can be loving. Love requires *praxis*.

The word "act" covers a range of behaviors, but love is intentional.

Love as Desire and Devotion

The most common alternative to my definition above and its emphasis on well-being is love as desire. This view is common among theologians and philosophers today, but love as desire is a minor theme in scripture. I explore this issue in later chapters, but it seems appropriate to address it briefly here. After all, "desire" is closely related to "acting intentionally." If desire is *simply* acting intentionally, desires

---

[20] A number of philosophers defend the importance and cogency of self-determination in terms of libertarian freedom. See especially William Hasker, *God, Time, and Knowledge* (Ithaca, N.Y.: Cornell University Press, 1989); Timothy, O'Connor, "Agent-Causal Theories of Freedom," in *The Oxford Handbook of Free Will,* 2nd ed., Robert Kane, ed. (Oxford: Oxford University Press, 2011), 309-328. See also Randolph Clarke, "Alternatives for Libertarians," in *The Oxford Handbook of Free Will,* 2nd ed., Robert Kane, ed. (Oxford: Oxford University Press, 2011), 329-348; Robert Kane, *The Significance of Free Will* (Oxford: Oxford University Press, 1998); Timothy O'Connor, *Persons and Causes: The Metaphysics of Free Will* (Oxford: Oxford University Press, 2000); Kevin Timpe, *Free Will: Sourcehood and its Alternatives,* 2nd ed. (New York: Bloomsbury, 2013).

[21] I explain "genuine but limited freedom" in "Genuine (but Limited) Freedom for Creatures and for a God of Love" in *Neuroscience and Free Will,* James Walters and Philip Clayton, eds. (Eugene, Or.: Pickwick, 2020). Daniel Day Williams makes this point in *The Spirit and Forms of Love* (New York: Harper and Row, 1968).

are present in all love. But love is more than acting intentionally and more than desire.

A long tradition going back as far as Plato understands love as desire. Thomas Aquinas understands love this way when he says, "every agent, whatever it be, does every action from love of some kind."[22] But ponder, for a moment, what Aquinas's words entail. If we accept his understanding, it seems every act of rape is in some sense an act of love. Every murder and theft, every act of torture and child slavery, every worship of dictators or destruction of ecosystems... *every* act, according to Aquinas, comes from love.[23] This way of understanding love might make sense within his philosophical argument, but it goes against common practice and meaning of the word and against the meaning of love in most of scripture.

Love as desire requires a modifier to provide clarity. So understood, love can be proper or improper, appropriate or inappropriate, ordered or disordered, and so on. If the action is morally positive, the actor loves properly. If the action is negative, the love is improper.

Those who define love as desire often fail to add modifiers, however. They say we should "love one another" and mean something positive, but they should actually have said we should "*properly* love one another." Or those who define love as desire may inconsistently add the modifiers necessary to provide clarity.

Defining love as desire has many disadvantages. The practice reinforces the popular view that sex and romance are always expressions of love, for instance.[24] If we understand love as desire, the one

---

[22] St. Thomas Aquinas, *Summa Theologica* (Westminster, Md.: Christian Classics, 1981), Part I-II, Q. 28, Art. 6. Aquinas offers various distinctions in his discussion of love. Love can be *amictia, amor, caritas,* or *dilectio.* Each love type involves action; their goals or aims differ. "By defining love as desire, Aquinas paints himself into a corner where he can be easily misunderstood in a way that leads to moral confusion or absurdity."

[23] Aquinas sometimes (and confusingly) uses "love" for those actions that promote well-being. See for instance, Aquinas's treatise on charity (*Summa Theologica,* IIA IIAE, Q.23. Craig A. Boyd, trans. In *The Altruism Reader: Selections from Love, Religion, and Science,* Thomas Jay Oord, ed. (Philadelphia: Templeton Foundation, 2008).

[24] Meredith F. Small equates sex and love in *What's Love God to Do with it? The Evolution of Human Mating* (New York: Anchor, 1995).

who desires sexual relations with another necessarily loves the other. But we know sexual desire does *not* always promote well-being. According to the desire view, logically even harmful sexual desires would be expressions of love. Most people would find this morally repugnant.

According to my definition, love is more than desire. This means, for instance, I can say harmful sex is not loving. The harmful desire for power, fame, or fortune is also not love. Acting to destroy the planet is not a way to love it. Love as I define it aims to promote well-being. Those who desire to harm do not love.

The problem with thinking love is simply desire can be made clear when we think about *wanting* something but not doing anything about that want. I might want or desire to help the homeless but never lift a finger. I might want or desire a healthy body but not love myself by exercising and eating well. Simply desiring is not an act of love.

Biblical writers do occasionally equate love with desire. In the vast majority of instances, however, biblical writers use "love" as something positive. When we understand love as action that aims to promote well-being, we make sense of biblical commands to love enemies, friends, strangers, family, other creatures, and oneself. I explore this issue in later chapters.

Theologians sometimes use other adjectives to preface love defined as desire. Those adjectives include "genuine," "sincere," "pure," and more. If we define love as I do, love cannot be insincere, disingenuous, or impure. Those adjectives suggest bad motives, but love, as I spell it out, by definition always has good motives.

To put it another way, love, according to my definition and as typically used in scripture, cannot be immoral. Adding adjectives like "proper" is unnecessary for indicating love's moral status. When we define love as acting intentionally, in relational response to God and others, to promote overall well-being, we overcome the confusion inherent in defining love as desire.

I don't dismiss all adjectives for love. Sometimes biblical writers and everyday speakers add adjectives to identify various forms of love. For instance, "self-sacrificial love" is a particular form, so is "neighbor love." Forms such as "friendship," "outsider" "compassionate," and more indicate particular forms of love among others.[25] And as we will see, *agape, philia,* and *eros* are forms of love.

Closely related to defining love as desire is defining it as devotion. To love God, say some, is to be committed to or worship God. God should be our priority, and to worship anything else is to idolize.[26] We find this language in the Bible, but it is not common.

Significant problems arise when we define love as worship or devotion. The oft-repeated biblical command to love one another, for instance, makes no sense if this means we should worship each other. The meaning of "devotion" is strained to its breaking point when equated with Jesus' command to love enemies. God does not call us to worship our enemies.

The Apostle Paul's injunction to "be devoted to one another in love" helps to clarify the relation between devotion and love. He recommends commitment in bonds of community, but "in love" clarifies that this commitment involves doing good or promoting well-being. We could imagine people being "devoted to one another in abuse," for instance, which would not be loving.

Desire, devotion, worship, and similar activities *may* accompany intentional responses, in relation to God and others, to promote overall well-being. But they may not. These activities undercut well-being when wrongly pursued. Therefore, we should not define love simply as desire, devotion, or worship.

It makes more sense to say love intentionally promotes well-being.

---

[25] Werner Jeanrond explores love's varieties in *A Theology of Love* (London: T & T Clark, 2010). See also *The Encyclopedia of Love in World Religions*, 2 Vol., Yudit Greenberg, ed. (Santa Barbara: ABC-CLIO, 2008).

[26] I could cite many theologians for this practice, but see James K. A. Smith, *You are What You Love: The Spiritual Power of Habit* (Grand Rapids, Mich.: Brazos, 2016), and *Desiring the Kingdom: Worship, Worldview, and Cultural Formation* (Grand Rapids, Mich.: Baker, 2009). I address James K. A. Smith's view of love as desire and it's similarities to Augustine's view in chapter four of this book.

Becoming Loving Persons and Communities

My definition of love points to actions, relations, and well-being. This focus is necessary, given the confusion surrounding love in everyday life, among scholars, and sometimes even in the Bible. My definition identifies an act of love. Without further clarification, however, this focus fails to account clearly for the development of loving people and communities.

While most biblical passages pertaining to love focus on actions, some also address what it means to become loving people and communities. Instead of love as an episode or moment, we should also identify love as a series of actions, a developmental process, a network of relations, or even a history. Books have been written on what it means to become a loving person and what loving communities look like. These issues are not my focus, but I want to address the connection between love as an act in a moment and what it means to become loving persons and communities over time.

Becoming a loving person is a process of frequently responding well to God and others to promote overall well-being. Repeated acts of love characterize those whom we consider habitually loving. A person who loves moment by moment in a consistent way develops a loving character. They become virtuous; Christians often call them "saints."

In Christian terms, those who repeatedly love "abide" in love. Jesus describes such people when he says, "if you keep my commandments, you will abide in my love, just as I have kept my Father's commandments and abide in his love" (Jn. 15:10). The virtuous person enjoys a personal history of frequent intentional responses to promote what is beneficial. They "abide" in love (John 15:9,10).

How frequently must a person love to develop a virtuous character? According to Jesus, the aim is perfection: invariably acting intentionally, in relational response to God and others, to promote well-being. Most Christians believe Jesus was perfect in this. Our loving as persistently as possible develops a loving character and provides a vision of what the afterlife might be like.

Practices, traditions, and habits play key roles in the development of loving people. And these loving ways emerge in communities and contexts.[27] Just as we consider those who love consistently to be loving persons, we should consider communities with a history of love to be loving communities. At their best, Christian communities bring together and inspire Christians to love one another, others, and the planet. These communities follow various practices that inculcate love. In the best of scenarios, loving communities teach themselves and others how to love.[28]

But practices, traditions, and habits can be positive or negative, loving or not. Christian communities have sometimes been catalysts for promoting well-being and sometimes catalysts for harm. Some of the most heinous crimes in history have been done by Christians claiming God's endorsement. Crusades, genocides, corruption, holocausts, slavery, sexual abuse, and more have been perpetrated by Christians in the name of God.

Relational networks can foster or hinder love. Networks that promote patriarchy or violence or undermine personal accountability hinder the work of love. Relational networks that encourage transparency, respect, and kindness enhance communities of love. When "love one another" goes macro, the possibility of loving civilizations can become a reality.[29] The kingdom of God emerges.

Loving persons and communities love consistently over time.

---

[27] On virtue ethics and related topics, see Craig Boyd, *A Shared Morality: A Narrative Defense of Natural Law Ethics* (Grand Rapids, Mich.: Brazos, 2007); Andrew Michael Flescher, *Heroes, Saints, and Ordinary Morality* (Washington, D.C.: Georgetown University Press, 2003); Alasdair MacIntyre, *After Virtue*, 2nd ed. (Notre Dame: University of Notre Dame Press, 1984); Ian Markham, *Do Morals Matter?* (London: Blackwell, 2007); William C. Spohn, *Go and Do Likewise: Jesus and Ethics* (New York: Continuum, 2000).

[28] For what love in community might look like, see Norman Wirzba, *The Way of Love: Recovering the Heart of Christianity* (New York: Harper One, 2016). See also Bishop Michael Curry, *Love is the Way: Holding on to Hope in Troubling Times* (London: Avery, 2020).

[29] See Oord, "A Loving Civilization (2021).

CONCLUSION

I have proposed a definition of love and explained its primary dimensions. I define love as acting intentionally, in relational response to God and others, to promote overall well-being. This definition plays a role in future chapters, as I give love pride of place in theology.

To say love acts intentionally is to say it is deliberate, has good motives, and is free. Love is more than desire or devotion, although it can include them. Those who love repeatedly develop loving characters, and relational loving networks make possible the emergence of loving communities.

The relational dimension of love identifies the necessity of give-and-receive influence. While love requires relationality, it is more than relationship alone. God is a necessary actor in loving relationships, and without divine action, creaturely love is impossible. Relational actors experience emotions which can be powerful forces for love. But sometimes we must love despite not feeling positive emotions or even when feeling negative emotions toward others.

Love's aim is well-being. It seeks to do good, be of benefit, or do what's positive. The justice of love reminds us that while our aim is often rightly directed at those who are near and dear, love seeks overall well-being. When we become aware that benefiting a few undermines the good of the whole, love demands we seek the common good.

3

Agape and Anders Nygren

*U*ntil the 20th century, *agape* was a word used only by Greek-speaking people and New Testament scholars. Today, many Christians know the word and use it, even some with scant biblical or theological education. For many, *agape* distinguishes Christian love from popular or secular loves. Some claim it's the only true love; others say *agape* is the highest or holiest of loves.

For many, *agape* is special.

Many Christians believe the Bible provides *agape's* definitive meaning, and this meaning connects closely to God. A careful look at biblical texts, however, reveals several meanings for *agape*. The word is not always connected to God or with what's good. The biblical witness to *agape* is mixed.

Agape as a verb ("to love"), noun ("love"), adjective ("beloved"), and other forms of speech occur 319 times in the New Testament.[1] Jesus uses *agape* in what he calls the first and second greatest love commands. The word features prominently in the Sermon on the Mount and Jesus' prayers. The Apostle Paul uses *agape* frequently, especially in his 1 Corinthians love hymn. He joins Jesus in saying *agape* fulfills the law. In his letters, John says, "God is *agape*," and the word plays a leading role in Johannine theology. James calls *agape* of

---

[1] Ceslaus Spicq, *Agape in the New Testament*, 3 vols. Sisters Marie Aquinas McNamara and Mary Honoria Richter, trans. (Eugene, Or.: Wipf and Stock, 2006 [1965]).

neighbor "the royal law." Although other New Testament words are also translated "love," *agape* is by far the most common.

The various meanings of *agape* in the New Testament prompt scholars to define the word. But their definitions vary widely. This variety reflects diverse theological, ethical, metaphysical, and anthropological intuitions. It also confuses those who want to know what *agape* means.

Consider the definitions below. *Agape* is…

"the simple yet profound recognition of the worthiness of and goodness in persons"[2]   —Bernard Brady

"ordinary human affection and compassion"[3]   —Don Cupitt

"a person's spending himself freely and carelessly for the other"[4]
                                                     —Paul Fiddes

"the principle of benevolence, that is, of doing good"[5]
                                              —William Frankena

"divine extravagance of giving without taking self into account"[6]
                                                    —Colin Grant

"unconditional willing of the good"[7]   —Timothy Jackson

---

[2] Bernard V. Brady, *Christian Love: How Christians Through the Ages Have Understood Love* (Washington, D.C.: Georgetown University Press, 2003), 268.

[3] Don Cupitt, *The New Christian Ethics* (London: SCM, 1988), 57.

[4] Paul Fiddes, *The Creative Suffering of God* (Oxford: Clarendon, 1988), 170.

[5] William K. Frankena, *Ethics* (Pearson Education, 1988), 44.

[6] Colin Grant, *Altruism and Christian Ethics* (Cambridge: Cambridge University Press, 2001), 188.

[7] Timothy Jackson, *Love Disconsoled: Meditations on Christian Charity* (Cambridge: Cambridge University Press, 1999), 15. Jackson defends what he calls "strong *agape*" in *The Priority of Love: Christian Charity and Social Justice* (Princeton: Princeton University Press, 2003).

"letting-be"[8] —John Macquarrie

"self-less altruism"[9] —Mike Martin

"the attribution to everyone an irreducible worth and dignity"[10]
—Gene Outka

"God giving himself" or "divine bestowal"[11] —Irving Singer

"value that x attributes to or creates in y"[12] —Alan Soble

to act "for the sake of the beloved"[13] —Edward Collins Vacek

"identification with the neighbor and meeting his needs"[14]
—Daniel Day Williams

This list gives a taste of the diverse definitions scholars have given *agape*. Some differences are subtle; others are stark.[15] There's a significant difference, for instance, between *agape* as "ordinary human love" and *agape* as "God giving himself." There's a difference between "letting be," which seems passive, and "selfless altruism," which suggests active self-sacrifice. There's a difference between *agape* as "attribution of irreducible worth" and "meeting needs." If

---

[8] John Macquarrie, *Principles of Christian Theology*, 2nd ed. (New York: Scribner's, 1977), 349.

[9] Mike W. Martin, *Love's Virtues* (Lawrence, Ks.: University Press of Kansas, 1996), 14.

[10] Gene Outka, *Agape: An Ethical Analysis* (New Haven: Yale University Press, 1972), 260.

[11] Irving Singer, *The Nature of Love*, vol. 1, 2nd ed. (Chicago: University of Chicago Press, 1987), 269.

[12] Alan Soble, *Agape, Eros, and Philia: Readings in the Philosophy of Love* (New York: Paragon, 1989), xxiv.

[13] Vacek, 157. Vacek writes elsewhere, "Agape is directed to the beloved's full value for the beloved's own sake" (179).

[14] Williams, *The Spirit and Forms of Love*, 262.

[15] Robert Merrihew Adams puts it this way, "*agape* is a blank canvas on which one can paint whatever ideal of Christian love one favors" (*Finite and Infinite Goods: A Framework for Ethics* [Oxford: Oxford University Press, 1999], 136).

we attribute irreducible worth to a needy person but fail to help, have we loved them?

Just as diverse meanings of "love" prompt some to neglect the word, the various meanings given *agape* also lead to its neglect. One rarely hears *agape* bantered about today at academic Bible conferences, for instance; it is more common in churches where there is less concern about definitional rigor. But good communication avoids muddled messages, and in some circles, *agape* has a communication problem.

Rather than abandoning the term *agape*, I want to salvage it. But doing so requires significant work interpreting biblical texts and *agape* theologies. Salvaging *agape* requires evaluating how it relates with love in general and other forms of love, like *eros* and *philia*. And it requires constructing an *agape* theology that makes sense of both scripture and lived experience.

In this chapter, my focus is the most influential book on *agape* in the 20th century: *Agape and Eros*, by Anders Nygren (1890-1978).[16] Nygren claims to provide the authentic biblical account of *agape*, and he offers a theology based on it. I will criticize his work. I will make my own claims about *agape*, without saying my account is the only authentic one. The Bible supports several definitions of *agape*, but I'll argue my account fits most biblical uses of the word and the general drift of scripture.

I don't pretend to be entirely objective. Like Nygren and everyone else, I have biases, and my life experiences incline me toward particular interpretations over others. I aim, however, to be open to what each text says. I want to think about love in ways consonant with the whole Bible, but especially *agape* in the New Testament.[17]

---

[16] Anders Nygren, *Agape and Eros*, tr. Philip S. Watson (New York: Harper and Row, 1957 [1930]). For scholarly responses to *Agape and Eros*, see Charles W. Kegley, ed., *The Philosophy and Theology of Anders Nygren* (Carbondale, Ill.: Southern Illinois University Press, 1970).

[17] For the meaning of *agape* in the Septuagint, New Testament, and beyond, see Oda Wischmeyer, *Love as Agape: The Early Christian Concept and Modern Discourse*, Wayne Coppins, trans. (Waco, Tex.: Baylor University Press, 2021).

I seek to be faithful to human experience and other dimensions of existence. And I strive for rational consistency.

The Bible has many voices and makes many claims. Most can be united in harmonious chorus, but some cannot. Scripture speaks of life in a time different from ours, although there are also remarkable similarities. Despite this, I believe the Bible's central ideas can help us understand God, ourselves, and how to live well. And *agape* can play a key role when constructing a theology of love.

Agape still matters.

(A word on grammar: I'll use "*agape*" for all instances in which forms of the word appear in scripture — whether as a verb, adjective, noun, etc. This approach should be less confusing than transliterating each form of speech *agape* takes, and less confusing than using the koine Greek alphabet. I also follow this practice for other Greek and Hebrew words. I have omitted diacritical marks that indicate vowel length and some conventions of transliteration. These decisions keep the reader's focus on the big ideas and avoid confusion.)

NYGREN AND *AGAPE*

"Whatever the reader may think of him," says Gene Outka of Anders Nygren, "one may justifiably regard his work as the beginning of the modern treatment of [*agape*]."[18] His volume *Agape and Eros* (published in English in 1957), provoked many criticisms and heated debates in the 20th century. His influence continues today. Surveying the broad-ranging discussion, Edward Collins Vacek concludes that Nygren's "insights are splendid, his mistakes are instructive, and his views are still very much alive."[19]

At the outset of *Agape and Eros*, Nygren states his purpose: "to investigate the meaning of Christian love" and "illustrate the main

---

[18] Outka, *Agape*, 1.

[19] Edward Collins Vacek, *Love, Human and Divine: The Heart of Christian Ethics* (Washington, D.C.: Georgetown University Press, 1994), 159.

changes it has undergone in the course of history."[20] If we can pin-
point "the distinctive character of the Christian conception of love,"
he says, we can discover how it differs from mistaken views.[21] Nygren's
investigation is both biblical and theological-historical.

According to Nygren, *agape* is the *only* Christian love. "Nothing
but that which bears the impress of *agape* has a right to be called
Christian love," he says.[22] In fact, "*agape* is the center of Christianity"
and "the Christian fundamental motif *par excellence*."[23] To be Christian is to express *agape*.

As Nygren sees it, *agape* has four essential aspects. It is 1) spontaneous and unmotivated, 2) indifferent to value, 3) creative, and 4)
the initiator of fellowship with God.[24] The first two aspects point to
God expressing *agape,* irrespective of creaturely value. *Agape* is un-
prompted; no creature and nothing in creation inspires it. Instead,
God seeks those who do not deserve love and can lay no claim to it.
Agape is unmerited.

The third and fourth aspects of *agape* underscore Nygren's view
of divine action. Only God expresses the creative and fellowship-en-
abling power of love. "God must Himself come to meet man," says
Nygren, "and offer him His fellowship."[25] When initiating right relationship, love creates value where there is none.[26]

Nygren gathers these ideas in a list describing the attributes of
agape. In his view, *agape*...

is sacrificial giving.

comes down from above.

---

[20] Nygren, *Agape and Eros*, 27, 39.

[21] Ibid., 29.

[22] Ibid., 92.

[23] Ibid., 48.

[24] Ibid., 75-81.

[25] Ibid., 81.

[26] Ibid., 78.

is God's way to man.

is God's grace: salvation is the work of divine love.

is unselfish love; it seeks not its own; it gives itself away.

lives for the life of God, therefore, dares to "lose it."

is freedom in giving, which depends on wealth and plenty.

is primarily God's love; "God is *agape*." Even when it is attributed to man, *agape* is patterned on divine love.

is sovereign in relation to its object and directed both to "the evil and the good;" it is spontaneous, "overflowing," "unmotivated."

creates value in its object.[27]

The Place of *Eros*

Anders Nygren rejects any legitimacy for the concept of *eros*. It is not a form of love equal to or complementary of *agape*. *Agape* and *eros* belong to two "entirely separate spiritual worlds," says Nygren, "between which no direct communication is possible."[28] According to him, *eros* has no place in the Christian's life of love.

Unfortunately, Nygren never gives a clear definition of what he means by *eros*. He uses the word to describe desire for what is valuable, a common way of understanding this form of love. He divides *eros* into two forms: earthly and heavenly. Earthly *eros* is found in the desire for what is sensual. Using a Johannine phrase, Nygren calls it "the lust and pride of life." Heavenly *eros* desires the world

---

[27] Ibid., 210.
[28] Ibid., 31-32.

beyond what we perceive. Plato originated this form when he argued humans should transcend sensual existence and strive for the good above this world.[29]

Earthly *eros* offers no challenge to *agape*, according to Nygren. It is clearly not essential to Christian faith. But heavenly *eros* is *agape*'s chief rival.[30] "When Christianity tried to express itself in Platonic terms," Nygren argues, "the *agape* motif inevitably underwent a transformation."[31] *Eros* draws us away from authentic love, which is *agape*.

Nygren offers the following characteristics of *eros*. Many stand in stark contrast with the characteristics he attributes to *agape*. In his view, *eros*...

is acquisitive desire and longing.

is an upward movement.

is man's way to God.

is man's effort: it assumes that man's salvation is his own work.

is egocentric love, a form of self-assertion of the noblest, sublimest kind.

seeks to gain its life, a life divine, immortalized.

is the will to possess, which depends on want and need.

is primarily man's love; God is the object of *eros*. Even when it is attributed to God, *eros* is patterned on human love.

---

[29] Ibid., 49-52.

[30] Ibid., 51.

[31] Ibid., 54.

is determined by the quality, beauty, and worth of its object; it is not spontaneous, but "evoked," "motivated."

recognizes value in its object.[32]

Nygren's theology of *agape* and *eros* presents a series of either/or options. In *agape,* God does all the work to "come down," he argues, and in *eros* humans do all the work to "move up" to God. In Nygren's view, divine *agape* acts irrespective of the value or lack thereof in others. By contrast, *eros* depends on the value in others for motivation. *Agape* is all about God; *eros* is all about creation. This is true of salvation too: *agape* means God does all the saving and humans play no role. *Agape* is God's love; *eros* is human love.

Nygren on Augustine and Luther

Several factors, says Nygren, led Christians to embrace *eros* rather than *agape*, or to embrace a mixture. In his view, Christian tradition played a crucial role in steering theology off track. Influential theologians confusingly connect the two loves when they should have kept them distinct. In fact, complains Nygren, distinguishing *agape* from *eros* seems unnatural to many Christians.[33]

Augustine gets the most blame in what we might call Nygren's History of Christian Love. Augustine assumes an illegitimate synthesis of *agape* and *eros*. In Augustinian theology, we find the Christian love command reinterpreted to answer philosophy's question of how to attain the highest good. We attain this good through a third love: *caritas* (charity).

In Augustine's thinking, the Greek words *agape* and *eros* are translated with the Latin word *caritas*. But this one word cannot contain what Nygren believes are radically divergent meanings of *eros*

---

[32] Ibid., 210.

[33] Ibid., 32.

and *agape*.[34] *Agape* is good and Godly; *eros* is neither. The two loves cannot be combined.

Martin Luther is the hero in Nygren's History of Christian Love. Luther and the Reformation marked a time in which Christian love was rightly elevated, because Luther smashed the illegitimate synthesis of *eros* and *agape*.[35] Along with elevating *agape*, he offers a theology that regards humans as without value, places all the work for salvation upon God, and transfers love from egoism to altruism.

"The deepest difference between Augustine and Luther can be expressed by the following formula," says Nygren. For Augustine, "fellowship with God is on God's own level, on the basis of holiness." For Luther, "fellowship with God is on our level, on the basis of sin." Augustine thinks "fellowship with God is motivated by some worth — produced, it is true, by the infusion of *caritas* — to be found in man." In Luther, "fellowship with God rests exclusively on God's unmotivated love," says Nygren, "justification is the justification of the sinner, the Christian is *simul iustus et peccator*" (simultaneously righteous and sinner).[36]

Because of their utter sinfulness, says Luther, humans cannot love God or neighbor.[37] Therefore, love must come from heaven/God.[38] God's *agape*, Nygren asserts, "seeks to make its way out into the world through the Christian as its channel."[39] Christians are like tubes through which love from above passes to neighbors below. The Christian contributes nothing.[40] When we see humans loving others, we *really* see God using humans as instruments. After all, argues

---

[34] Ibid., 30-34.

[35] Ibid., 692.

[36] Ibid., 690.

[37] Ibid., 476-532.

[38] Ibid., 733.

[39] Ibid., 218

[40] Ibid., 735, 741.

Nygren, "the Christian is not an independent center of power along-side God."[41]

Right relationship with God, says Nygren, relies on "a purely theocentric love, in which all choice on man's part is excluded."[42] That creatures have no role to play affirms "the profound significance of the idea of predestination: man has not selected God, but God has elected man."[43] God's love has no place for human freedom, says Nygren, because God's *agape* "made him a slave to God."[44]

Given Luther's low view of creaturely value, it comes as little surprise that he rejects self-love. In fact, he thinks self-love is the foundation of sin and should be annihilated.[45] In Nygren's view, Luther brilliantly ousts *caritas* while building up *agape* as selflessness. True Christian love is free from desire and ego.

LOVE AND THE OLD TESTAMENT

Nygren claims his view of *agape* and theology comes from scripture. But we need to look at the Bible to assess the accuracy of such claims. We should ask about the meanings of *agape* and other loves in the whole Bible.

Agape is a Greek word, so it's not found in the Hebrew-language portion of the Bible. At least not the word itself. One might argue that a book whose title has two Greek words — *Agape and Eros* — can avoid Christian scripture written in Hebrew. But this argument weakens when we remember it's the *meaning* of *agape* and *eros* that concerns Nygren, not just the words.

Nygren asks little about what Old Testament writers say about love. There's no discussion of *hesed* or *ahavah*, two prominent Hebrew words translated "love." Christians who believe this portion

---

[41] Ibid., 734.

[42] Ibid., 213.

[43] Ibid., 214.

[44] Ibid., 94.

[45] Ibid., 709, 713.

of the Bible should be considered when constructing a theology of love should be alarmed by his neglect. The Old Testament is twice the size of the New Testament, and its ideas should contribute to the meaning of Christian love.

Nygren's avoidance of the Old Testament reflects his belief that *agape* theology is "a new creation of Christianity."[46] "The history of the Christian idea of love," he says, "begins with an entirely new and peculiarly Christian fundamental motif of religion and ethics — the *Agape* motif."[47] This means Christianity is "something altogether new and different in kind from Judaism."[48] Judaism tended "to make love central in ethical and religious relationships," Nygren says,[49] so the meaning of Christian *agape* differs from love's meaning in the Old Testament.[50] The love spoken of in the Hebrew-language scriptures was for particular people who kept covenants.[51] *Agape* is for all.

We can detect problems with Nygren's theology here. Most Christians will believe God's love is universal in some ways, but particular in others. Old Testament passages speak of a special love between God and Israel (e.g., Hosea 11:1), but they also speak of God's love for aliens and strangers (Deut. 10:18-19). In fact, the Lord commands Israel to love strangers "as yourself" (Lev. 19:33-34). Unlike Nygren, Christians generally have seen continuity between these two portions of the Bible, although there are differences.

---

[46] Ibid., 48.

[47] Ibid., 53.

[48] Ibid., 67.

[49] Ibid., 62.

[50] Nygren argues that the word *agape* is only found scattered throughout ancient Greek literature and the Septuagint. Catherine Osborne points out, however, that its use is more extensive than Nygren realizes. The frequency of *agape* in the New Testament reflects the authors' ties and familiarity with the Septuagint, instead of Nygren's claim that *agape* identifies unique theological concerns entertained first by New Testament writers (Catherine Osborne, *Eros Unveiled: Plato and the God of Love* [Oxford: Clarendon, 1994], 2). A. H. Armstrong also argues that Nygren's reading of love in non-biblical history is erroneous ("Platonic *Eros* and Christian *Agape*," *Downside Review* 79 [Spring 1961]: 106-120).

[51] Nygren, *Agape and Eros*, 63.

Nygren admits Old Testament writers witness to some of what he means by *agape*. God demonstrated *agape*, for instance, in response to Israelites who broke covenants (e.g., see Exodus and Hosea). He also admits the Old Testament supports *eros* theologies. For instance, God desires Israel to act in particular ways (e.g., Ex. 34:14; Dt. 5:9; Is. 58:6-7; Hos. 6:6, 11:8). In Nygren's mind, the presence of *eros* meanings counts against the legitimacy of an Old Testament theology of love.

Nygren doesn't mention that Old Testament writers also use *philia* love language. Classic examples are the friendship love between God and Moses (Ex. 33:11) and between God and Abraham (II Chron. 20:7; Is. 41:8).[52] This form of love also appears in other passages, including the friendship love between David and Jonathan (1 Sam. 20). If we understand *philia* to describe loving friendship, covenants, and cooperation, the Old Testament speaks often and approvingly of this form of love.

Nygren fails to develop the connection between the two great love commands emphasized by Jesus and their origin in the Old Testament (Leviticus 19:2, 18, 33-34). He admits these commands would be a natural place to reflect on the meaning of Christian love.[53] But he says starting with Jesus' love commands would "bar our own way to understanding" *agape*, because the great love commands come from the Old Testament.[54]

My Response to Nygren's Use of the Old Testament

Many Christians will probably join me in alarm that Nygren fails to take as central the commandments Jesus regarded as the greatest of all (Mt. 22:36, 37; Mk. 12:29, 31).[55] This alone might be grounds to

---

[52] John Burnaby argues that friendship love is common both to the Old and New Testaments and not restricted to mutual love between humans (*Amor Dei*, 18 & elsewhere).

[53] Nygren, *Agape and Eros*, 61.

[54] Ibid.

[55] For a thorough discussion of each gospel's record of the great commandments, see Paul Victor Furnish, *The Love Command in the New Testament* (Nashville: Abingdon, 1972), ch. 1.

reject Nygren's theology. He's so committed to the novelty of New Testament *agape* and inferiority of the Old Testament that he cannot privilege the love commands Jesus prized as the core of Christian love.

Nygren cannot embrace Jesus' love commands because his assumptions prevent such an embrace. Not only do the love commands originate in the Old Testament, but they also require human love of God. Creatures must love their Creator. But Nygren thinks authentic love only comes from God, and nothing comes from us.[56]

We should wonder why Jesus — the centerpiece of Christianity — would advocate love commands that by their plain meanings oppose the "new religion" Nygren thinks Jesus initiates. Nygren actually admits his views "admittedly strain" the love commandments in the Old and New Testaments "almost to their breaking-point."[57] But surely something is amiss when a theology of love strains the commands Jesus himself most emphasized.

Instead, Jesus' own view of love should reign in a Christian theology of love.

Nygren fails to account for the diversity of love portrayed in the Old Testament. This diversity comes in both the Hebrew love words and the diverse forms of love we find in the texts. Love in Hebrew-language scriptures takes the form of friendship, romance, sacrifice, covenant, forgiveness, delight, sensuality, loyalty, and more.[58]

Although Nygren may think diverse forms of love in the Old Testament strengthen his claim that *agape* is original to Christianity,

---

[56] Nygren, *Agape and Eros*, 127-132.

[57] Ibid., 93

[58] Among the many texts that explore love in the Old Testament, see especially Michael J. Chan and Brent A. Strawn, eds., *What Kind of God? Collected Essays of Terence E. Fretheim* (Winona Lake, IN: Eisenbrauns, 2015); Terence Fretheim, *The Suffering of God: An Old Testament Perspective* (Philadelphia: Fortress, 1984); Joel S. Kaminsky, *Yet I Loved Jacob: Reclaiming the Biblical Concept of Election* (Nashville: Abingdon, 2007); Brad E. Kelle and Stephanie Smith Matthews, eds., *Encountering the God of Love: Portraits from the Old Testament* (Kansas City, Mo.: Foundery, 2021); Jon D. Levenson, *The Love of God: Divine Gift, Human Gratitude, and Mutual Faithfulness in Judaism* (Princeton: Princeton, 2016); Marty Alan Michelson, *The Greatest Commandment: The LORD's Invitation to Love* (Oklahoma City, Ok.: Dust Jacket, 2012); J. Richard Middleton, *The Liberating Image: The Imago Dei in Genesis 1* (Grand Rapids, MI: Brazos, 2005).

I think they should prompt him to reconsider his views. It should prompt him to celebrate how the two canonical Christian testaments and two faith traditions — Judaism and Christianity — are remarkably similar, despite their differences.

Nygren's failure to consider what I am calling pluriform love in the Old Testament undermines his claim to conform to scripture.

NYGREN ON *AGAPE* IN THE NEW TESTAMENT

Anders Nygren argues for his *agape* theories based on the New Testament. Our investigation of love's meaning in those writings requires exploring what Jesus, Paul, John, and other New Testament writers have to say. And an adequate investigation needs to explore the meanings not just of *agape*, but also other forms of love.[59]

The New Testament meaning of love, says Nygren, "has as its prototype the *agape* manifested by God." This means it "must be spontaneous, unmotivated, uncalculating, and unconditional."[60] Love for God cannot include desire (*eros*) or friendship (*philia*). Desiring love is improper, says Nygren, because it makes God "the means for the satisfaction of man's desire." God should not be a means to any end. Friendship love is improper, because it "presupposes an equality between Divine and human love which does not exist."[61] *Eros* and *philia*, says Nygren, are "excluded in the sovereignty of divine love."[62]

The distinctive character of Christian love, says Nygren, is found in Jesus' words: "Love your enemies" (Mt. 5:44; Lk. 6:27).[63] Jesus represents God's love when he fellowships with the sinful. He "came not

---

[59] For diverse ways Christians throughout the centuries have understood Christian love, see Bernard V. Brady, *Christian Love: How Christians Through the Ages Have Understood Love* (Washington, D.C.: Georgetown University Press, 2003); Carter Lindberg, *Love: A Brief History Through Christianity* (Oxford: Blackwell, 2008); David P. Polk, *God of Empowering Love* (Anoka, Mn.: Process Century, 2016); Brent J. Schmidt, *Relational Grace* (Provo, Ut.: BYU Press, 2015).

[60] Nygren, *Agape and Eros*, 91.

[61] Ibid.

[62] Ibid.

[63] Ibid., 66-70.

to call the righteous, but sinners" (Mark 2:17).[64] Nygren believes this biblical statement confirms his view that humans have nothing of value to motivate divine love.

As Nygren sees it, Jesus offers fellowship to the unrighteous, while the righteous go away empty.[65] God does not love sinners because they are better, however. Humans have nothing to offer, so fellowship with God depends exclusively upon initiating *agape*. God, in sovereignty, loves considering no action by or value of the recipient.

Jesus and Sinners

The bulk of Nygren's argument for *agape* rests on how he interprets the sentence, "I did not come to call the righteous, but sinners." It fits his conviction that humans have nothing valuable to offer God and play no role in salvation. Nygren reads the New Testament through a lens that says humans are depraved and passive. They cannot love; God uses them as instruments.

An examination of the New Testament shows otherwise, however. When Nygren quotes Jesus saying, "I did not come to call the righteous, but sinners," for instance, he skips other statements in the same context. Jesus says, "Go and learn what this means, 'I desire mercy, not sacrifice.' For I have come to call not the righteous but sinners" (Mt. 9:13). These words explicitly refer Jesus' hearers to Old Testament texts (Hosea 6:6; Micah 6:6-8), although Nygren wants to paint *agape* as Christianity's innovation. But Nygren's proof text actually comes from Judaism.

Matthew's words also undermine Nygren's rejection of *eros*. According to Jesus, God has desires: "I desire mercy." Isn't that *eros*? In addition, creaturely actions play a role in fulfilling those desires: Creatures fulfill God's desires when they show mercy. Matthew's text

---

[64] Ibid., 68.

[65] Ibid., 72.

implies that rather than being mere instruments, humans can love and thereby satisfy God's *eros*.

Nygren's *agape* proof text fails to support his *agape* theology.

Jesus' Parables

Nygren thinks Jesus' parables support God's *agape* as spontaneous, creative, and the initiator of fellowship. He says the parables show unmotivated divine love. "It is futile to try to find a motive for God's love for the lost," says Nygren.[66] God's *agape* makes a mockery of all attempts at divine motivation.[67]

According to Nygren, four parables illustrate this. Jesus' parable of the prodigal son shows the Father's *agape* has no rational ground (Lk. 15:11ff).[68] The parable of the vineyard and laborers upends the law of equal pay for equal work (Mt. 20:1ff). The master gives all workers the same wage, and those who think they deserve more wages refuse to accept unmotivated love.[69] The parable of the sower illustrates God's free and unmotivated love to all (Mk. 4:3ff). Just as the sower spreads seeds with no regard for where they land, God loves others without regard for their value.[70] Finally, the parable of the unmerciful steward shows an *agape* ethic (Mt. 18:23ff): The servant whose debt was forgiven should show unmotivated mercy toward his peer.[71]

A closer look at the parables, however, shows they *do not* support Nygren's *agape* theory. At least not fully. In the prodigal son story, for instance, the father does not do *all* the work to reestablish fellowship with the son. The son's choice to return home plays a crucial part of the story; he contributes to re-establishing fellowship. The wayward

---

[66] Nygren, *Agape and Eros*, 88.

[67] Ibid., 82.

[68] Ibid., 86.

[69] Ibid., 88-90.

[70] Ibid., 90.

[71] Ibid., 91.

son realizes he would be better off as his father's servant than destitute in a foreign land and chooses to find a way to reunite with his
father.

Had Nygren chosen the two "lost" stories preceding the prodigal
son story, he would have better grounds for his view that the lost play
no role in being found. The lost seem to be passive like a coin and
sheep. But those stories explicitly affirm that the lost object's worth
motivates searchers. If God is a like a shepherd seeking a valuable
sheep or a woman seeking a valuable coin, God must consider lost
people valuable too.

The parable of the vineyard workers also fails to support Nygren's
agape proposals. While the master gives workers the same wage no
matter the amount of work, he rewards them. He gives them something for their labor; their actions motivate the master. Applied to
God's love, we might say that what creatures do at least partly motivates divine love. And creatures play a role in *how* God loves.

Nygren refers to the parable of the sower to argue that God, like
the extravagant sower, spreads love no matter the status of those who
receive it. Scripture supports the idea that God loves the righteous,
the unrighteous, and all creation, so Nygren has good grounds for
touting universal divine love. But Nygren ignores outright Jesus' explanation of the story: "The measure you give will be the measure
you get" (Mk. 4:24). Either the disciples' love of others should motivate their spread of the gospel, or what the disciples do motivates the
measure of blessing God gives. Either claim undermines Nygren's
view that *agape* has nothing to do with motivation.

The parable of the unmerciful steward is equally problematic.
Nygren refers to it to argue the steward's mercy for neighbor should
be the same as the king's mercy for the steward. But the king's last
act was to hand over the steward for torture. The steward's failure to
show mercy motivated the king's merciless response. This implies
God's activity, like the king's, is at least partially motivated by others.
Divine love has a responsive element.

Nygren does not address at all the story Jesus specifically tells to
explain *agape* of neighbor: the parable of the good Samaritan (Lk.

10:25-37). Christians often cite it as crucial for understanding how Jesus thought about love. In the story, Jesus says a neighbor's condition (a victim of beating and theft) motivates a foreigner to express love. The stranger has compassion for the victim. In the story, needs motivate *agape*.

Nygren often criticizes *eros* as a love motivated by the object or person loved. If we accept this understanding of *eros*, Jesus' parables seem to tell us God's love involves *eros*, even if that word is not used in the text. God *eros* loves humans, because God values them. In fact, Jesus says God values humans more than sheep or birds (Mt. 6:26;10:31;12:12; Lk. 12:7, 24). Although writers don't put the word *eros* in Jesus' mouth, he preaches divine desire.

Jesus also urges listeners to strive for what is good. They should, for instance, "strive first for the kingdom of God and his righteousness" (Mt. 6:33; Lk. 12:31). Jesus refers to the Kingdom of heaven as a treasure one desires to obtain as a fine pearl, the purchase of which requires sacrificing other things (Mt. 13:44, 46). In these instances, Jesus expects lovers to be motivated to get what is valuable. This opposes Nygren's *agape* theology, which says authentic love is unconcerned with the value of what is loved.

Jesus' parables do not support Nygren's *agape* theology.

The Apostle Paul

Nygren thinks the Apostle Paul's writing provides the strongest support for his views.[72] "No words are too strong for him," he says, "to press home [*agape*'s] spontaneous and unmotivated character."[73] But just as Nygren fails to present the full picture of how Jesus understands love, he fails to present Paul fully.

---

[72] Although I recognize that some of the New Testament letters attributed to Paul were likely not written by him, I will refer to these writings as the Pauline letters for sake of convenience.

[73] Ibid., 155.

A feature "especially characteristic of the Pauline idea of *agape*," Nygren says, is its "opposition to all that can be called 'self-love.'"[74] To illustrate his point, Nygren quotes Paul's words in 1 Corinthians 13:5: "Love seeks not its own." But Nygren fails to note that in other writing, Paul endorses healthy self-love. Paul commands men in Ephesus to *agape* their own bodies, for instance (Eph. 5:28, 33).[75]

Building from Luther's theology, Nygren says the proper human response to God is not love but faith. "There is no question of Paul's wishing to eliminate the spiritual reality denoted by the phrase 'love towards God,'" says Nygren. Paul "merely seeks to give it its proper name, which he calls 'faith.'"[76]

While Paul often speaks of faith *in* God, he also uses *agape* to describe human love *for* God. "Anyone who loves (*agape*) God is known by him," he tells Corinthian readers (1 Cor. 8:3). We find *agape* in Paul's reference to "those who love God" (Rm. 8:28); he says God prepares good things "for those who *agape* him" (1 Cor. 2:9).

Nygren prefers Pauline writings, in part because he thinks Paul "knows nothing of any distinction between true and false *agape*."[77] Nygren believes Paul always uses *agape* to identify proper love. A look at scripture shows, however, that Paul occasionally refers to false *agape*. Paul says Demas deserted him because he was "in love (*agape*) with this present world" (2 Tim. 4:10).

Not even the Apostle Paul is a consistent advocate for Nygren's *agape* theories.[78]

---

[74] Ibid., 130.

[75] This assumes, of course, that Paul was the author of Ephesians. Nygren makes this assumption.

[76] Nygren, *Agape and Eros*, 127.

[77] Ibid., 156.

[78] James D. G. Dunn explores the Apostle Paul's views on love and raises them to prominence. See *The Theology of Paul the Apostle* (Grand Rapids, Mich.: Eerdmans, 1998). See also J. Paul Sampley, *Walking in Love: Moral Progress and Spiritual Growth in the Apostle Paul* (Minneapolis: Fortress, 2016).

Johannine Writings

A look at John's New Testament writings shows them to be even more detrimental to Nygren's ideas. Nygren acknowledges the problems, but he does not reformulate his views.

The only Johannine statement Nygren strongly endorses is "God is *agape*" (1 John 4:8, 16).[79] This sentence only fits his *agape* theology, however, if interpreted in a way that does not align with most scriptural statements on God and love. Nygren packs into this three-word pronouncement all the theological ideas I've been criticizing.

According to Nygren, a "doubleness" of meaning is present in John's gospels and epistles. Nygren admits John claims God is *agape*, but also that creatures can *agape* God. "The Johannine idea agrees with the Synoptic idea of *agape* in that it represents Christian love as manifested in two directions: towards God and towards men," he says.[80] Rather than accept John's use of *agape*, however, Nygren dismisses human love for God.

John uses *agape* to describe mutual love of those in the community. People should *agape* those with whom they have close relations. This use does not fit Nygren's view that *agape* only comes down from Heaven and is oriented toward sinners. Rather than embrace the legitimacy of friendship or communal love among humans, Nygren confines *agape* to fellowship within God and ignores some biblical passages.[81]

John speaks of a special *agape* between God and Jesus. In a prayer, Jesus says, "you loved me before the foundation of the world" (Jn. 17:24; cf. 3:35; 5:20; 15:9). *Agape,* in this instance, cannot have the meaning Nygren gives it. After all, according to Nygren, *agape* can only be expressed for sinners and those without value. Jesus never sinned. Even if we say Jesus took up sin on the cross, Jesus speaks of God's *agape* "before the foundation of the world."

---

[79] Nygren, *Agape and Eros*, 147.

[80] Ibid., 148.

[81] Ibid., 154.

Nygren realizes problems arise when saying Jesus loves God, and God loves Jesus. "If the eternal love of the Father and the Son is the prototype of all that can be called *agape*," he confesses, "the question inevitably arises: Does *agape* here keep its original character? Is it still absolutely unmotivated?" Wouldn't it be the case "that the inherent worth of the Son is what makes Him the object of the Father's love?"[82] Interestingly, he does not answer his own question.

John also uses *agape* in ways that suggest *eros* meanings. The Father will love the disciples, says John, *because* they keep Jesus' word (Jn. 14:23). The Father loves Jesus *because* he lays down his life (Jn. 10:17). In these cases, God's love is motivated in some sense.

After examining the Johannine literature, Nygren admits a mingling of the *eros* and *agape* senses of love in it. God's love for sinners and God's love of Jesus implies *agape* may or may not be motivated.[83] But rather than reconsider his view, Nygren concludes that John — the disciple whom Jesus loved and whose writings are saturated with love language — misunderstands *agape*.

For these reasons, I believe Nygren misunderstands the meanings of biblical *agape*.

PHILIA AND EROS IN THE NEW TESTAMENT

I've focused primarily upon Nygren's claims about *agape*. I shift now to show how *philia* is also present in the New Testament. In fact, the verb and noun forms of *philia* appear 30 times. Most occur in the gospels.

The way biblical writers use *philia* undermines Nygren's *agape* theology. Nygren knows this, and he regrets that writers use *philia* in positive ways.[84] In John's gospel, for instance, Jesus says the Father

---

[82] Ibid, 152.

[83] Ibid., 151-59.

[84] Ibid., 153-55.

expresses *philia* for the Son and for disciples (5:20; 16:27).[85] In the gospels of Matthew and Luke, Jesus responds to those who accuse him of expressing *philia* for sinners, and his response implies his accusers are correct (Mt. 11:19; Lk. 7:34).

Writers of scripture use *philia* to speak of love as doing good or benefiting. Jesus expresses *philia* for those of ill-repute (Lk 7:34; Mt. 11:19). Peter admonishes readers to *philia* (1 Pt. 3:8; 4:9; 2 Pt. 1:7). The writer to the Hebrews commands *philia* toward those in the fellowship and toward strangers (Heb. 13:1, 2). James says Moses was a friend of God and uses a *philia* derivative to say this (Js. 2:23). Each instance undercuts Nygren's claim that *agape* is the only authentically Christian love.

Even the Apostle Paul — whom Nygren praises as endorsing his thesis that *agape* is the only authentically Christian love — uses *philia* to talk about Christian love. Paul says Christian leaders should *philia* what is good (Tit. 1:8) and *philia* others (1 Tim. 3:2). He says *philia* is one mark of the true Christian (Rom. 12:10; 12:13). Paul refers to *philia* for God (2 Tim. 3:4) and says God expresses *philia* for humans (Tit. 3:4). In fact, Paul places a curse on those who do not *philia* the Lord (1 Cor. 16:22).

The biblical authors furthermore use *agape* and *philia* in ways that appear identical. John uses both *agape* and *philia* to talk about God's love for Jesus (Jn. 3:35; 5:20). The story of the raising of Lazarus uses both *agape* and *philia* (Jn. 11), with no apparent difference in the meaning. John is called "the one whom Jesus loved," and forms of both *agape* and *philia* are used. Writers use both *agape* and *philia* to describe (1) the Father's love for the Son, (2) the Lord's love for humans, (3) Jesus' love for humans, (4) human love for Jesus, and (5) human love for humans.[86]

---

[85] Passages in John's writings in which a form of *philia* occurs: John 5:20; 11:3, 36; 12:25; 15:13-15, 19; 16:27; 20:2; 21:15-17; 3 John 15; Revelation. 3:19. John also records Jesus' saying that the Son *agapes* the Father (Jn. 14:31).

[86] Roy F. Butler, *The Meaning of Agapao and Phileo in the Greek New Testament* (Lawrence, Kans.: Coronado, 1977), 70, 86-87.

Commentators are mixed in opinions on why both *agape* and *philia* are used in Jesus' questions for Peter: "Do you love me?" (Jn. 21:15-19). Because John often uses the two words interchangeably, there is likely no special meaning when Jesus shifts from *agape* to *philia*.

In a minority of instances, *philia* is not a positive love. Jesus says hypocrites "*philia* to pray" to attract attention (Mt. 6:5) and "*philia* the place of honor" (Mt. 23:6). Scribes "*philia* to be greeted with respect in the marketplaces" (Lk. 20:46). Jesus says those who "*philia* father or mother more than me is not worthy of me" (Mk. 10:37). But even with these exceptions, *philia* is predominantly used to describe action that promotes well-being.

Anders Nygren fails to afford *philia* the legitimacy it deserves.

The word "*eros*" is not present in the New Testament at all. Neither are other Greek words we might translate as "love," including *storge*, *ludus*, *epithymia*, and more.[87] But if *eros* means something like "desire" or "attraction to what's valuable," its meaning is certainly present in scripture.

Scholars speculate as to why some Greek words for love are present in the New Testament and others are not. New Testament scholar James Moffatt thinks, for instance, that Paul avoided *eros* because his readers might identify it with lust and immorality.[88] Catherine Osborne argues that the widespread use of *agape* instead of *eros* or other Greek love words reflects a cultural-linguistic trend more than a theological concern.[89] All of this is conjecture.

Even though Paul does not use the word *eros*, he uses language with *eros* meanings. He commands Philippians, for instance, to seek an *eros* orientation. "Beloved," Paul says, "whatever is true, whatever is honorable, whatever is just, whatever is pure, whatever is pleasing,

---

[87] C. S. Lewis explores *agape, eros, philia,* and *storge* in *The Four Loves* (Glasgow: Collins, 1981).

[88] James Moffatt, *Love in the New Testament,* (London: Hodder and Stoughton, 1929), 35. Moffatt notes that Christians following the first century were quick to use *eros* to talk about appropriate love (39).

[89] Catherine Osborne, *Eros Unveiled: Plato and the God of Love* (Oxford: Clarendon, 1994).

whatever is commendable, if there is any excellence and if there is anything worthy of praise, think about these things" (4:8). Following this list of values, Paul says, "keep doing" these things (4:9).

Biblical translators often render *agape* with *eros* meanings. *Agape* can be translated "to long for" (2 Tm. 4:8), "to prefer" or "to desire" (2 Tm. 4:10; Jn. 3:19; 12:43), "to prize" or "to value" (Hb. 1:9; Rv. 12:11), and "to be fond of" (Lk. 7:5).[90] These English words and phrases have *eros* elements because they point to desire for what is valuable, beautiful, or worthwhile.

From the absence of the word in the New Testament, however, Nygren argues that God does not *eros* humans and humans should not *eros* God. In Nygren's view, creatures have nothing of value for God to desire, and humans should have faith in God rather than love. I have shown though that scripture speaks positively of human love for God. And God desires positive relationships with humans.[91]

The *meaning* of *eros* is in scripture, even though the word does not appear.

CONCLUSION

I have presented some of the main ideas in the 20th century's most influential book on *agape*, *Agape and Eros* by Anders Nygren, strongly criticizing Nygren's analysis of *agape*. He fails to account well for the diverse understandings of love in the biblical text. I largely reject his theology as well.

Nygren fails to take love in the Old Testament seriously, at least in terms of how it dovetails with New Testament views of love. He does not champion the *agape* commandments Jesus himself thought most important, which are found in Hebrew scriptures.

---

[90] For an examination of these meanings, see Moffatt, *Love in the New Testament*, 48-51. See also Francis Watson, *Agape, Eros, Gender: Towards a Pauline Sexual Ethic* (Cambridge: Cambridge University Press, 2000).

[91] On the good life as conceived by biblical writers, see Brent A Strawn, ed., *The Bible and the Pursuit of Happiness* (Oxford: Oxford University Press, 2012).

Nygren fails to account well for *agape* in the gospels, in Paul's letters, in the Johannine writings, and more. He ignores the diverse meanings of *agape* in scripture. And he fails to acknowledge *philia*, *eros*, and other forms of love as legitimate.

The Bible does not support Nygren's *agape* theology.

This chapter has largely been critical. I presented Nygren's widely influential *agape* claims and showed their inadequacy. This work of deconstruction will set the stage for positive reconstruction to come.

4

Doing Good, Essentially Loving, and "In Spite of" Love

*A*lthough *agape* has many meanings in the New Testament, biblical writers overwhelmingly use the word to describe action to do what is positive, good, or beneficial. I've shown *agape* and the other biblical love words refer primarily to promoting well-being. Love does good and seeks flourishing.

While Nygren's proposals have problems, they alert us to the fact that theologies of love make claims about God, creation, value, freedom, power, and more. Christians cannot account for love, and *agape* in particular, through a word study alone. Words are not isolated repositories of absolute meaning. We must explore the various facets of theology these words imply in context, including how God and creatures act, relate, experience well-being, and...love.

Nygren's theology derives primarily from his belief that God loves sinners. Most Christians would agree, perhaps citing the Apostle Paul who writes, "God proves his love for us in that while we were still sinners, Christ died for us" (Rom. 5:8). It's not controversial to say God loves sinners, or that God loves everyone. "God so loved the world..." states one of the Bible's most famous verses.

But Nygren adds other claims. He says humans cannot express authentic love, for instance, unless God expresses it for them. Creatures are passive instruments without power independent from God. Nygren says humans are valueless in themselves, and God's love does not desire or respond to creaturely value. He claims *agape* is always self-sacrificial and opposes self-love. Humans cannot be friends with God. Nygren thinks God sovereignly controls humans, predestining them.

The Bible does not support these additional claims, at least not very well. They reflect Nygren's embrace of Luther's theology of human depravity and his rejection of Augustine's theology of desire.

An adequate theology of love, I will argue, says God always loves creatures *and* creatures have intrinsic value. Love is sometimes self-sacrificial but sometimes acts for the good of the self. An adequate theology says God is the source and power of creaturely loving without portraying creatures as passive tubes God controls. Creatures love freely. The theology I propose affirms giving-and-receiving relationships between God and creation, including friendship. It builds from love witnessed in the Old and New Testaments, seeing them as more continuous than Nygren does.

In the first portion of this chapter, I return to what the New Testament says about *agape*. I aim to show 1) that *agape* overwhelmingly means promoting well-being, and 2) the ways *agape* promotes well-being vary. *Agape* takes an assortment of forms.

In the latter parts of the chapter, I pick up key theological ideas that emerge in a biblical exploration of *agape*. I will argue that God by nature — necessarily — loves creatures. God initiates relationship with creatures and is the source of their love. I propose a particular meaning for *agape* as one form of love among others. *Agape* responds to enemies, harm, or foreigners by acting to promote well-being.

EXPLORING *AGAPE* IN THE SYNOPTIC GOSPELS

In the overwhelming majority of cases, biblical writers use *agape* to describe actions that promote well-being. But the forms *agape* takes when doing this vary. *Agape* points to the general meaning of love but also identifies specific expressions.

In the Sermon on the Mount recorded by Matthew, Jesus tells listeners to *agape* both neighbors and enemies. If we help only those who help us, he says, we do not love rightly. God helps everyone, which includes sending rain and sun to the righteous and wicked alike. Jesus' final charge to "be perfect as your heavenly father is perfect" means we should imitate God by doing good to neighbors and enemies (Mt. 5:43-48). As a form of love, *agape* helps both friends and foes.

Matthew, Mark, and Luke each use *agape* when quoting the love commands Jesus considered greatest. "*Agape* the Lord your God with all your heart, and all your soul, and with all your mind," writes Matthew, quoting Jesus. And "*agape* your neighbor as yourself." Jesus says the law and prophets hang on these two commands (22:37-39). Mark records Jesus saying, "There is no commandment greater than these" (12:31).

Luke explains what it means to *agape* by telling a story. In it, a foreigner helps a beaten man laying along the road (10:25-37). In this case, to *agape* one's neighbor is to do good to the injured stranger. The foreigner puts a beaten man on a donkey, takes him to receive health care, and pays his expenses. *Agape* acts for well-being by help-ing the injured and needy.

The Sermon on the Mount in Luke's gospel uses *agape* to address what it means to do good when others do harm — cursing, mistreat-ing, slapping cheeks, or taking coats. Jesus tells listeners to *agape* en-emies, just as God is kind to the ungrateful and wicked.[1] In this case, *agape* takes the form of being kind to those who harm us.

Luke tells a story about a Centurian's *agape*. The Centurian ex-pressed *agape* by building a synagogue for Israel at his own expense (7:5). In the story, the Centurian comes to Jesus seeking help. His servant, whom he "valued highly," was sick. Luke chooses the Greek word *entimos*, translated "valued highly," to express the Centurian's esteem for this servant. He reserves *agape* for describing the Centurian's doing good — building a synagogue at his own expense. *Agape* takes a form of love that benefits others at some cost to oneself.

---

[1] In Luke's telling of the Sermon the Mount, Jesus shifts from *agape* to *oiktirmones*: "be mer-ciful as your Father in heaven is merciful" (36). *Oiktirmones* is a rarely-used Greek word. We also find it in James, when he says the Lord is merciful (5:11). Luke's point in the passage seems to be that both *oiktirmones* and *agape* do good even to those who harm.

In a story about Jesus and the "scandalous woman," Luke uses *agape* three times (7:31-50). Two people are forgiven their debts, and Jesus says the one forgiven the larger debt shows greater *agape*. Then Jesus forgives a scandalous woman, and she expresses *agape* in response. In these passages, *agape* takes the form of grateful love.

Jesus criticizes Pharisees for paying "a ten percent income tax on mint and rue and herbs of all kinds, and neglect[ing] justice and the *agape* of God" (Lk. 11:42). Jesus' point seems to be that some follow rules but ignore the broader work of promoting overall flourishing. God wants well-being established more than the rules followed.

In a few instances, *agape* pertains to priorities rather than to doing good. "No man can serve two masters," says Jesus. "A slave will either hate the one and *agape* the other or be devoted to the one and despise the other" (Mt. 6:24; Lk. 16:13). Pharisees have *agape* of places of prestige (Lk. 11:43). In about five percent of the Gospel instances of the use of *agape*, it describes priorities rather than promoting well-being.

When Jesus is called "beloved" at his baptism (Mt. 3:17; Mk. 1:11; Lk. 3:22) and the transfiguration (Mt. 17:5; Mk., 9:7), a form of *agape* is also used. In Matthew's account of the transfiguration, the voice that calls Jesus "beloved" adds these words: "with whom my soul is well pleased." This mirrors a passage in Matthew's gospel that connects Jesus to Isaiah: "Here is my servant, the one I have chosen, the one I *agape*, in whom I delight" (Mt. 12:18).

Are these phrases "with whom I am well-pleased" and "in whom I delight" restating the meaning of *agape*? Or does *agape* mean something more? When Jesus is called "beloved" and "the one I love," does *agape* mean God *likes* Jesus or *does good* to him? If *agape* in these instances means God *likes* Jesus, the phrases "in whom I am well pleased" and "in whom I delight" are redundancies. But if *agape* means God acts for Jesus' well-being, the phrases add information. God is pleased/delighted with Jesus *and* acts for his good. The latter interpretation makes more sense. God both likes Jesus *and* acts for his well-being.

AGAPE IN JOHN'S WRITINGS

In his epistles and gospel, the Apostle John uses *agape* often. He apparently calls himself the disciple Jesus' loved with *agape*. John typically uses *agape* to mean promoting well-being. His *agape* statements provide ideas a theology of love should embrace.

Jesus explains to Nicodemus what it means to be born again. This explanation includes a passage explaining God's love: "For God so *agaped* the world that he gave his only Son, that everyone who believes in him may not perish but may have eternal life" (Jn. 3:16). God's *agape* does good. It is not restricted to a few; it provides the opportunity for eternal life to everyone. In this case, *agape* takes the form of life-giving love available to all.

In the thirteenth chapter of John's gospel, we find Jesus saying, "This is my commandment: that you *agape* one another as I have *agaped* you. No one has greater *agape* than this, to lay down one's life for one's friends" (Jn. 15:12-13). Earlier, in chapter 13, we find Jesus praying, "Just as I have *agaped* you, you should *agape* one another. By this everyone will know that you are my disciples: if you have *agape for* one another" (Jn. 13:34-35). Promoting well-being may involve laying down one's life for the good of others. *Agape* sometimes takes the form of self-sacrifice.

In various Johannine passages, Jesus ties *agape* to obedience. "If you *agape* me, you will keep my commandments," he says. "They who have my commandments and keep them are those who *agape* me...Those who *agape* me will keep my word, and my Father will *agape* them...Whoever does not *agape* me does not keep my words" (Jn. 14:15, 21, 23-24). "To *agape* God is to keep his commandments," writes John in his first letter. "Let us *agape* one another. And this is love, that we walk according to his commandments; this is the commandment just as you have heard it from the beginning — you must walk in it." (2 Jn. 5b-6). In these passages, *agape* involves obedience to God's commands, and those are given for the good of creatures and creation.

Commanding *agape* and linking it to obedience raises questions. Can love *be* commanded? If love is primarily a matter of feelings and if feelings are not entirely within our control, it's difficult to see how love can be commanded. Healthy commands assume those commanded can obey. So if love is primarily about action that promotes well-being and we decide our actions to some degree, it seems love can be commanded.[2]

Love can primarily be about action *and* involve emotions. Positive, negative, or otherwise neutral emotions accompany love.[3] Sometimes, emotions play a leading role in deciding to love. We can also cultivate positive emotions, which then help us love more consistently.[4] Rather than say love is *only* about decisions or *only* about feelings, it would be better to say emotions accompany actions. And emotions can aid or fail to support decisions to love.

John's Love Theology

John's longest epistle offers profound *agape* theology. Readers have heard "from the beginning," he writes, they should "*agape* one another" (3:11). That's what God's children do: they "*agape* their brothers and sisters" (3:1, 10). *Agape* here takes the form of familial love.

The one who expresses *agape* abides in light and has no cause for stumbling (1 Jn. 2:10). Those who do not *agape* walk in darkness (1 Jn. 2:10-11). Those who *agape* pass from death to life (3:14). In these

---

[2] Jacob Milgrom asks the questions of obedience and love in *Leviticus 17-22* in *Anchor Bible* (New York: Doubleday, 2000), 1653.

[3] Lovers do not simply feel in one moment and simply choose in the next. Feelings and choices intertwine. Sometimes feelings dominate, however, but other times decisions dominate. As Stephen Post puts it, "co-primacy between emotion and reason is the fitting alternative to those who would diminish the importance of either capacity" (*Unlimited Love: Altruism, Compassion and Service* [Philadelphia: Templeton, 2003], 67).

[4] I'm grateful to Shai Held for helping to clarify in my mind the relationship between commanding love and the emotions that accompany love. For an exploration of the relation of emotions to reason, see Samuel M. Powell, *The Impassioned Life: Reason and Emotion in the Christian Tradition* (Minneapolis: Fortress, 2016).

cases, *agape* takes the forms of enlightenment and life, and it benefits those expressing it.

If someone has material possessions but doesn't help those without, asks John rhetorically, "how does the *agape* of God abide in that person?" (3:17) *Agape* helps the needy "in truth and actions" (3:18). We know what *agape* looks like, because we see it when Jesus laid down his life for us. We ought to imitate this *agape* (3:16). *Agape* here takes the form of generosity and self-sacrifice that promotes well-being.

In the fourth chapter of this epistle, John explains connections between *agape*, God, and creation. The passage deserves quoting at length to note the theological themes in it:

> Beloved, let us *agape* one another, because *agape* is from God; everyone who *agapes* is born of God and knows God. Whoever does not *agape* does not know God, for God is *agape*. God's *agape* was revealed among us in this way: God sent his only Son into the world so that we might live through him. In this is *agape*, not that we *agaped* God but that he *agaped* us and sent his Son to be the atoning sacrifice for our sins. Beloved, since God *agaped* us so much, we also ought to *agape* one another. No one has ever seen God; if we *agape* one another, God lives in us, and his *agape* is perfected in us. (4:7-12)

A few verses later, John continues his focus on the primacy of *agape*:

> So we have known and believe the *agape* God has for us. God is *agape*, and those who abide in *agape* abide in God, and God abides in them. *Agape* has been perfected among us in this: that we may have boldness on the day of judgment, because as he is, so are we in this world. There is no fear in *agape*, but perfect *agape* casts out fear; for fear has to do with punishment, and whoever fears has not reached perfection in *agape*.

We *agape* because he first *agaped* us. Those who say, "I *agape* God," and hate their brothers or sisters, are liars; for those who do not *agape* a brother or sister whom they have seen, cannot *agape* God whom they have not seen. The commandment we have from him is this: those who *agape* God must *agape* their brothers and sisters also. (4:16-21)

The meaning of *agape* in these verses coincides with my claim that love seeks well-being. God's sending the Son was motivated by a divine desire for our good. We cannot both *agape* God and hate brothers and sisters. *Agape* drives out fear God will punish.

According to John, our *agape* relies upon divine *agape*. Humans can *agape* because God first *agapes* them. John says his readers did not *agape* God, but God expresses *agape* for them. John later speaks approvingly of human *agape* for God. He says expressing *agape* for brothers and sisters, whom we can see, is only possible if we *agape* God, whom we cannot see. I interpret John's initial denial that humans can *agape* God as denying that humans first *agape* before God *agapes* them. His point seems to be that God is the source of *agape*.

Although humans rely upon God, these verses give no sense that God uses them as mere instruments or tubes. God enables human *agape*. In fact, some may choose not to *agape*: "whoever does not *agape* does not know God." Humans have the power of choice to *agape*.

Jesus plays an atoning role and is the one in whom we have confidence. "*Agape* has been perfected among us...because as he is, so are we in this world." Throughout scripture, Jesus shows love at all times and to all people. Human *agape* takes the form of Christlikeness.

The twice-repeated phrase, "God is *agape*," can be interpreted in many ways. I'll argue later that we best interpret it to mean God necessarily, by nature, loves others. I'll wait to explain this more fully.

To conclude my exploration of *agape* in the Johannine literature, I note John occasionally uses the word to mean "desire." He says, "do not *agape* the world or the things in the world. The *agape* of the Father is not in those who *agape* the world; for all that is in the world—the desire of the flesh, the desire of the eyes, and the pride in riches — comes not from the Father, but from the world" (1 Jn. 2:15-16). Jesus says people "*agape* darkness rather than light, because their deeds were evil" (Jn. 3:19). And people "*agaped* human glory more than the glory that comes from God" (Jn 12:43).

Agape as desire occurs in less than ten percent of John's writing about love. He most often uses the word to describe promoting well-being. Why he uses *agape* to talk about love as desiring or evil is a question I cannot answer. But I note that John uses *agape* in this negative way more than other New Testament writers. His writings were likely completed by followers near the end of the first century, and their language shows the influence of Greek philosophy and mysticism. Or, given that Greek thinkers often identified love with desire, it could be that Greek culture and philosophy exerted greater influence upon John's writing. But this is speculation.

AGAPE IN PAULINE WRITINGS

In the vast majority of instances, the Apostle Paul uses *agape* to mean love that does good. *Agape* builds up (1 Cor. 8:1, 3; Eph. 4:16), is generous to those in need (2 Cor. 8:24), and serves others (Gal 5:13). *Agape* spurs us to humility, meekness, patience, unity, and peace (Eph. 4:2). *Agape* nourishes and cherishes others rather than hating them (Eph. 5:29).[5]

Agape does no evil to the neighbor, says Paul, it does good. Consequently, *agape* fulfills the commandments and law (Rom. 13:8-10). The goodness of *agape* binds and perfects compassion, kindness, humility, forgiveness, meekness, and patience. Therefore, we should clothe ourselves with *agape* (Col. 3:14).

"The fruit of the Spirit is *agape*," says Paul. He lists other characteristics as either *agape*'s expressions or sitting alongside it as virtues: joy, peace, patience, kindness, goodness, faithfulness, gentleness,

---

[5] I will refer to all the books traditionally identified as from the pen of Paul as "Pauline writings." I recognize that many are disputed and some likely were not written by Paul.

and self-control (Gal 5:22). *Agape's* ways of well-being stand in contrast to the ways of ill-being, such as idolatry and sexual immorality. The ways of evil are not part of God's kingdom (Gal. 5:19-21). *Agape* avoids selfish ambition and conceit, and it looks to meet the interests of others (Phil 2:1-2).

The *agape* Paul describes to his Roman readers comes with a list of positive expressions. *Agape* hates evil and clings to good, is devoted to others, honors others above oneself, shares with those in need, practices hospitality, blesses instead of curses, rejoices with those who rejoice, mourns with those who mourn, lives in harmony with one another, associates with people of low position, is not conceited, does not repay anyone evil for evil, does what is right, lives at peace as far as possible, does not take revenge, feeds the hungry, gives drink to the thirsty, and overcomes evil with good (9:9-21). The requirements of *agape* mean not injuring the weaker believer (Rom. 14:15).

Paul uses *agape* to describe over two dozen forms of love.

Jesus' *agape* benefits us, says Paul, because Jesus sacrificed himself for our good (Rom. 5:8; Gal. 2:20). God's *agape* provides the good life we experience in Christ (Eph. 2:4). Divine *agape* does good by encouraging, giving hope, and making us steadfast in good deeds and words (2 Thess. 2:16). God blesses those who *agape* (1 Cor. 2:9) and "pours" *agape* into them through the Holy Spirit (Rom. 5:5).

The Apostle Paul also sees a cosmic dimension to *agape*. God *agapes* all creation (1 Thess. 1:4; 2:13). Nothing can separate us from God's *agape*, says Paul (Rom. 8:35, 39). He wants readers to "be rooted and grounded" in *agape*, and he hopes they can grasp the height, depth, breadth, and length of Christ's *agape* (Eph. 3:16-19). *Agape* inclines God to bless us before we are even born (Eph. 1:4). God's inclusive *agape* does good even to those once not considered God's people (Rom. 9:25).

Agape can involve special expressions of well-being for those near and dear. Husbands should *agape* their wives rather than being harsh (Col. 3:19); they should *agape* wives as Christ *agapes* the Church (Eph. 5:25). Paul's *agape* benefits people in Corinth (2 Cor.

11:11). He "spends himself" in *agape* to help them, even when they fail to help in response (2 Cor. 12:15). Paul praises readers for the "*agape* you have for the saints" (Col. 1:4). *Agape* is a positive trait in the exemplary pastor (1 Tim. 4:12; 2 Tim. 2:22) and a positive activity children of God pursue (1 Tim. 6:11).

The paragraph above explicitly describes humans expressing *agape*. There is no hint of God using them as passive tubes or sovereignly controlling them. Paul makes the point powerfully when he writes to those in Ephesus, "Be imitators of God, as beloved children, and live in *agape*, as Christ *agapes* us…" (5:1-2a). According to these lines, creatures can love like God does. They imitate God when they *agape*, and Jesus is their primary example of what *agape* looks like.

The Apostle Paul uses *agape* as a noun far more than any New Testament writer.[6] We find it as a noun more than a dozen times in 1 Corinthians 13, although Paul clearly thinks *agape* should be expressed in an action-oriented way. We should "pursue *agape*," he says in conclusion (14:1). The forms of *agape* promote well-being. Paul says *agape* is greater than faith or hope (13:13), and he launches his praise of *agape* by calling it "the most excellent way" (12:31).

In the definition of love offered, I said love requires good motives. Actions that get positive results despite evil motives are not expressions of love. In his letter to Timothy, Paul associates *agape* with good motives and a pure heart (1 Tim. 1:5). He also tells the Philippian church that envy, rivalry, partisanship, and harm motivates some preachers. But those who preach with good intentions do so from *agape* (Phil 1:16).

One difficult Pauline *agape* phrase is rendered in English "the love of God" (e.g., 2 Thess. 3:5; 2 Cor. 13:13). Does this phrase refer to a love humans have *for* God? Or does it refer to God's love *for* humans? For instance, Paul says "the *agape* of Christ compels" him to

---

[6] *Agape* is used only twice as a noun in the synoptic Gospels. In one instance, "love grows cold" (Mt. 24:13). In another, Jesus criticizes Pharisees for not paying attention to "love for God" (Lk. 11:42).

benefit his readers (2 Cor. 5:14). Is he saying his own desire for Christ motivates? Or does he mean Christ's loving activity empowers Paul to benefit others?

Augustine would interpret Paul as referring to our desire *for* God. Nygren would interpret Paul as describing God working through us. I can accept either interpretation, so long as one doesn't say God controls us or that love is simply desire. The broader point of the passage is that *agape* compels Paul to help his readers, which fits the common biblical view that love aims to promote well-being.

Paul even makes summary commands in relation to *agape*. "Let all that you do be done in *agape*" (1 Cor. 16:14). And "let your conduct be guided by *agape*" (Eph. 5:2). These passages indicate that love should be the overarching category for all actions that promote well-being. Love is the virtue encompassing all virtues. They also indicate that human beings can choose and act.

Agape Elsewhere in the New Testament

After looking at the gospels, the Johannine literature, and Paul's writings, not much remains in the New Testament. But writers of the remaining books do use *agape*, and they typically mean by it promoting well-being.

Jude speaks of *agape* feasts, which apparently nourish body and spirit (12). Peter says the goodness and hospitality of *agape* covers a multitude of sins (1 Pt. 4:8). He mentions the practice of an *agape* kiss, which apparently functions as a positive greeting (1 Pt. 5:14). Referring to Jesus, the writer of Revelation says the one who expressed *agape* "freed us from our sins" and "made us to be a kingdom" (1:5, 6). James says *agape* is "the royal law" (2:8), indicating it as the supreme way of living.

In one instance, Peter uses *agape* in a negative sense. He says Balaam expressed *agape* for the wages of wickedness (2 Pt. 2:15).

As I transition to a new set of issues, let me summarize what I've said. Using the biblical text, I've demonstrated that contrary to

Nygren, *agape* has many meanings, because love takes many forms.[7] Over ninety percent of the time, *agape* refers to promoting well-being. Although the forms vary — from self-love to neighbor-love to foreigner-love to enemy-love and more — *agape* aims in various ways to good, benefit, or be a blessing.

Love is pluriform.

GOD AS ESSENTIALLY LOVING

Some of Anders Nygren's intuitions, if articulated differently, should be included in a theology of love. For instance, he often claims God's love is unmotivated and unmerited. He calls it "spontaneous," because it does not depend on creaturely value (or lack thereof). God loves even though all have sinned (Rom. 3:23).

Many today call this "unconditional love." Nygren gets this right when he talks about God's nature. To the question, "Why does God love?" he says, "there is only one right answer: Because it is His nature to love."[8]

I agree, in part.

I think God's eternal nature is love. God inevitably loves no matter the condition of creatures and creation, because love is an aspect of God's essence. God is essentially loving. This means God *must* love; God cannot not love. To quote a line from a Charles Wesley hymn, "God's nature and name is love."[9]

I interpret John's three word-statement, "God is *agape*" (1 John 4:8, 16), as saying love is essential to God. To put it another way, love is an essential aspect of God's nature. The Apostle Paul says God

---

[7] Colin Grant makes a partial defense of Nygren's claims for *agape*, but I find this defense unconvincing. See Colin Grant, *Altruism and Christian Ethics* (Cambridge: Cambridge University Press, 2001).

[8] Ibid., 75.

[9] This line comes from a Charles Wesley hymn by the same name. It also serves as the title of the book, *Thy Name and Thy Nature is Love: Wesleyan and Process Theologies in Dialogue*, Bryan P. Stone and Thomas Jay Oord, eds. (Nashville, Tenn.: Kingswood, 2001).

"cannot deny himself" (2 Tim. 2:13), which points to aspects of the divine nature even God can't change. Hosea says God's nature is love such that God cannot abandon loved ones. And because God loves, God cannot destroy the beloved (Hos. 11:8-9).

Philosophers often use the word "necessary" for the idea that an attribute is essential to an object. Roundness is a necessary attribute of circles, for instance. Oxygen is a necessary attribute of water. With God, I would assert that love is a necessary attribute in the divine nature. There are no circumstances in which God exists and does not love. I agree with Nygren, therefore, when he says it's God's nature to love.

God is essentially loving.

Related to this, I also believe love is the *logically primary* attribute of God's nature.[10] This means God must love and cannot choose to do otherwise. It also means we best understand other divine attributes in light of love. Because love comes first logically, we should start with love when making sense of God's power, relationality, creating, experience, knowledge, and more. God does not have the power *not* to love.

Love is logically primary in God's essence.

In another sense, God's love is conditional. While God is essentially loving, God expresses love in particular ways. The forms that God's love takes depend on the particularities of the creatures and situations. The particular form of love seeks to promote well-being in a particular situation or for a specific creature. In another situation or for another creature, God's love will take a different form.

It helps to differentiate between love's *modes* and *forms*. With God, love is essential. Loving is a *necessary* mode of activity, so God always loves. You and I do not always love. We love in the mode of contingency: *whether* we love is contingent on our choice. Love is not essential to human nature, because sometimes humans choose to harm, hurt, and sin.[11]

---

[10] I address this issue in various books, including *The Uncontrolling Love of God*, ch. 7.

[11] Since Darwin, it has become less common to think humans have a nature. I am skeptical of the category "human nature." But I refer to it here to show the contrast between God,

God and creatures express multiple love forms. I have identified many in the biblical text, but there are many, many more. I join scholars who focus on three broad forms of love, identified by the Greek words *agape, eros,* and *philia.* But all forms of love promote well-being — if they are expressions of love as I have defined it.

Distinguishing between love as essential to God's nature and also as various forms helps us to untangle problems Nygren presents in relation to creaturely value. He rightly says God is essentially loving, which means God will love no matter the condition of creatures. But he then adds that creatures have no value. It's one thing to say God loves creation based on no merit in creation. It's another thing to say creation has no intrinsic value.

An adequate theology of love says God essentially loves creatures *and* they are valuable. God loves necessarily despite sin, *and* God loves in particular ways that appreciate and enhance creaturely value. God encourages us to love ourselves, as we affirm our own value and appropriately enhance our well-being. Considering God's love as necessary *and* as taking various forms makes better sense of both "God is love" and the biblical witness to pluriform love.

God is essentially loving, but the ways God loves are pluriform.

GOD INITIATES RELATIONSHIP AND INSPIRES OUR LOVE

An ongoing debate in Christian theology pits God against humans on the question of salvation. On one side, some theologians claim God does all the work. Nygren, for instance, says God initiates and sovereignly determines fellowship.[12] He thinks "all choice on man's part is excluded."[13] He affirms a Calvinist view of predestination in

---

by nature, expressing love and creatures expressing love contingently. For a discussion of what it means to be human, see Anne L.C. Runehov, *The Human Being, the World, and God* (Switzerland: Springer, 2016).

[12] Nygren, *Agape and Eros*, 75. See also 76-81.

[13] Nygren, *Agape and Eros*, 213.

which humans play no role in salvation.[14] Instead of the relational love language of child and *Abba*, the intimate word for father, Nygren opts for the domination language of slave and master.[15] As we saw in the first chapter, Mildred Erickson fills in details about the idea that God sovereignly does all the work in salvation.

Saying God does *all* the work in salvation leads to many problems for a theology of love. It guts Jesus' greatest commandments, which assume creatures contribute. Jesus says to "love the Lord your God" and "love your neighbor as yourself" (Mt. 22; Mk. 12; Lk. 10), which require human responses. If God alone establishes and maintains fellowship with creatures, God should not fault them for failing to love. Entirely determined creatures are not morally responsible. The God who predestines some to everlasting damnation does not love all people nor love steadfastly. A controlling God is also culpable for failing to prevent evil.

Saying God alone decides salvation undermines the logic of love.

Theologians on the other side of the debate say humans play a role in their salvation. But according to one interpretation, humans initiate relationship with God. Salvation begins with creatures, according to this view, although God plays a role in ongoing relationship. This has its own problems. To say creatures take the lead in salvation often generates unhealthy pride, which is a form of sin. Or it leads to despair, because some humans recognize they are incapable of love without help from a Source beyond themselves.[16]

To say salvation depends on our initiating right relations puts the onus on us.

An attractive theology of love affirms a God-creation relationship in which God moves first to establish a right relationship with

---

[14] Ibid., 214.

[15] Ibid., 94.

[16] John B. Cobb, Jr. argues that humans require divine grace in "Human Responsibility and the Primacy of Grace," *Thy Nature and Thy Name is Love*, Bryan P. Stone and Thomas Jay Oord, eds. (Nashville, Tenn.: Abingdon, 2001), ch. 4.

creatures. Because God is essentially loving, God *always* initiates relationship, moment-by-moment. But God's initiating is a relational
invitation.[17] God empowers creaturely response rather than coerc-
ing. For the relationship to flourish and love to thrive, creatures must
cooperate with God. The idea that God lovingly acts first but creatures must respond is often called "prevenient grace."[18]

God's love comes first in each moment, but it requires free creaturely response.

John's gospel teaches that God is the ultimate source of love. Not
only should we say, "God is love," we should also say, "we love, because he first loved us" (1 Jn. 4:19). Other biblical writers agree. For
instance, James says every generous act of giving, with every perfect
gift, comes from a loving God (Ja. 1:17). These and other biblical passages point to God as the source of love.[19]

In an adequate theology of love, creatures utterly depend, moment by moment, upon God as the source of love. They can love
because God makes loving possible. But God's specific calls to love
are tailormade for each creature in light of various relations, forces,
factors, and actors. Creatures love when acting intentionally in a

---

[17] John Wesley expresses this well when he says God does not "take away your liberty, your power of choosing good or evil." And "[God] did not *force* you, but being *assisted* by [God's] grace you, like Mary, *chose* the better part." In "The General Spread of the Gospel," Sermon 63, *The Works of John Wesley*, vol. 2 (Nashville: Abingdon, 1985), 281 (italics in original).

[18] See Barry L. Callen, *God as Loving Grace: The Biblically Revealed Nature and Work of God* (Nappanee Ind.: Evangel, 1996); John B. Cobb, Jr., *Grace and Responsibility* (Nashville: Abingdon, 1995); Kenneth J. Collins, *The Theology of John Wesley: Holy Love and the Shape of Grace* (Nashville, Tenn.: Abingdon, 2007); H. Ray Dunning, *Grace, Faith, and Holiness: A Wesleyan Systematic Theology* (Kansas City, Mo.: Beacon Hill, 1988); Randy L. Maddox, *Responsible Grace: John Wesley's Practical Theology* (Nashville, Tenn.: Abingdon, 1994); Thomas Jay Oord and Michael Lodahl, *Relational Holiness: Responding to the Call of Love* (Kansas City, Mo.: Beacon Hill Press of Kansas City, 2005); Johan Tredoux, *Mildred Bangs Wynkoop: Her Life and Thought* (Kansas City, Mo.: Foundery, 2017); Mildred Bangs Wynkoop, *A Theology of Love: The Dynamic of Wesleyanism* (Kansas City: Beacon Hill, 1972).

[19] Michael Lodahl argues that God is the source of creaturely love in *God of Nature and of Grace: Reading the World in a Wesleyan Way* (Nashville: Abingdon, 2003).

particular moment, in relational response to God's call and to the influence of others, to promote overall well-being.[20]

God is love's source, and God empowers creatures to respond.

AGAPE AS *IN SPITE OF* LOVE

The idea that *agape* is the only authentic love collapses under the witness of scripture. Biblical writers use *agape* to describe various forms of love. They use *philia* to describe love too. The meaning of *eros* is present in scripture even though the word does not appear. Love in scripture is pluriform.

How should we then use the word *agape*?

Even Christians with little to no theological training prize *agape*. But common views of *agape* fail to match the diverse biblical witness. Scholars give multiple and contrary definitions for *agape*. Given this confusion, it's tempting to discard *agape* on the pile of overused and misunderstood words.

To salvage *agape*, overcome confusion, and provide it a coherent role in a theology of love, I propose we start with a general definition of love. I propose that we define love as acting intentionally, in relational response to God and others, to promote overall well-being.

The second step to salvaging *agape* involves identifying the particular forms love takes.[21] *Agape* is as one form of love among others. It differs from other forms, such as *philia*, *eros*, compassion, sex/romance, attraction, family affection, and so on. All forms of love, however, align with the general definition of love I have offered. As

---

[20] Many scholars explore what it means to perceive God's call. I have been influenced by theologians like John B. Cobb, Jr., who speaks of "nonsensory perception of God" and "nonsensuous experience of the divine presence in our lives" (*Grace and Responsibility: A Wesleyan Theology for Today* [Nashville, Tenn.: Abingdon, 1995], 75). I propose a theory in "A Postmodern Wesleyan Philosophy and David Ray Griffin's Postmodern Vision," *Wesleyan Theological Journal* 35:1 (2000): 216-244.

[21] For diverse notions of *agape* and their implications for theologies of love, see Craig A. Boyd, *Visions of Agape: Problems and Possibilities in Human and Divine Love* (Burlington, Vt.: Ashgate, 2008).

a form of love, *agape* promotes well-being in a specific way. Let's examine that now.

The biblical witness offers many ways to identify *agape* as a form of love. But I suggest we particularly identify it with action that promotes well-being when responding to that which is harmful, threatening, or strange. So understood, *agape* as a form of love repays evil with good, as Jesus, Paul, and Peter put it (Lk. 6:27-31, Rom. 12:21, 1 Thess. 5:15, 1 Pt. 3:9). *Agape* helps enemies and aliens. It turns the other cheek and gives aid to foreigners. As a form of love, *agape* promotes, extends, or establishes *shalom* in response to that which promotes death and destruction. *Agape* responds to curses with blessings.

To use an accessible phrase, we might say *agape* is "in spite of" love. *Agape* promotes overall well-being *in spite of* negativity, harm, or unfamiliarity. It does good *in spite of* evil or when encountering aliens. Just as God loves us *in spite of* our sin, we ought to love others and ourselves *in spite of* whatever harm we or they have done.

In spite of harm, conflict, or unfamiliarity, *agape* promotes good.

In future chapters, I'll define *eros* and *philia* as forms of love. They also align with the general definition of love I've provided. While love takes a myriad of forms, our focusing primarily upon *agape*, *eros*, and *philia* provides a helpful approach to identifying key themes in a robust theology of love.

Conclusion

I have examined in this chapter how biblical writers use *agape*. Two major conclusions have emerged. First, more than nine times out of ten, the writers of scripture use *agape* to talk about promoting well-being. Second, the specific ways *agape* promotes well-being varies. This Greek word identifies many ways both God and creatures express love.

My exploration of *agape* leads to several theological proposals. God is essentially loving, I have argued, in the sense that God loves by nature. God necessarily loves, because God *is* love. But how God chooses to love in each moment is conditioned by creatures and circumstances. God loves necessarily, but love expression is tailormade for each recipient.

God initiates relationship with all and is the source of love. Creatures can love, because God first loves them. Humans are not controlled by God; they freely choose whether to love in response to divine empowering. They are more than mere tubes or channels through which God works. They have real agency and intrinsic value. Humans should love themselves, in the sense of acting to promote their own well-being.

Agape is one form of love beside others. While the biblical witness gives it various meanings, I identify *agape* with a form of love that does good to enemies, strangers, and those who harm. For ease of reference, I call it "in spite of" love. *Agape* seeks overall well-being in spite of obstacles, evil, and threats.

In the next chapter, I explore perhaps the most influential theologian in history: Augustine. Insights gained in previous chapters — especially those related to the biblical meanings of love — will help us analyze Augustine's theology.

5

Eros and Augustine

Saint Augustine of Hippo (354-430) has probably influenced more Christians than anyone whose writings are not in the Bible.[1] Anders Nygren thinks this influence surpasses even the Apostle Paul's, at least when it comes to love. Augustine's theology continues to shape Christian theology and philosophy today.

Augustine's most sustained exposition of love comes in his book *Teaching Christianity (De Doctrina Christiana)*.[2] He began writing it early in life but completed it nearly 30 years later. In this chapter, I explore the meaning of love in that book, referring occasionally to statements in Augustine's other writings.

Nygren was partly right: Augustine thinks of love as desire. Because the Greek word *eros* is typically associated with desire, and because Augustine has been so influential, I begin by examining the concept of *eros* with his thought.

Augustine's views offer both assets and obstacles for a Christian theology of love.

---

[1] Among the many helpful books on Augustine, see Eugene TeSelle, *Augustine the Theologian* (Eugene, Or.: Wipf and Stock, 2002). See also John Burnaby, *Amor Dei: A Study of the Religion of St. Augustine* (London: Canterbury Press, 1938. Reprint, Eugene, OR: Wipf and Stock, 2007).

[2] I use the New City Press translation: Augustine, *Teaching Christianity* (De Doctrina Christiana), ed. John E. Rotelle, O.S.A, trans. Edmund Hill, O.P. (Hyde Park, N.Y.: New City, 1996).

LOVE IS DESIRE, ACCORDING TO AUGUSTINE,
NOT PROMOTING WELL-BEING

Augustine makes a claim at the outset of *Teaching Christianity* that sets the stage for his theology. He says there are two ways of relating to people and things: we either use them or enjoy them.

"There are some things which are meant to be enjoyed, others which are meant to be used, yet others which do both the enjoying and the using," he says. "Things that are to be enjoyed make us happy; things which are to be used help us on our way to happiness."[3] In the Latin terms Augustine uses, *frui* means to enjoy something as an end, for its own sake. *Uti* means to use something for the sake of something else.

This distinction between using and enjoying is central to Augustine's views on love. "Enjoyment consists in clinging to something lovingly for its own sake," he says, "while use consists in referring what has come your way to what your love aims at obtaining. Provided, that is, it deserves to be loved."[4]

We naturally wonder what we should enjoy and what we should use. One might wonder, for instance, if we should use or enjoy rocks, horses, and friends. Should we use or enjoy the earth? Should we use or enjoy enemies? And what about ourselves?

Augustine answers in a section heading: "God Alone is to be Enjoyed."

Only God is worthy of our desire. Therefore, we should only seek to enjoy deity. "Among all the things there are," says Augustine, "those alone are to be enjoyed, which we have noted as being eternal and unchanging. The rest are to be used in order that we may come at last to the enjoyment of [that which is eternal and unchanging]."[5] "If we wish to return to our home country where alone we can be truly happy," Augustine says, "we have to use this world, not enjoy it." We

---

[3] Ibid., Book 1, paragraph 3.

[4] Ibid., Book 1, paragraph 4

[5] Ibid., Book 1, paragraph 22.

use creatures and creation "so that we may proceed from temporal and bodily things to grasp those that are eternal and spiritual."[6]

The idea we ought to use rocks seems harmless enough, although our use has implications for life overall. But the idea we should use people opposes what we typically think love does. Doesn't love help others rather than use them? Can't we enjoy our friends in themselves? Does love require using children?

Augustine realizes the idea we should use people seems inappropriate. "We have been commanded, after all, to love one another," he says. "But the question is whether people are to be loved by others for their own sake, or for the sake of something else." If we love others for their own sake, we enjoy them. If we love people for the sake of something else, we use them.

That which is worthy of love for its own sake, says Augustine, "constitutes the life of bliss." Because creatures cannot bring true bliss — including children, neighbors, strangers, and ourselves — he thinks, we should use them.[7] Only love for God brings bliss; only God deserves love.

Some will find offensive the idea that we use them instead of enjoying them for their own sake. But they "must not take offense," says Augustine, "if you also love them for God's sake and not their own."[8]

Augustine's claims about love as use and enjoyment assume that love is desire. We love something if we desire it. "Love is a kind of craving," he explains,[9] or what some call "acquisitive desire."[10] Augustine uses words like "cling" and "obtain" as synonyms with love. To love someone or something is to be inclined toward it, yearn

---

[6] Ibid., Book 1, paragraph 4. Many have criticized Augustine for his views of sex. For a sustained theological criticism, see Werner Jeanrond, *A Theology of Love* (London: T & T Clark, 2010).

[7] Ibid., Book 1, paragraph 20.

[8] Ibid., Book 1, paragraph 21.

[9] Augustine, *Eighty-Three Different Questions*, 35, 2.

[10] See, for instance, Paul Ramsey, *Basic Christian Ethics* (Chicago: University of Chicago Press, 1950), 122. See also Paul Avis, *Eros and the Sacred* (Harrisburg, Penn.: Morehouse, 1989).

for it, or seek satisfaction in it. Such love can also include devotion and worship.

For Augustine, to love is to desire.

Augustine uses what I earlier called the proper/improper language of love. According to it, love itself is neutral. Love may intentionally do evil or intentionally do good. It may be appropriate or inappropriate.[11] Augustine says a miser can love gold, for instance, "with an evil as well as with a good love: it is loved rightly when it is loved ordinately; evilly when inordinately."[12]

Two Latin love words describe proper and improper desire, according to Augustine. Charity (*caritas*) desires something or someone for God's sake. Cupidity (*cupiditas*) desires for the sake of something other than God. "What I mean by charity is any urge of the spirit to find joy in God for his own sake, and in oneself and one's neighbor for God's sake," he explains. "By cupidity, [I mean] any impulse of the spirit to find joy in oneself and one's neighbor, and in any kind of bodily thing at all, not for God's sake."[13] The difference between *caritas* and *cupiditas* is not one of kind. Both are desires. It is a difference in object.

"Love, but see to it *what* you love," says Augustine.[14]

My Response to Love as Desire

Even the novice will think Augustine's claims sound strange, if not outright wrong. Using people does not seem right, let alone using ourselves. Love helps people in need, establishes friendship, forgives

---

[11] Hannah Arendt explores Augustine's view that love can be true or false, good or bad in *Love and St. Augustine* (Chicago: University of Chicago Press, 1998).

[12] Augustine, *City of God*, Book 15, chapter 22

[13] Augustine, *Teaching Christianity*, Book 3, paragraph 16.

[14] Augustine, *Commentaries on the Psalms*, 90, 31, 5. When *frui and uti* are combined with *cupiditas* and *caritas* four possible relations emerge: (1) right enjoyment (of God); (2) wrong enjoyment (of the world); (3) right use (of the world); and (4) wrong use (of God) (*City of God*, 11, 25).

wrongs, and more. Using people to enjoy God seems opposed to the recurring New Testament charge to "love one another."

I've noted that New Testament writers rarely use "love" to talk about desire. This is true of Old Testament scripture too. Most biblical authors reserve "love" for talking about promoting well-being in some way. To love is to show compassion, be kind, offer salvation, help enemies, be generous, or do something good. It's hard to overstate the difference between the way biblical writers typically understand love and Augustine's understanding.

Love in Scripture typically pertains to doing good and seldom to desire.

While I think Augustine makes a huge mistake in defining love as desire, I'm not rejecting desire. While desire itself is not love, when understood as a factor in acting intentionally, I believe that desire plays a role in loving activity. The emotional content in desire can also play a role. As we saw in earlier discussions, emotions can help or hinder decisions about whether and how to promote well-being.

Desire plays a role in love, but it is not love itself.

Problems arise when theologies reject desire entirely. We saw this in Nygren's *agape* theories. He rightly rejects Augustine's view that love is desire alone. But he goes further and separates desire *entirely* from love. This is a mistake, and it leads him to commit three errors.

First, Nygren eliminates creaturely decision and intentionality in love. This is an error because love requires intentional decisions. To intend to do something, broadly speaking, is to desire to do it. Rejecting desire in this way leads Nygren to reject free creaturely responses to God's calls. Predestination and divine control follow.

Second, although Nygren correctly rejects the idea of love as mere desire, he wrongly thinks creatures and creation have no value in themselves. He rightly thinks God by nature loves creatures. But he wrongly thinks this means creatures have no intrinsic value. This, in turn, leads Nygren to reject self-love.

The third error Nygren commits is rejecting *eros* as a form of love. As a form, *eros* finds value in others and appreciates that value or seeks to enhance it. When aligned with a broader definition of love, *eros* promotes well-being in response to what is valuable. Like Nygren, Augustine doesn't affirm *eros* as one form of love beside others. But instead of rejecting it, he makes it primary. He regards love as desire itself and then says God is the only value worth enjoying.

While Augustine's language runs contrary to the primary way biblical writers understand love, it has another problem. It's confusing. When Augustine says, "love one another," we naturally think he means we should do good to others. But what he really means is "properly desire others as instruments to desiring God." "Love your enemies," to Augustine actually means "properly desire your enemies as instruments to desiring God." "Love the sick and destitute" really means "desire the sick and destitute as instruments to desiring God." And so on.

Those who think of love as proper or improper desires should always add modifiers when they use the word "love." But Augustine and others often do not. More confusion follows. Without modifiers, this love language lacks clarity. We wonder, is it proper or improper to love ourselves? Can we appropriately love enemies and friends? Can we love God improperly? Is it proper or improper to love amoeba?

Misunderstanding proliferates.

AUGUSTINE'S ORDER OF LOVES

Augustine thinks we should prioritize our loves (desires). He calls this "the right order of love." When "love of God is put first," says Augustine, "everything else is to converge on it."[15] Wisdom calls us to arrange our desires.

Knowing how our desires ought to be prioritized requires "one to be capable of an objective and impartial evaluation of things; to love things, that is to say, in the right order." A person should do this, says Augustine, "so that you do not love what is not to be loved, or fail to love what is to be loved, or have a greater love for what should

---

[15] Augustine, *Teaching Christianity*, Book 1, paragraph 28.

be loved less, or an equal love for things that should be loved less or more, or a lesser or greater love for things that should be loved equally."[16] We must discern.

The ordering of loves only makes sense, says Augustine, if love for creatures is *actually* love for God. "Every human being, precisely as human, is to be loved on God's account," says Augustine. "All things are to be loved for God's sake."[17] God "takes pity on us, so that we may enjoy him, while we take pity on each other, again so that we may all enjoy him, not one another."[18] "When you enjoy a human being in God," says Augustine, "you are really enjoying God rather than the human being."[19]

Instead of enjoying creatures as ends in themselves, we ought to take pity on them as means to enjoying God. This is love rightly ordered, according to Augustine.

Contemporary theologian James K. A. Smith uses Augustine's language of love. We see this when Smith titles his influential book, *You Are What You Love*. That book makes accessible some material in his more academic writings, including *Desiring the Kingdom*. In both books, Smith identifies love with desire.

Smith begins *You Are What You Love* with this question: "What do you *want?*"[20] He proceeds by saying, "our wants and longings and desires are at the core of identity, the wellspring from which our actions and behavior flow." This means discipleship is a way "to be attentive to and intentional about what you love," says Smith. Jesus "forms our very loves," he argues, and Jesus "is after nothing less than your wants, your loves, your longings."[21]

---

[16] Ibid.

[17] Ibid.

[18] Ibid., Book 1, paragraph 29.

[19] Ibid., Book 1, paragraph 37.

[20] James K. A. Smith, *You Are What You Love: The Spiritual Power of Habit* (Grand Rapids, Mich.: Brazos, 2016), 1. A mid-twentieth century writer who makes arguments similar to Smith's is Martin C. D'Arcy, *The Mind and Heart of Love, Lion and Unicorn: A Study in Eros and Agape* (Cleveland: World, 1964).

[21] Ibid., 2.

Smith turns to Augustine's views to make his case. We are "fundamentally *erotic* creatures," says Smith, and *eros* "signals a desire and attraction that is a good feature of our creaturehood." Consequently, "we could think of *agape* as rightly ordered *eros*," and this means "rightly ordered desire for God." To summarize his reasoning, Smith says, "You are what you *desire*."[22]

In *Desiring the Kingdom*, Smith says Christians ought to develop positive habits, embrace a Christian worldview, and be oriented toward what is divine and good. The Christian life is not primarily about thinking rightly; it's "a matter of being the kind of person who *loves* rightly."[23] Our "love can be misdirected," says Smith, and "aimed at the wrong things."[24] Christians should consider "ultimate loves… what we desire above all else, the ultimate desire that shapes and positions and makes sense of all our penultimate desires and actions."[25]

Smith says we should desire God first and order other desires accordingly.

My Response to Ordering Loves and Desires

There is much to affirm in Smith's arguments about priorities, discipleship, and developing positive habits. And there is much to embrace in the longstanding work by Christians on these issues. But we must keep separate two meanings of "ordering loves" (desires).

The first way to order loves pertains to our obligations, as finite creatures, to promote well-being.[26] This task assumes the meaning of love common in the Bible. In a world of limited time and resources,

---

[22] Ibid., 9-10.

[23] James K. A. Smith, *Desiring the Kingdom: Worship, Worldview, and Cultural Formation* (Grand Rapids, Mich.: Baker, 2009), 32.

[24] Ibid., 52.

[25] Ibid., 53.

[26] For instance, Garth L. Hallett, *Priorities and Christian Ethics* (Cambridge: Cambridge University Press, 1998); Stephen J. Pope, *The Evolution and Ordering of Love* (Washington, D. C.: Georgetown University Press, 1994).

to order loves means we sometimes help some instead of others, in the sense of promoting the well-being of some over others.

We should admit, for instance, we have special obligations to help our own children or life partners more than a stranger, kangaroo, or insect. Affirming special commitments does not mean we can neglect strangers entirely or unnecessarily harm other creatures. But our current locations, past commitments, and various relationships mean we are sometimes rightly promoting the good of one or some over the good of others.[27]

As an example, consider a mother's obligation to love her newborn. She should help her child in ways she is not obliged to help others. This specific infant relies upon this specific adult, and specific responsibilities follow.

Acting for the good of one or a few, of course, often overlaps with promoting the common good. Raising a socially mature child, for instance, is good for the child and for society. In an interconnected world, the good of one often coincides with the good of others. But we sometimes act for the good of one or some more than others.

This approach to ordering understands love as promoting well-being. It's not about desires or devotion, at least not primarily. Ordering loves pertains to *whose* well-being we should promote, given various limitations, relations, and commitments.

The second way to talk about ordering loves is better called prioritizing desires rather than ordering loves. We may rightly desire or devote ourselves to friends more than a complete stranger, for instance. We might rightly desire friendship over isolation or devote ourselves to children more than video games. We are rightly devoted to God rather than idols.

The work to order our desires and devotion makes sense. We ought to orient our lives around that which gives life and does good and orient ourselves away from that which destroys and does evil.

---

[27] Gary Chartier makes this move in *The Analogy of Love: Divine and Human Love at the Center of Christian Theology* (Charlottesville, VA: Imprint Academic, 2007). See also Chartier, *Loving Creation: The Task of the Moral Life* (Minneapolis: Fortress, 2022).

James K. A. Smith's writings, among others, offer powerful insights for the ordering of desires and devotion.

Ordering desires, however, isn't the same as ordering love when love is understood as promoting well-being. They're different. Ordering devotion isn't the same as asking whose well-being we should promote, given various limitations. We can devote ourselves to our favorite baseball team and think little about the well-being of the team members.

Desiring God or the good is not the same as promoting well-being. We can long for God but kill our enemies. We can "put God first" while simultaneously destroying the creatures God cares about.

The Apostle James points this out. He criticizes those who have the right priorities and want what is good but fail to love by helping the needy. "If a brother or sister is naked and lacks daily food, one of you says to them, 'Go in peace; keep warm and eat your fill,' and yet you do not supply their bodily needs, what is the good of that?" (2:15-16)

The Apostle Paul argues similarly. To praise God in utmost desire, we may "speak in the tongues of mortals and of angels" (1 Cor. 13:1). But if we do not love, we are "a noisy gong or a clanging cymbal." In utter devotion, we may "give away all [our] possessions" or "hand over [our] body to be burned." But if we do not love, we "gain nothing" (1 Cor. 13:3).

To desire or be devoted is not the same as promoting well-being.

Based on scriptural use and everyday meaning, we should reserve "love" for actions that seek to promote well-being. The work of ordering love, therefore, should mean discerning or prioritizing who we help, in any moment, as finite creatures with limited resources. We should use phrases like "ordering our desires" or "prioritizing our devotion" to explore the issues Smith and others raise.

Smith's book should be titled, "You Are What You Desire."[28]

---

[28] Even this alternative title would fail to account well for what "you" become. Many factors outside your control influence who you become. Some factors affect you unconsciously. You are more than what you desire, so the title is problematic either way.

AUGUSTINE MANGLES THE LOVE COMMANDS

One might read the previous paragraphs and ask, "Is this merely a fight over language?" Are criticisms of Augustine and Smith merely semantics? No.

Convoluted love language yields convoluted theologies of love.

Let's return to Augustine. He builds from Jesus' first love commandment to support his belief that nothing other than God should be loved (desired), at least not in itself. "This is the rule of love that God has set for us," he says: "*You shall love your neighbor as yourself.*" Then Augustine adds, quoting Matthew's version of the command, "[You shall love] God, however, *with your whole heart and your whole soul and your whole mind.*"[29]

Augustine's interpretation of "whole" proves crucial. "All your thoughts and your whole life and all your intelligence," he says, "should be focused on him from whom you have received the very things you devote to him." Jesus "did not leave out any part of our life, which could be left vacant, so to speak," says Augustine, "and [Jesus did not] leave room for wanting to enjoy something else." Anything other than God, he says, "must be whisked along toward that point to which the whole impetus of your love is hastening."[30]

Augustine understands proper love as devotion to God.

This view affects how Augustine interprets Jesus' second love command. Christians typically think of loving neighbors as helping, supporting, assisting, or promoting their well-being. We should do good to others like we do good to ourselves. But that's not what Augustine thinks the second love command means.

Augustine interprets "love your neighbor as yourself" as enfolded into what it means to love God wholly. "All who love their neighbors in the right way ought so to deal with them that they too love God with all their heart, all their soul, all their mind. By loving

---

[29] Augustine, *Teaching Christianity*, Book 1, paragraph 21.

[30] Ibid., Book 1, paragraph 21.

them, you see, in this way as themselves, they are relating all their love of themselves and of the others to that love of God."[31]

This interpretation applies to self-love, according to Augustine. Those who love themselves for their own sakes "are not relating themselves to God," he says. "In turning to themselves, they are not turning to anything unchangeable." To orient oneself toward what is changeable is to orient toward the defective, he thinks. People ought to orient themselves toward God, "the unchangeable good."[32]

According to Augustine, therefore, we should not love neighbors for their own sakes. Nor should we love ourselves for our sakes.[33] We rightly love (desire) others and ourselves only as conduits for love (desire) of God. To love others as ends in themselves divides our allegiance. Our love (allegiance) should only be to God.

My Response to Augustine and the Love Commands

I understand why many Christians at least initially accept Augustine's interpretation of Jesus' first love command. When he focuses on "whole," readers might think the passage teaches full devotion to God. Saying we should love God with our whole heart/mind/soul/ strength aligns with the biblical command to avoid idolatry. Without additional reflection, few will object to interpreting "love God" to mean desiring God above others.

The problem with this interpretation becomes clear when we move to the second command: We ought to love our neighbors as ourselves. Christians naturally think, in this instance, that love means promoting well-being. To love the neighbor is to do good to them. Like the language of love in most scripture, we naturally interpret the

---

[31] Ibid., Book 1, paragraph 20.

[32] Ibid., Book 1, paragraph 21.

[33] Oliver O'Donovan identifies the shifting meaning of self-love in Augustine's thought in *The Problem of Self-Love in St. Augustine* (Eugene, Or.: Wipf and Stock, 1980).

second command as acting to benefit others as ourselves. Few will interpret it as commanding us to *desire* our neighbors and ourselves as means to desire God.

Shifting love's meaning from "promoting well-being" to "desire" or "devotion" twists the meaning of the second command. Instead of saying, "help others as we help ourselves" or something similar, it means "desire others as we desire ourselves." Augustine adds, "desire others as a means to desiring God."

Augustine's language mangles Jesus' second command.

Interpreting love as desire or devotion also mangles the meaning of the first command. We should interpret "love" in it like we interpret love in the second command. There is no sign Jesus intends a change in meaning. Rather than a shift, the meaning of love as promoting well-being should remain consistent.

The result of interpreting love consistently is that the command to love God with our whole heart/mind/soul/strength means promoting God's well-being. Love for God, neighbor, and ourselves involves promoting the well-being of God, neighbors, and ourselves.

It may surprise some to hear that obeying the first love command means doing good to God. But biblical writers often say creatures increase God's happiness, bliss, or joy. Over and over, the psalmist speaks of our ability to bless God, for instance (e.g., Ps. 103). The writer of Hebrews tells us that Enoch pleased God (Heb. 11:5). And the greatest lover of all — Jesus — increased God's happiness as the one whom the voice from heaven called "son" and said, "in him I am well pleased" (Mt. 3:17; 17:5; Mk. 1:11: 3:17; Lk. 3:22; 1 Pt. 1:17).

Well-being-enhancing-love enhances God's well-being too.

Augustine saw a conflict between loving God with all we are and loving neighbors as ourselves. How can *every* desire be for God, but we also desire others as ourselves? His "solution" denies we should desire anyone but God. We only desire God entirely if we desire God when desiring creatures as means to another end. According to Augustine, love for creatures isn't *really* love for them; it's *actually* love for God.

We should interpret Jesus' love commands differently than Augustine did. Jesus calls us to promote God's well-being. "And the second command is like the first," Jesus says in Matthew's gospel (22:39). There is no contradiction between promoting God's well-being and promoting the well-being of neighbors as ourselves.

If we define love as promoting well-being, the two commands complement one another rather than require a radical shift in meaning. We can embrace Jesus' commands in a way that also fits love's meaning in the vast majority of scripture. When we love our neighbors and ourselves in terms of promoting their well-being, we also love God in terms of promoting God's well-being.

The ability to love others, ourselves, and God simultaneously is possible because God is omnipresent. God is always present to neighbors, us, and all creation. And as I will argue in future chapters, we should believe the omnipresent God is also relational. What we and others do affects God. Consequently, we promote the well-being of an omnipresent, relational God when we promote the well-being of neighbors, ourselves, and creation.

To put it another way, loving neighbors and ourselves for their own sakes aligns well with loving God. For instance, helping the helpless affects their well-being and the well-being of an omnipresent and relational God. Rejoicing with those who rejoice positively affects both them and God. Befriending strangers, caring for infants, doing good to enemies, cooperating with constructive activism, engaging in self-care, and so much more positively affects a universal God whose well-being can be influenced.

Even solitary prayer promotes the good of creation and Creator.[34] As interrelated beings, we are never *truly* solitary. We always affect ourselves and others, even in our thoughts. Our communication with God can promote God's well-being, and it does not compete with our love for others or ourselves.

---

[34] On the efficacy of prayer, see Mark Gregory Karris, *Divine Echoes: Reconciling Prayer with the Uncontrolling Love of God* (Orange, Ca.: Quoir, 2018) and chapter two of Thomas Jay Oord, *Questions and Answers for God Can't* (Grasmere, Id.: SacraSage, 2020).

Rather than desiring God alone, love seeks the good of God, others, and ourselves.

AUGUSTINE'S GOD DOESN'T LOVE US

My discussion of Jesus' love commands reveals that my differences with Augustine are more than semantics. How we understand love affects how we interpret Jesus' understanding of love. But there are other issues at stake. My differences with Augustine are also evident in the Christian claim that God loves us and all creation.

Another subsection of *Teaching Christianity* is entitled, "God Does Not Enjoy Us, But Makes Use of Us." The first phrase in the title aptly describes Augustine's view. The second phrase is more confusing, because he doesn't mean this — at least not in the usual sense of "use." Both statements have disturbing implications for Augustine's theology of love.

To say God *uses* us seems contrary to Jesus' words: "For God so loved the world that he gave his only Son…" (Jn. 3:16). It seems to oppose the Apostle Paul's words that "God proves his love for us in that while we still were sinners, Christ died for us" (Rm. 5:8). It seems in opposition to the Psalms, which speak of God's steadfast love (*hesed*) for creation. These passages and many more say the world and its creatures benefit from divine love. God wants to promote our good, not use us.

To explain his view, Augustine reminds us of what he considers love's true object. "There still seems to be some uncertainty about what we have been saying," he admits, "that we enjoy that thing which we love for its own sake."[35] And we should use what does not make "us perfectly happy or blissful," he says. Then Augustine poses a question to himself: "How does [God] love us?"

According to Augustine's categories, he's asking, "Does God use or enjoy us?" If God "enjoys us," says Augustine, "it means he is in need of some good of ours, which nobody in his right mind could

---

[35] Augustine, *Teaching Christianity*, Book 1, paragraph 31.

possibly say. Every good of ours, after all, is either God himself, or derived from him."[36] To enjoy us, we must be able to contribute something God finds worth enjoying. Augustine thinks we have nothing of value to offer because God has all values eternally.

The only way God can love (desire) us, according to Augustine's categories, is to use us. "He does not enjoy us, but makes use of us," he states. "Because if he neither enjoys us nor makes use of us, I cannot find any way in which he can love us."[37] Augustine's love categories paint him into a corner! Because God needs nothing, God cannot really love us in either sense.

If we do not treat people at least sometimes as ends in themselves, it's hard to see how we promote their well-being. We may treat people as both ends and means, of course. We might act for their good and for the good of God and others. But using people *only* for the sake of something else contradicts what it means to love them, in terms of promoting their good. Although biblical writers say God created us and all creation "very good" (Gen. 1:31) and God desires a loving relationship with us, Augustine's God doesn't enjoy creation for its own sake. So, says Augustine, God must use us.

Augustine can't say God loves us for our own sakes.

After saying God uses us, Augustine realizes he faces another problem. His notion of use implies God needs something. But this cannot be true, according to his theology. He believes God is the only one with ultimate value, and God has no needs. What use is creation to an entirely self-sufficient God?

Augustine admits his problem. God "does not make use of us, either" he confesses. At least not "in the same way as we use things." He explains: "Our making use of things is directed to the end of enjoying God's goodness." But "God's making use of us is directed to his goodness."[38]

---

36 Ibid.

37 Ibid., Book 1, paragraph 32.

38 Ibid.

I'll address the line "in the same way as we use things" in the next chapter when I talk about analogies between God's love and ours. I'll just note here that even God's using us has God's own good in mind. But God has no needs whatsoever, according to Augustine. So his saying God uses us makes no sense, and he ultimately admits this.

God cannot enjoy us for our own sake nor use us; God only loves Godself.

Creatures may benefit when God uses them as means to enjoying Godself.[39] But this does not mean God loves creatures in themselves. Augustine's God doesn't intend to promote creaturely well-being, which is what most of the Bible says love does. God is concerned only with the divine life, because only that which is eternal and unchanging deserves concern.

We briefly encountered the idea God only loves Godself when discussing Millard Erickson's theology. Like Augustine and many theologians in what many call "classical theism," Erickson thinks God can only love Godself.[40] The logic at play assumes love is desire and God is unaffected by creation. God has no needs. We'll address these issues in the next chapter, but I mention them to illustrate the continuing influence of Augustine's theology today.

When reflecting on the Trinity, Augustine says God ceaselessly loves Godself. This love is contemplation and enjoyment of the divine life.[41] His appeal to intra-Trinitarian love, however, does not solve his problems regarding God's love for creatures and creation. God simply doesn't love them. God neither loves creatures by enjoying them or using them — except insofar as in using them, God loves Godself. And God does not intend to promote their well-being.

Augustine's God does not love the world.

---

[39] Ibid.

[40] Paul Tillich follows Augustine on this and in many ways. Tillich says, "man's love of God is the love with which God loves himself." See *Systematic Theology*, Vol. 1 (Chicago: University of Chicago Press, 1951), 282.

[41] Augustine, *On the Trinity*, 9, 2.

My Response to God Not Loving Us

On this matter, it's hard to voice my opposition strongly enough!

It's a significant error when Augustine defines love in a way contrary to the vast majority of scripture. His definition also runs contrary to how many today understand love, which promotes well-being in some way. It's a greater error to interpret Jesus' love commands in confusing ways. Those interpretations prevent Augustine from recognizing Jesus' call to love God, neighbors, ourselves, and all creation by promoting their well-being.

Augustine even denies the Christian claim, "God so loved the world" — at least if this means God loves the world for its own sake. He must deny it to follow his logic of love. God doesn't love us by promoting our well-being, which is what I and most biblical writers regard as loving.

For Augustine (as for other theologians that have followed his lead through the centuries), God only loves Godself. Divine desires are only for God's own good. Only by loving Godself in creatures does God have any reason to interact with them. And even "interact" is not the right word for Augustine's God, as we will see in the next chapter.

To put it in contemporary terms, Augustine's God is the ultimate narcissist.

CONCLUSION

Using *Teaching Christianity*, I have explored what Augustine says about love. He defines it differently from most biblical writers. For him, to love is to desire, but it can also involve devotion. I argue that love is better understood as acting intentionally, in relational response to God and others, to promote overall well-being. The latter definition fits most references to love in scripture.

The problems with Augustine's views involve more than semantics. He interprets Jesus' love commands to mean we should desire God entirely and only desire neighbors and ourselves as means to enjoying God. Jesus' love commands are better understood, I have said, as calling us to promote the well-being of God, others, ourselves, and all creation. We can love creation and Creator simultaneously, I add, because God is omnipresent and relational. Our love for others positively affects God.

Augustine instructs his audience to order their loves. By this, he means ordering their desires in relation to God. I point out that ordering desires is important, but it's not the same as deciding whose well-being we should promote in any moment, given our limitations, relations, and commitments. I conclude Augustine's thought is useful for understanding desires and prioritizing devotion. It's not helpful for making sense of love.

As we have seen, Augustine cannot say God loves us or the world. God does not love us for our own sake. Augustine believes we should never love neighbors or ourselves for their or our own sakes. Consequently, he cannot affirm what I and most Christians believe stands as a central claim in scripture. Augustine's logic leads him to say God only loves Godself.

Many of Augustine's views should not be adopted in a Christian theology of love.

6

Classical Theism and "Because of" Love

We might wonder why Augustine would adopt views that don't align well with love in scripture. Or why he would have such a strange interpretation of the love commands Jesus thought greatest. We might wonder why Augustine denies we should love others for their sakes and ourselves for our sakes. We might object to his view that God cannot love creatures or creation, neither enjoying nor using them — at least in any way we understand those words. We might reject Augustine's claim God can only love Godself. We might see problems with defining love as desire, rather than doing good.

Why would Augustine embrace such beliefs?

The answer, I suggest, comes from the philosophy he embraces. A particular philosophical framework affects Augustine's views of divine and creaturely love. It shapes how he thinks about the value of the world and God. It affects his views of agency, causation, time, relationality, change, and more. We need to examine the assumptions undergirding Augustine's theology.

Philosophy always plays a role in Christian theology. This isn't a bad thing; philosophy isn't inherently evil. We're all philosophers, in the general sense of thinking about things, and all theologies have philosophical assumptions. In fact, every statement about love — scholarly or not — incorporates philosophy, at least in the broad sense.

Some philosophies do better than others at elucidating love, however. Some better fit the way biblical writers portray God and creation. Some better fit our experience of the world, aligning better with contemporary science, personal experiences, art, and culture. Some philosophies are more plausible, in the sense of cohering with what we know about life. And some are more internally consistent.

The test of a philosophy's adequacy for a Christian theology of love is the measure to which it illumines the way God loves and calls us to do the same. We should avoid philosophies that cannot help us talk coherently about love. We should shun philosophies that make little or no sense of love.

While exploring Augustine's philosophical assumptions, I will address what many today call "classical theism." Classical theists share most of Augustine's views. I will argue neither Augustine nor classical theism helps us understand love as portrayed in the Bible and in our lives. We need alternative views, and I suggest replacements. I will close by suggesting *eros* as a form of love that appreciates value and, in doing so, promotes well-being.

Rightly understood, *eros* plays a role in a Christian theology of love.

AUGUSTINE AND CLASSICAL THEISM

Augustine read widely in philosophy, including the works of Aristotle, the Neoplatonists (e.g., Plotinus, Porphyry), the Stoics, and others. Many scholars note the influence these philosophies had on his theology. Adolf Harnack (1851-1930) is often cited as the first to decry Greek philosophy's influence upon Augustine and Christian theology. Harnack called it "the Hellenic spirit" and many today call this the "Hellenization" of Christian thought.[1] These philosophical

---

[1] Adolf Harnack, *History of Dogma*, Neil Buchanan, trans. (London: Williams and Norgate, 1897). Many others have made this argument. See Hubertus R. Drobner, "Christian Philosophy," in *The Oxford Handbook of Early Christian Studies* (Oxford: Oxford University Press, 2008). 672–90; Helmut Koester, *History, Culture, and Religion of the Hellenistic Age* in *Introduction to the New Testament*, 2nd ed. (Berlin: Walter de Gruyter, 1995). Sometimes

traditions still influence Christian theologians and philosophers today.

Many use the label "classical theism" to describe ideas endorsed by Augustine and theologians he influenced, such as Anselm, Thomas Aquinas, John Calvin, and Martin Luther. "Classical" doesn't necessarily mean old. Nor do only theologians who lived long ago embrace these ideas; some scholars embrace them today.[2] And not every theologian of yesteryear embraced so-called classical theism. Theological diversity existed then as it does now.

Augustine and classical theism affirm at least four unique ideas about God, ideas intricately connected to Platonic and Neo-Platonic views about the superiority of what is changeless. They say God is 1) timeless, 2) immutable, 3) impassible, and 4) simple.[3] To a great extent, these four ideas are mutually reinforcing, and each has implications for a theology of love.

1. Augustine Believes God is Timeless

Just about every Christian believes God had no beginning and will have no end. But classical theism understands this belief in a particular way. It says God experiences no succession of moments. God is timeless. There is no "before" or "after" in God because God is non-temporal. Deity does not experience moment by moment.

---

the Hellenism thesis is taken too broadly, as Paul Gavrilyuk has argued (*The Suffering of the Impassible God: The Dialectics of Patristic Thought* [Oxford: Oxford University Press, 2004]).

[2] For examples, see James E. Dolezal, *God without Parts: Divine Simplicity and the Metaphysics of God's Absoluteness* (Eugene, OR: Pickwick, 2011); H. J. McCann, *Creation and the Sovereignty of God* (Bloomington: Indiana University Press, 20212).

[3] On this designation for classical theism, see Ryan T. Mullins, "Classical Theism," in *T & T Clark Handbook of Analytic Theology*, James M. Arcadi and James T. Turner, Jr., eds. (London: Bloomsbury, 2021), 85-100; T. Williams, "Introduction to Classical Theism," in J. Dillerand A. Kasher, eds., *Models of God and Alternative Ultimate Realities* (New York: Springer, 2013), 95-7.

Augustine affirms this divine timelessness view.[4] "In the sub-limity of an eternity which is always in the present," he says, God is "before all things past and transcends all things future."[5] In fact, God created time, according to Augustine. "What time could there be that you had not created?" he asks rhetorically of God. "You are the Maker of all times…No time is co-eternal with you."[6]

Because time had a beginning, Augustine says, we should not ask what God was doing before creating.[7] That question is nonsensical, because there was no time before God created it. In fact, Augustine admits he can't really talk about time at all. "If I wish to explain it to one who asks," Augustine says, "I know not [how]."[8]

Scholars propose various ways God might relate to time. Two pro-posals dominate. The divine timelessness view we find in Augustine says God experiences no succession of moments. God has no expe-rience. Many use the word "eternal" to identify this view, although in popular vernacular, some say God is "outside time."

The other dominant way to think about God and time is often called the "everlasting" view.[9] It says God experiences a succession of moments, and this succession had no beginning and will have no end. But God experiences the ongoing flow of time. Past moments preceded each moment of God's everlasting life, and God will expe-rience moment by moment everlastingly into the future. The ever-lasting God is the "living God," to use a common biblical phrase, in the sense of experiencing time's ongoing succession.

---

[4] Augustine, *On the Trinity*, 5, 17; *Confessions*, 13, 38, 53; *City of God*, 11, 8; 22, 30.

[5] Augustine, *Confessions*, XI. xiii (16).

[6] Ibid.

[7] Ibid.

[8] Ibid.

[9] Translations of scripture rarely indicate what view of time the writer holds. Biblical transla-tors sometimes use the word "eternal" to describe what is likely the "everlasting" view and vice versa. Note, for instance, various translations of the conclusion to John 3:16. Some say God gives "eternal" life and other say "everlasting" life.

In short, to say God is "eternal" means God is timeless or non-temporal. To say God is "everlasting" means God continually experiences and is pantemporal.

My Response to a Timeless God

It is difficult to align the dominant portrait of God in scripture with Augustine's and classical theism's portrait. The God described in the Old and New Testaments interacts with creatures, moment by moment. This involves time sequences. The living God of interactive love has "befores" and "afters," making promises about what God will do and responding to what creatures have done. In the Bible, God plans for the future, talks about past events, and acts alongside creatures in the present. Biblical writers typically describe God as one who experiences time's flow.

Old Testament writers use the word *olam* to describe God's relation to time. This Hebrew word connotes long duration, antiquity, and futurity rather than timelessness. *Olam* describes the remote past or future, but also the notion of perpetuity.[10] When used with reference to God, *olam* better describes God as everlastingly experiencing rather than as timelessly not experiencing. Many scholars also say the timeless view of God is absent in the New Testament.[11]

According to this reasoning, passages that appear to support divine timelessness are better interpreted as identifying God's faithfulness. God is lovingly faithful *through* time, not outside it. C. R. Schoonhoven states the case bluntly: "In the understanding of the writers of the Old Testament and New Testament, eternity is not timelessness but endless time."[12] The God of the Bible "lives in time,"

---

[10] F. Brown, S. R. Driver, and C. A. Briggs, *A Hebrew and English Lexicon* (London: Oxford University Press, 1906), 761.

[11] Oscar Cullmann, *Christ and Time*, F. V. Filson, trans. (London: SCM, 1951[rev. ed. 1962]), 69-80. This is the conclusion of many New Testament scholars, including Eldon G. Ladd (*A Theology of the New Testament* [Grand Rapids, Mich.: Eerdmans, 1974], 47).

[12] C.R. Schoonhoven, "Eternity" *International Standard Bible Encyclopedia*, vol. 2, ed. G. W. Bromiley (Grand Rapids, Mich.: Eerdmans, 1982), 162-164.

says John Goldingay.[13] "Neither timelessness nor the simultaneity of past, present, and future," says Terence Fretheim, "would represent the view of any biblical tradition."[14]

An everlastingly time-full God interacts with time-full creatures in a time-full universe.

The timeless view presents problems for a theology of love. From everything we know, love requires time-full giving and receiving. Love is interactive and experiential, which implies influencing and being influenced moment by moment. The love of a timeless God would be nondurational, which makes no sense with love as we know it.

If the divine timelessness view is true, many biblical passages would be meaningless. John's claim that we love because God *first* loved us (1 Jn. 4:19), for instance, would be incomprehensible. A timeless God doesn't act prior to our actions. If God is nontemporal, John should have said we and God love simultaneously. Creatures would not need a timeless God to act first on their behalf.

Or take the biblical view that God redeems.[15] To say God, in love, redemptively responds to sin makes no sense if God is timeless. A timeless God has no time to redeem, because an eternal God does not respond to what occurs in time's flow. Nicholas Wolterstorff puts it nicely: "God the Redeemer cannot be a God eternal."[16] A redeeming God must be everlasting, which means responding moment-by-moment to creation.

One of the most profound expressions of divine love is forgiveness. God responds to sin by forgiving the offender. "If we confess our sins," writes John, "he who is faithful and just will forgive us our

---

[13] John Goldingay, *Israel's Gospel*, Vol. 1 of *Old Testament Theology* (Downers Grove, Ill.: Intervarsity, 2003), 64.

[14] Terence E. Fretheim, *God and the World in the Old Testament: A Relational Theology of Creation* (Nashville: Abingdon, 2005), 303.

[15] Richard Holland Jr. offers a strong argument for why a timeless God cannot be incarnate. See *God, Time, and the Incarnation* (Eugene, Or.: Wipf and Stock, 2012).

[16] Nicholas Wolterstorff, "God Everlasting," in *God and the Good*, ed. Clifton J. Orlebeke and Lewis B. Smedes (Grand Rapids, Mich.: Eerdmans, 1975), 182.

sins" (1 Jn. 1:9). But forgiving love makes no sense if God is time-less, because a nontemporal God cannot respond. Forgiveness is a time-oriented form of love.

Love requires time, and Augustine's God doesn't have any.

2. AUGUSTINE BELIEVES GOD IS IMMUTABLE

Closely related to God as timelessly eternal is the view God cannot change.[17] "We have God within us," says Augustine, "and there all that we love is fixed and changeless."[18] "[God] is the one who supremely and primordially is," he says, "being absolutely unchanging."[19] "There is no modification in God," says Augustine, "because there is nothing in him that can be changed or lost…he remains absolutely unchangeable."[20] People ought to orient themselves toward God who is "the unchangeable good."[21]

Like Platonic and Neo-Platonic philosophers, Augustine worries about transience. He thinks the permanent and eternal are ultimately good but what changes is not. "Those alone are to be enjoyed which we have noted as being eternal and unchanging," he says.[22] The problem with loving ourselves and other creatures, according to Augustine, is that we "are not turning to anything unchangeable." Humans should "proceed from temporal and bodily things to grasp those that are eternal and spiritual."[23]

Classical theism says God never changes in relation to creation or within Godself. Even the Father, Son, and Holy Spirit "possess the same eternity," says Augustine, "the same unchangeableness."[24]

---

[17] Augustine, *On the Trinity*, 5, 17; *Confessions*, 13, 38, 53; *City of God*, 11, 8; 22, 30.

[18] Augustine, *De Musica*, vol. 6, xiv, 48.

[19] Augustine, *On the Trinity*, 9, 2.

[20] Augustine, *Teaching Christianity*, Book 5, paragraph 5.

[21] Ibid., Book 1, paragraph 21.

[22] Ibid., Book 1, paragraph 22.

[23] Ibid., Book 1, paragraph 4.

[24] Ibid., Book 1, paragraph 5.

As timeless, God is unchanging in all respects. This only makes sense if, as Augustine and classical theism think, God never experiences moment by moment.

Divine immutability is typically linked to a particular understanding of divine perfection and God's enjoyment of values.[25] Augustine thinks God has all values in Godself. Nothing can be added to God, and nothing could be lost. Divine perfection, in this view, entails divine immutability.[26] Perfection cannot be improved.

My Response to an Immutable God

Love requires change. Giving and receiving love assume a moment in which the gift is not yet given and a subsequent moment when it is. Love assumes a change in the receiver from not having received the gift to receiving it. Unchanging beings cannot give and receive love. An immutable God cannot love, at least in the way we know love.

The biblical witness affirms God's immutability *and* mutability. Consequently, the theology of love I propose says, that in one sense, yes, God's love changes. But in another sense, no, it does not. Divine love is immutable in one aspect but mutable in another.

Take Malachi 3:6 as an example, because many quote this passage to support divine immutability. "For I the Lord do not change," it reads. The very next verse, however, indicates God can change: "Ever since the days of your ancestors," the Lord continues, "you have turned aside from my statutes and have not kept them. Return to me, and I will return to you" (3:7). For God to return is to change from one relational state to another. That's divine mutability.

Another passage often cited to affirm immutability says, "God is not a human being that he should lie, or a mortal that he should

---

[25] For other examples of this view of divine perfection, see Stephen Charnock in, eds. Samuel Renihan, *God Without Passions: A Reader* (Palmdale, Fl.: Reformed Baptist Academic, 2015), 144-154; Carl F. H. Henry, *God, Revelation, and Authority: The God who Stands and Stays, Part One*, vol. 5 (Waco, Tex.: Word, 1982), 304.

[26] K. A. Rogers, *Perfect Being Theology* (Edinburgh: Edinburgh University Press, 2000), 47.

change his mind" (Num. 23:19). Other Old Testament passages say God changes, however. In Exodus, we read, "The LORD changed his mind about the disaster that he planned to bring on his people" (32:14). According to Jonah, "When God saw what they did, how they turned from their evil ways, God changed his mind about the calamity that he had said he would bring upon them; and he did not do it" (3:10). These and other passages say God changes.[27]

The book of James offers perhaps the most cited New Testament passage supporting immutability. "Every generous act of giving, with every perfect gift, is from above," James writes, "coming down from the Father of lights, with whom there is no variation or shadow due to change" (1:17). While this verse says in God "there is no variation or change," it also says "every generous act of giving, with every perfect gift" comes from God. According to classical theism, a timeless and unchanging God never acts more than once. Multiple acts require change. So this verse in James supports *both* divine change and changelessness.

We make best sense of scripture if we distinguish between God's nature and God's experience. Love in God's nature is unchanging. The forms of love God expresses change as God acts moment by moment.

We can agree with Augustine if we say God's *essence* is unchanging. Biblical passages saying God never changes are best interpreted as meaning God's essence is immutable. In terms of love, this means God *always* loves, because love is logically primary in God's nature. Because God's essence is immutable, we can count on God's love. God is faithful.

At the same time, Scripture writers describe God as an experiencing individual, and the divine experience changes moment by moment. God lives. In interactive love relationships, God chooses

---

[27] On Old Testament statements about God repenting, see Terence Fretheim, *The Suffering of God*; Michael J. Chan and Brent A. Strawn, eds., *What Kind of God? Collected Essays of Terence E. Fretheim* (Winona Lake: Eisenbrauns, 2015), ch. 2; R. W. L. Moberly, *Old Testament Theology: Reading the Hebrew Bible as Christian Scripture* (Grand Rapids, Mich.: Baker Academic, 2013), ch. 4.

to love variously in one moment, in a particular circumstance, or in relation to this creature compared to others. Because God's love is tailormade for each creature in each moment, it changes to suit the recipient and situation. The *experience* of a perfectly loving God changes in ongoing love relationships.[28]

I call these two aspects the "divine essence-experience binate." Others call it dipolar theism.[29] God's essence-experience binate affirms both an eternal and unchanging divine essence *and* an everlasting and changing divine experience. These are not two parts of God; they describe two aspects.

How God loves in one moment can differ from how God loves in the next. The divine experience changes in the interest of diverse creatures and complex creation. Divine love is pluriform: God loves in numerous ways to promote the well-being of people, other creatures, and all creation. *The fact that* God loves, however, is eternal and immutable. God never transitions from loving to unloving or from unloving to loving. God *always* loves because God's nature is love. In short, the divine essence-experience binate entails that:

God's loving essence is unchanging, but God's loving experience changes.

Affirming God's essence-experience binate allows us to accept two forms of divine perfection.[30] God is perfectly immutable, in the sense that the divine essence never changes. Essences don't increase or decrease; they cannot be added to or subtracted from. But God's experience is perfectly mutable, in the sense that the divine

---

[28] Peter Forrest makes this case in *Developmental Theism: From Pure Will to Unbounded Love* (Oxford: Oxford University Press, 2007).

[29] Charles Hartshorne raised "dipolar theism" to prominence. See his essay "The Dipolar Conception of Deity," *Review of Metaphysics* 21:2 [1967], 273-89) and Donald Viney's explanation in "Hartshorne's Dipolar Theism and the Mystery of God" *Philosophia*, 35 (2007), 341-350.

[30] Charles Hartshorne should be given credit for being the first to articulate well this expanded view of divine perfection. Among his many books, see *Man's Vision of God and the Logic of Theism* (Chicago and New York: Willett, Clark, and Co., 1941), 348.

experience changes moment by moment. The divine experience is added to and increases perfectly.[31]

God's essence-experience binate is doubly perfect.

3. AUGUSTINE BELIEVES GOD IS IMPASSIBLE

The two classical claims that God is timeless and immutable in all respects fit naturally with a third affirmation: God is impassible. Creatures cannot influence God, and God needs no one. Many today call this "nonrelational" theology because it says God is not related to and not influenced by others.[32]

If God "enjoys us," reasons Augustine, "he is in need of some good of ours." But this is preposterous, he says: "nobody in his right mind could possibly say" this.[33] God needs nothing, so creatures have nothing to offer.

Augustine uses the philosophical category of "accidents" to describe what an impassible God neither has nor experiences. Accidental properties "can be either lost or diminished," he explains, or they exist "in relation to something." Examples of accidental properties, says Augustine, include "friendships, relationships, services, likenesses, equalities, and anything else of the kind." They include "places and times, acts and passions."[34]

---

[31] Charles Hartshorne argues this point in several books, especially *The Logic of Perfection* (LaSalle, Ill.: Open Court, 1962).

[32] Jürgen Moltmann, for instance, is well known for emphasizing God's suffering. See, especially, *The Crucified God* (London: SCM, 1974). See also Richard Bauckham, *Jesus and the God of Israel: God Crucified and Other Studies on the New Testament's Christology of Divine Identity* (Grand Rapids, Mich.: Eerdmans, 2008); William Placher, *Narratives of a Vulnerable God: Christ, Theology, and Scripture* (Louisville, Ky.: Westminster John Knox, 1994); Alan Torrance, "Does God Suffer? Incarnation and Impassibility," in ed. Trevor A. Hart, *Christ in Our Place: The Humanity of God in Christ for the Reconciliation of the World* (Eugene, Or.: Wipf and Stock, 1989).

[33] Augustine, *Teaching Christianity*, Book 1, paragraph 31.

[34] Augustine, *Trinity* V:17.

"In God," Augustine says, "*nothing* is said to be according to accident."[35] This means God can't act, relate, be a friend, experience time, or be like creatures. Those are accidental properties, and God does not have them.

To say God is impassible means creatures cannot influence or affect deity. God is not really related to creatures or the universe in the sense of undergoing causal influence. God has no experience *of* anything beyond the divine self. Ancient people used the word "suffer" to describe experiencing a feeling or being affected in relationship. Augustine's God never suffers.[36]

Divine impassibility is connected to classical theism's claim that God has no emotional responses to creatures.[37] God cannot experience pain or joy, for instance, in reaction to what creatures do. God has no empathy or compassion, in the sense of responding to a creature's experiential state.[38] God only experiences happiness by enjoying Godself.

---

[35] Ibid.

[36] Thomas Aquinas thought God was not affected by creatures. "A relation of God to creatures is not a reality in God," he writes. In this way of thinking, God knows creatures as ideas without being causally affected by them. Influencing relations with creation "are not really in Him," Aquinas says, and "are ascribed to him only in our understanding." In other words, we only *imagine* God gives and receives in loving relationship. See Thomas Aquinas, *Summa Theologica*, I (Westminster, Md: Christian Classics, 1981), q. 6, a.2, ad 1; *Summa Contra Gentiles* II (Notre Dame, Ind.: University of Notre Dame Press, 1981), 13-14.

[37] Thomas Aquinas argues against the idea God has emotions, based on his view that God is bodiless. "Every passion of the appetite takes place through some bodily change," said Aquinas about emotions. "None of this can take place in God, since He is not a body." Aquinas, *Summa Contra Gentiles*, I, 89, 3. I have argued that God doesn't need to have a divine body to feel emotion. See Thomas Jay Oord, "Strong Passibility," and "My Response," in *Four Views of Divine Impassibility*, Robert Matz, ed. (Downers Grove, Ill.: Intervarsity, 2019).

[38] "How are you compassionate, and at the same time passionless?" Anselm asks rhetorically. "For if you are passionless, you do not feel sympathy. And if you do not feel sympathy, your heart is not wretched from sympathy for the wretched. But this it is to be compassionate." In response to his own question, Anselm says, "When you behold us in our wretchedness, we experience the effect of compassion, but you do not experience the feeling. Therefore, you are both compassionate, because you do save the wretched and spare those who sin against you, and not compassionate, because you are affected by no sympathy for wretchedness." So we *think* God is compassionate, according to Anselm, when God is actually not. See St. Anselm, *Proslogium*, tr. Sidney Norton Deane (La Salle, IL, 1951), 13-14.

My Response to an Impassible God

Contemporary theologians know the problems with divine impassibility well. The classic view matches neither the biblical witness nor love as we understand it.[39] An impassible God can't love relationally.

But the God of the Bible is relational, being affected by creatures. Scripture writers describe God as compassionate, for instance, which involves divine emotions and feelings in response to creatures.[40] Creation causally influences deity, and scripture writers depict God as experiencing anger, joy, sadness, and other emotions in response.

Only relational beings can love. Love requires experiencing others, in the sense of affecting and being affected. Love responds. Lovers often also experience emotions in relation to what occurs. Without emotional experiences, God could not feel empathy, joy, or sadness and express love in response.

The covenants described in scripture are primary examples of divine relationality. God initiates these covenants, and they require ongoing commitments and responses. We judge the ongoing actions of covenant parties as we evaluate whether promises are kept. This

---

[39] A host of Old Testament scholars argue in favor of divine passibility. For examples, see Walter Brueggemann, *Theology of the Old Testament: Testimony, Dispute, Advocacy* (Minneapolis: Fortress, 1997); Terence Fretheim, *God and the World in the Old Testament*; *The Suffering of God*; *What Kind of God?*; John Goldingay, *Old Testament Theology*, vol. 1 (Downers Grove, Ill.: InterVarsity, 1993); Abraham Heschel, *The Prophets* (New York: Harper and Row, 1962).

[40] Among the many theologians who argue that God is passible, see Dietrich Bonhoeffer, *The Cost of Discipleship* (New York: Macmillan, 1949); Gregory A. Boyd, *Is God to Blame?* (Downers Grove, Ill.: InterVarsity, 2003); John B. Cobb, Jr., *God and the World* (Philadelphia: Westminster, 1969); H. Ray Dunning, *Grace, Faith, and Holiness* (Kansas City, Mo.; Beacon Hill, 1988); Paul Fiddes, *The Creative Suffering of God* (Oxford: Oxford University Press, 1988); Catherine Keller, *From a Broken Web* (Boston: Beacon, 1986); Kazoh Kitamori, *Theology of the Pain of God* (Richmond: John Knox, 1965); Jung Young Lee, *God Suffers for Us* (Netherlands: Martinus Nijhoff, The Hague, 1974); Jeff Pool, *God's Wounds: Hermeneutic of the Christian Symbol of Divine Suffering*; John Sanders, *The God Who Risks: A Theology of Divine Providence* (Downers Grove, Ill.: Intervarsity Academic, 2007); Nicholas Wolterstorff, "Suffering Love," in *Philosophy and the Christian Faith*, Thomas V. Morris, ed. (Notre Dame: University of Notre Dame Press, 1990); and others noted in footnotes throughout this book.

evaluating assumes covenant partners are relational and assumes the reality of time's flow.

One of the best ways to describe love's relationality is to say it involves giving and receiving. Love gives and, in doing so, hopes to promote well-being. It receives from those with whom the lover relates. A gift of love is most effective when the giver has previously gathered information.[41] Blind love, in the sense of having little to no information, is often ineffective. We can love well those we know well, but this knowing requires receiving information, relational input, and empathetic influence. A loving God who receives from all creation can love all creation perfectly.

Relationships are essential to love.

4. AUGUSTINE BELIEVES GOD IS SIMPLE

It's common for Christians to say God is one, in the sense of having no divine parts. God's oneness dovetails with the common view that God has no body. God doesn't have a divine liver and heart, no divine fingernails or claws. God is incorporeal. The divine mind is unified. Although God has various thoughts, makes plans, and recalls past events, God does not struggle with split-personality disorder.

God has essential unity and is simple in this sense. How God is also triune, of course, involves additional speculation. But if divine simplicity means God has no parts, no body, and no mental diffusion, most Christians will affirm it.

Classical theism, however, adds additional claims to the notion of divine simplicity. According to it, God's attributes are identical to one another.[42] God's omnipotence, for instance, is identical to God's

---

[41] On love as gift, see Risto Saarinen, *God and the Gift* (Collegeville, Mn.: Liturgical, 2005).

[42] Ryan T. Mullins offers a convincing criticism of divine simplicity he calls "the problem of modal collapse." If God intentionally acts to create a world and God's acts are identical with God's necessary nature, the world's existence is necessary. But classical theists want to say the world does *not* exist necessarily. Furthermore, the world must necessarily be as it is; it could not be otherwise. See Mullins, "Classical Theism," 85-100.

love and knowledge. Divine attributes are identical to one another in God's nature, and God's nature is identical to God's existing.[43]

We might put this in a formula: Divine Attributes = Divine Nature = Divine Existence. God exists all at once — as a whole — without material or conceptual parts. Deity is purely actual without potential, which means God is timelessly unified.

"There is a good which is alone simple and therefore unchangeable," says Augustine explaining divine simplicity, "and this is God." God's nature "is called simple," he says, "because it has not anything which it can lose, and because it is not one thing and its contents another." In the simple God, "substance and quality are identical."[44] "God has no properties but is pure essence," says Augustine, and God's attributes "neither differ from his essence nor do they differ materially from each other."[45]

If we accept divine simplicity as understood by Augustine and classical theism, we must not talk about God's power *and* knowledge. They're identical. Nor can we say that God is creator *and* redeemer. We should not say God acts *and* responds. We can't even claim God once created or is now creating. The simple God of classical theism neither acts, nor feels, nor relates, nor starts to create. The best one can say is "God is."

Distinctions in God have no place in classical theism's view of divine simplicity.

My Response to Divine Simplicity

Of the four hallmarks of classical theism, this is the most confusing. It asks us to collapse all references to divine attributes into one flat language about God's nature and existence. Divine simplicity, as

---

[43] E.g., see Aquinas *Summa Theologica*, English Dominican Fathers, trans. (London: Burns, Oates, and Washbourne, 1936) I, Q10; James E. Dolezal, *All That Is in God: Evangelical Theology and the Challenge of Classical Christian Theism* (Grand Rapids, Mich.: Reformation Heritage, 2017).

[44] Augustine, *City of God*, Book 11, paragraph 10.

[45] Augustine, *On Trinity*, Book 6, paragraph 7.

Augustine understands it, eliminates all distinctions in God, which means the biblical language describing a personal, active, relational, and thinking God must be false.

Divine love makes no sense if Augustine's view of divine simplicity is true. If love, by definition, requires actions, relations, freedom, intentions, and the aim to promote well-being, and if those requirements involve real distinctions, the simple God cannot love. A simple God cannot respond, redeem, forgive, or even decide to be generous. Augustine's view of divine simplicity is incompatible with love as described by biblical writers.

Classical theism's view of divine simplicity is incompatible with every definition of love I know, and incompatible with my own definition. If his view of simplicity is true, in fact, not even Augustine himself can talk coherently about divine love. After all, he claims God enjoys Godself. But this implies a distinction between subject and object and between divine states of existence. Such distinctions are impossible if classical divine simplicity is true.

A simple God cannot do what love requires.

Divine simplicity makes it difficult, if not impossible, to talk coherently about God. Augustine realizes this problem and admits it. "God is inexpressible," he says. Even saying this goes too far. So, Augustine corrects himself. "God is not to be called inexpressible," he says. "When this is said about him, something is being expressed." So what solves this problem of language for Augustine? "This battle of words should be avoided," he advises, "by keeping silent."[46]

Augustine doesn't follow his own advice. "While nothing really worthy of God can be said," he continues, "[God] has accepted the homage of human voices and has wished us to rejoice in praising him with our words."[47]

But this explanation makes no sense, given divine simplicity. A simple God can't "accept the homage of human voices." Nor can this God "wish us to rejoice in praising him with our words."

---

[46] Augustine, *Teaching Christianity*, Book 1, paragraph 6.
[47] Ibid.

Accepting and wishing are actions a simple God can't do in response to creatures.

We simply cannot fathom how a simple God loves.

TALKING WELL ABOUT DIVINE AND CREATURELY LOVE

Augustine's theology and classical theism draw from Platonic and Neo-Platonic categories not in harmony with how scripture typically describes God or love. Neither are these categories in harmony with our personal experience of love. Love, in Augustine's theology, has little or no similarity to love as we know it.

The key problem in Augustine and classical theism's love language is the claim God utterly transcends creation, in the sense of being unlike creatures in just about every way possible. Their philosophical categories prevent them from saying Creator and creatures have anything in common. God has no "likenesses," "relations," "actions," or "equalities" with creatures, says Augustine.[48] Those traits are accidents, and God has none of them. God does not act, relate, or feel like creatures do, because Creator differs from creatures in these respects.[49]

I noted this problem briefly in the last chapter when we saw Augustine says God can't enjoy us. Instead, God uses us. But because God has no needs, God "does not make use of us either," says Augustine. God does not use us "in the same way as we use things." He explains: "Our making use of things is directed to the end of enjoying God's goodness." But "God's making use of us is directed to his goodness."[50]

---

[48] Augustine, *Trinity* V:17.

[49] Thomas Aquinas suffers from this language problem as well. For his discussion of God's perfections and the creature's relation to them, see *Summa Theologica* (Westminster, Md.: Christian Classics, 1981), I, Q. 4, arts. 1-3. See also Etienne Gilson, *The Christian Philosophy of St. Thomas Aquinas* (Notre Dame: University of Notre Dame Press, 1956), 103-110; E. L. Mascall, *Existence and Analogy: A Sequel to "He Who Is"* (London: Longmans, Green, and Co., 1949), ch. 5.

[50] Augustine, *Teaching Christianity*, Book 1, paragraph 32.

It's hard to imagine what it means for a God with no relations, actions, or passions to *use* creation for God's own sake. Using, as we know it, assumes relations, actions, and passions. Divine using, therefore, must be entirely different from ours. We use things for some purpose, relating to it and having desires for something we do not already have. Augustine says God uses us for what God already has, and that makes no sense. There is no similarity between creaturely use and divine use.

Without similarities between us and God, our theological language cannot be meaningful.[51] If God is utterly dissimilar to creatures, divine love is utterly incomprehensible. Absolute apophatic theology cannot communicate anything true about divine love.

Classical theists like Augustine insist God is timeless, impassible, immutable, and simple. But when they consider God's love, relations, feelings, or actions, they say God utterly transcends human language. God doesn't have those accidental properties. Divine love is a mystery, in this view, but divine timelessness is not. If God utterly transcends human language, I ask, how can we then insist on the truth of human concepts like timelessness, impassability, immutability, and simplicity?[52]

It stands to reason that classical theists should either 1) affirm absolute mystery about God, which means also rejecting all claims about God being timeless, impassible, immutable, and simple (affirming absolute mystery also means, as Augustine realized, remaining utterly silent); or they should 2) reject divine timelessness, impassibility, immutability, and simplicity. This second path allows one to embrace common language for divine and creaturely love.

---

[51] George M. Newlands puts it nicely: "If there is to be genuine communication, there must be some sort of analogical relationship between God and our language about him" (*Theology of the Love of God* [Atlanta: John Knox, 1980], 53). See also Eberhard Jungel, *God as the Mystery of the World: On the Foundation of the Theology of the Crucified One in the Dispute between Theism and Atheism*, trans. Darrell L. Gruder (Grand Rapids, Mich.: Eerdmans, 1983), 281.

[52] Charles Hartshorne argues similarly in *The Divine Relativity: A Social Conception of God* (New Haven: Yale University Press, 1948), 26.

Doing so could produce a theology that fits the biblical witness and human experience.

A plausible theology assumes love's meaning applies to creatures and Creator. It points to connections between divine and creaturely love. And it assumes we can speak positively about God.

Robust theologies of love affirm analogies between Creator and creatures. These analogies are bi-directional, in the sense of saying the Creator is like creatures in some ways and creatures are also like their Creator.[53] Bi-directional analogies assume that some ontological categories apply to both God and creation.[54] They provide a conceptual basis, for instance, to say God and creatures act, relate, feel, and love.[55]

The most likely path for Christians to identify similarities between divine and creaturely love begins with scripture. As I've shown in previous chapters, biblical writers talk well and often of love, both creaturely and divine. The parables of Jesus, the poetry in the Psalms, the vision of John, Paul's epistles, and many other biblical writings use bi-directional analogies for love expressed by God and creatures.

---

[53] Normally, analogies are bi-directional. But many classical theists, such as Thomas Aquinas, think of Creator-creation analogies as uni-directional. Aquinas affirms such analogies when he says creature are like God, but God is not like creatures (*Summa Contra Gentiles* [London-New York: 1928 & 1929], I: 29). Aquinas also affirms a *via negativa,* insofar as "we cannot grasp what God is, but what He is not" (Ibid., II, 21). In terms of love, this means the love that creatures express is like God's love, but God's love is *not* like creaturely love. And we cannot grasp divine love. My love analogies reject uni-directional analogies and a *via negative,* at least in the sense Aquinas uses it.

[54] Daniel Day Williams says this well: "On the strictest biblical terms, there must be something in common between the words we use to speak about God's being and about our being" (*The Spirit and the Forms of Love* [New York: Harper and Row, 1968], 123). Such analogies offer conditions for "appropriate human discourse on God," as Eberhard Jungel puts it, and "the point of departure for an ethical theory for Christian faith" ("La signification de l'analogie pour la theologie" in *Analogi et dialectique,* ed. J. L. Marion [Geneve, 1982], 250). For a discussion on Jungel and analogy, see Philip A. Rolnick, *Analogical Possibilities: How Words Refer to God,* AAR Series, no. 81 (Atlanta: Scholars, 1993).

[55] Gary Chartier puts this nicely, "To understand God using the analogy of love is to allow our convictions to be shaped by a complex interplay of the church's narrative and affirmations about God on the one hand and our own experiences and reflection on the other" (*The Analogy of Love: Divine and Human Love at the Center of Christian Theology* [Charlottesville, VA: Imprint Academic, 2007], 13).

"Be imitators of God, as beloved children," says Paul, for instance, "and live in love..." (Eph. 5:1). This command makes no sense if Paul thought God's love was utterly dissimilar to human love. If creaturely love is entirely different from divine love, Jesus' command to "be merciful, just as your Father is merciful" (Lk. 6:36) would also be meaningless.

Insofar as Jesus provides the fullest revelation of God's love and insofar as humans can love like he did, Jesus's love identifies similarities between divine and creaturely love. "We know love by this," says John, "that he laid down his life for us." So "we ought to lay down our lives for one another" (1 Jn. 3:16). This passage and many others provide grounds for believing self-giving is one form of love both Creator and creature can express. According to the revelation of Jesus Christ, we can love like God, at least in some ways.

Another path showing connections between divine and creaturely love points to how God has been revealed in "the things he has made" (Rm. 1:20). God is like a hen lovingly gathering chicks, for instance (Mt. 23:37) or an eagle protecting its nest (Dt. 32:11). Because humans have been created in God's image, this motherly love presumably tells us something about God's love (Gen. 1:26). In fact, biblical writers often express the activity and character of God in analogies about masters and servants, grooms and brides, husbands and wives, and fathers and sons.[56] They also employ metaphor, simile, and other positive language to describe love, creaturely and divine.

Because God shares similarities with us, God's love and ours have similarities.

---

[56] For an extensive discussion of New Testament analogies, see Herbert M. Gale, *The Use of Analogy in the Letters of Paul* (Philadelphia: Westminster, 1965). For a philosophical explorations of the analogies of love, see Robert Merrihew Adams, *Finite and Infinite Goods: A Framework for Ethics* (Oxford: Oxford University Press, 1999) and Paul Ricoeur, "Naming God," in *Figuring the Sacred*, Mark Wallace, ed. (Minneapolis: Fortress Press, 1995).

SIMILARITIES AND DIFFERENCES BETWEEN DIVINE AND CREATURELY LOVE

Every theology assumes philosophical ideas. We can't go through life without philosophy, even though many people do not consciously evaluate their philosophical assumptions. I believe a robust Christian theology of love ought to adopt assumptions consonant with scripture, human experience, and the knowledge we find in various disciplines.

The theology of love I propose affirms philosophical ideas that lie in stark contrast to ideas Augustine and other classical theists embrace. But such contrast is necessary, I believe, if we are to construct a viable Christian theology of love. Good philosophical assumptions support basic analogies vital to a coherent theology.

Let me spell out briefly some basic analogies of love I find helpful and that point to similarities and differences between God and us.[57] While these statements do not exhaust all analogies between God and creation, the assumptions of each stand in contrast to Augustine's assumptions.[58] These statements also better fit love expressed by God and creatures as portrayed in scripture.

1. Creator and creatures give and receive in loving relationship.

Both God and creatures are relational. They affect others and are affected; their love is giving and receiving. God and creatures are passible, to use the ancient language. Instead of accepting classical theism's claim that God only gives, we should affirm that God and

---

[57] On analogies of love, see Thomas Jay Oord, "Analogies of Love between God and Creatures: A Response to Kevin Vanhoozer," In *Love, Human and Divine: Contemporary Essays in Systematic and Philosophical Theology* (London: T & T Clark, 2020).

[58] For more helpful philosophical frameworks to make sense of Christian love, see David Ray Griffin, *Reenchantment without Supernaturalism: A Process Philosophy of Religion* (Ithaca, NY: Cornell University Press, 2001); Keith Ward, *The Christian Idea of God: A Philosophical Foundation for Faith* (Cambridge: Cambridge University Press, 2017).

creatures give and receive love in relationship. Creator and creatures are alike in this way.

God differs from creatures, however, by giving and receiving perfectly. God is the ideal contributor and ideal receiver; creatures do not always give and receive ideally.[59] Only God loves perfectly at all times. Creator and creatures differ in this way.

2. Creator and creatures love in the ongoing flow of time.

Both God and creatures love moment by moment. The timeless, eternal God of classical theism cannot love this way, but an everlasting God can. Rather than acting all at once, God loves moment by moment, like creatures do. This love responds to what happened in the past and acts to promote good in the present. The future depends, in part, on the love Creator and creatures express now. Creator and creatures are alike in time-full love.

God differs from creatures, however, by loving everlastingly. There is no beginning and no end to divine love. Creatures have a beginning and have not always loved. The steadfast love of the Lord endures forever. Creator and creatures differ in this way.

3. Creator and creatures love by promoting overall well-being.

Both God and creatures love by aiming to promote overall well-being. In fact, my definition of love — to act intentionally, in relational response to God and others, to promote overall well-being — applies both to Creator and creatures. Both God and creatures can act in ways that engender flourishing. The love of both aims to promote overall well-being.

God differs from creatures by promoting overall well-being directly as the omnipresent Lover. The love creatures express can

---

[59] For what it means that God is an ideal contributor and receiver, see *Defining Love*, ch. 6. See also Daniel Day Williams, *The Spirit and the Forms of Love*, 10; Mark Lloyd Taylor, *God is Love: A Study in the Theology of Karl Rahner*, AAR Academy Series 50 (Atlanta: Scholars, 1986), 304.

contribute to overall well-being as they act locally, but an omnipresent God directly and universally promotes well-being. The God who loves all creation directly can act directly for the good of a worm in Japan and a horse in Guatemala. Divine and creaturely loves differ in scope.

4. Creator and creatures love as experiencers.

Both God and creatures are experiencers. To be loved is to experience well-being; to love is to act as an experiencer who seeks to enhance the experiences of others. Because love is inherently experiential, both Creator and creatures must experience.[60] Creator and creatures are alike in this way.

God differs from creatures as the omnipresent experiencer. As one who loves from complete social awareness, God experiences the values of *all* pleasures and *all* pain. The Creator is the omni-experiencer, in the sense that God feels alongside all creaturely experiencers. Creatures love from limited awareness as localized experiencers with localized bodies.[61] They experience *some* pleasures and pains. God and creatures differ in this way.

5. Creator and creatures are agents who love freely.

Both God and creatures make choices about how to love. As free agents, their choices are not entirely determined by past, present, or future. Although Nygren and Augustine thought otherwise, I'm

---

[60] David Ray Griffin defends a version of panpsychism he calls "panexperientialism." It says all existing beings and entities — from God to quarks — are experiential. See *Unsnarling the World-Knot: Consciousness, Freedom, and the Mind-Body Problem* (Berkely: University of California Press, 1998). Joanna Leidenhag defends a similar view, although embracing a more traditional theology. See *Minding Creation: Theological Panpsychism and the Doctrine of Creation* (London: T & T Clark, 2021).

[61] For more on my view of panexperientialism/panpsychism, see Thomas Jay Oord and Wm. Andrew Schwartz, "Panentheism and Panexperientialism for Open and Relational Theology," in *Panentheism and Panpsychism: Philosophy of Religion Meets Philosophy of Mind*, Godehard Brüntrup, et. al., eds., (Mentis Verlag/Brill, 2020).

claiming Creator and creatures have genuine but limited freedom.[62] Both freely decide what forms of love to express. While creatures rely upon their Creator to empower and inspire love, both Creator and creatures are alike in loving freely.

Creatures differ from God in that creatures can choose *not* to love. God must love because God is essentially loving. Creatures do not have eternal natures of love, so their love is erratic. They sometimes freely sin, which is not loving. Creatures differ from God by choosing whether to love, whereas God loves necessarily.

6. Creator and creatures have the needs of love.

Love cannot occur in isolation. Lovers need a beloved; the beloved needs those who love them. Both God and creatures have needs inherent in what it means to love.[63] We don't have to understand God as entirely egoistic; we can also affirm God as altruistic. Creatures don't have to be entirely egoistic; they can also act altruistically. The loving Creator and loving creatures are alike in needing others to love.

God differs from creatures in that while God needs others to love, God exists necessarily. Creatures do not exist necessarily. God both exists necessarily and needs creatures to love. This will sound odd to some, but I'll explain it further in an upcoming chapter. The point: Creator and creatures both have the needs of love, but they differ in what they need to exist.

---

[62] How Augustine understands intentionality and agency is another matter. Much of his thought implies that creaturely agency does not include genuine freedom vis-à-vis God. According to Augustine, "however strong the wills either of angels or of men, whether good or evil, whether they will what God wills or will something else, the will of the Omnipotent is always undefeated" (*Enchiridion*, paragraphs 95 & 100). Augustine shifted to what seems to be determinism. See *To Simplician — One of Various Questions* in *Augustine: Earlier Writings*, John H. S. Burleigh trans. (Philadelphia: Westminster, 1953), 370-406. On these issues, also see also Kenneth Wilson, *Augustine's Conversion from Traditional Free Choice to "Non-free Free Will"* (Tübingen: Mohr Siebeck, 2018).

[63] On God having the needs of love, see Vincent Brümmer, *The Model of Love* (Cambridge: Cambridge University Press, 1993), ch. 9.

7. Creator and creatures are valuable in themselves.

Both God and creatures are inherently valuable.[64] Both can be valued for their own sakes. As experiencers, in fact, both the well-being of God and the well-being of creatures can be enhanced when others love them. But both also are intrinsically valuable. Creator and creatures are alike in being valuable.

God differs from creatures by enjoying the greatest values possible and by being supremely valuable. Creatures have limited abilities for enjoyment.[65] And although intrinsically valuable, they are not equal in value with God. God transcends creatures both by being the most valuable and by appreciating all of creation's value. Creator and creatures differ in these respects.

Some similarities and differences in the analogy of love require more explanation.[66] I will do so in future chapters as I explore open and relational theology. My purpose in these brief statements is to show analogies between God's love and ours. These analogies sharply distinguish the theology of love I propose from Augustine's.[67] The

---

[64] For an analysis of value in God and creation, see Andrew M. Davis, *Mind, Value, and Cosmos* (Lanham, Md.: Lexington, 2020); Rem B. Edwards, *An Axiological Process Ethics* (Claremont, Ca.: Process Century, 2014);

[65] Keith Ward has written well and often about the importance of values for theology. Among his books, see especially *Morality, Autonomy, and God* (London: One World, 2013).

[66] To stress God's omnipresence but keep a distinction between God and creation, many embrace panentheism: all things are *in* God. I believe panentheism is best understood as saying all of creation is in God's experience. I prefer a form of panentheism I call "theocosmocentrism." It says adequate theologies place creation and God at their center, but God comes first conceptually. Theocosmocentrism affirms Terrence Fretheim's observation that "God and creation must be considered together, because again and again the texts keep them together." See *God and the World in the Old Testament: A Relational Theology of Creation* (Nashville: Abingdon, 2005), xvi. For an account of the diverse meanings of panentheism, see Philip Clayton and Arthur Peacocke, eds., *In Whom We Live and Move and Have our Being* (Grand Rapids, Mich.: Eerdmans, 2004). For more on the meaning of theocosmocentrism, see Thomas Jay Oord and Wm. Andrew Schwartz, "Panentheism and Panexperientialism for Open and Relational Theology," in *Panentheism and Panpsychism: Philosophy of Religion Meets Philosophy of Mind*, Godehard Brüntrup, et. al., eds., (Mentis Verlag/Brill, 2020).

[67] Jordan Wessling does something similar when he affirms "the similarity thesis." See *Love Divine: A Systematic Account of God's Love for Humanity* (Oxford: Oxford University Press, 2020), 12.

analogies of love I offer provide a framework and language for love without appealing to or resulting in absolute mystery or incoherence.

We *can* talk coherently about love, creaturely and divine.

EROS AS BECAUSE OF LOVE

Despite its deficiencies, Augustine's theology rightly states that theologies of love make claims about value. Love is a value-laden activity. I've argued that well-being is love's goal, and this involves seeking flourishing, peace, nourishment, blessedness, and more. I've said God and creation are intrinsically valuable. But when loved, they both increase in well-being.

Anders Nygren denied humans were free or could desire God. He thought creatures were passive tubes through which divine love moves without creaturely contribution. Christian love, he said, is entirely God's action, and God can give value to creatures not otherwise valuable. In Nygren's view, any talk of humans choosing to love God is illegitimate.

Augustine thought humans ought to desire God as the ultimately valuable one or highest good. Love, in his view, *is* desire, and humans order their desires toward God. But Augustine denies that humans love creatures or themselves for their own sakes. And he believes God only desires what is supremely valuable: Godself. Deity cannot love creatures for their own sakes. Nygren and Augustine are mistaken in many ways.

Eros is the Greek love word usually identified with desiring what is valuable. Although defined variously, *eros* points to love that appreciates, delights, esteems, cherishes, prizes, admires, and more. *Eros* values.

To offer a coherent theology of love, I offered a definition of love and said love takes various forms. Love has one general meaning, but it is pluriform in expressions. A good definition of *eros* as a form of love, therefore, will align with my general love definition. It includes love's essential elements: acting intentionally, relational response to God and others, and promoting overall well-being. But as a form of love, *eros* differs from *agape, philia,* compassion, generosity, and so on.

I propose we understand *eros* as a form of love that appreciates value. It acts intentionally, in response to God and others, to promote overall well-being when appreciating what is beautiful, worthwhile, or valuable. [68] It affirms what is good and enhances well-being in positive response. The ways *eros* appreciates value vary.

We find the values *eros* appreciates in other creatures, creation, and God. All creaturely existence is intrinsically valuable because God creates and calls it all "good" (Gen. 1). And God is good. This means creatures can *eros* God, others, and themselves, for their own sakes. And God can *eros* us, creation, and Godself, for their own sakes. Despite the sin and evil that sometimes occur, creation remains intrinsically good. Encounters with intrinsically valuable others can prompt lovers to express the *eros* form of love.

A robust theology of love says both God and humans can express *eros*.

Some theologians qualify *eros* with adjectives. They speak of "proper *eros,*" "perfect *eros,*" or "holy *eros.*" These adjectives, however, imply *eros* can be improper, imperfect, or unholy. My definition of love eliminates the need for those qualifying adjectives. Every form of love — properly defined — seeks well-being, including *eros*. Qualifiers are redundant when one defines love sufficiently and designates *eros* as a form of love in general.

In an earlier chapter, I said we more easily remember the meaning of *agape* as *in spite of* love. Here I propose we call *eros* the *because of* form of love. *Eros* appreciates value and promotes overall well-being *because of* the value it encounters. *Because of* value present in others, creation, and God, lovers can express *eros*.

Eros enjoys values and promotes well-being when doing so.

---

[68] For a powerful argument that God enjoys creation and creatures ought to enjoy in response, see Elaine Padilla, *Divine Enjoyment: A Theology of Passion and Exuberance* (New York: Fordham University Press, 2015). Rita Nakashima Brock offers an erotic theology in *Journeys By Heart: A Christology of Erotic Power* (New York: Crossroads, 1988).

We promote overall well-being when we love with *eros*. Sometimes, the well-being of the lover herself is primarily promoted. The pleasures that come from enjoying a conversation, watching a glorious sunset, listening to beautiful music, adoring a child's laughter, tasting a delicious meal, smelling the air after a hard rain, satisfying sexual intercourse, and more promotes well-being for the one enjoying these values. As part of the whole, personal enjoyment contributes to the good of the whole.

But *eros* need not be entirely about the one. *Eros* promotes the well-being of others too. The well-being of the chef is enhanced as he watches guests enjoy his mouthwatering meal. The artist feels great satisfaction knowing others find her art exciting. The sexual partner can enjoy pleasure both as one enjoying intercourse and knowing the sexual experience is enjoyable for the other partner. The sidewalk chalk artist gets a kick out of knowing others will be thrilled by her creativity. *Eros* can promote the well-being of many as part of promoting well-being overall.[69]

The God who loves with *eros* both enjoys for God's immediate experience of value and enjoys in response to creaturely enjoyment. As the perfect altruist and egoist, God urges creatures to enjoy positive values. God enjoys alongside creatures and enjoys God's own good. Divine *eros* is good for God and creation.

Eros is "because of" love.

CONCLUSION

Augustine's philosophical assumptions cannot support well an adequate Christian theology of love. They do not fit the dominant view of love in scripture, nor the way we understand love in personal experience.

---

[69] Werner Jeanrond addresses the *eros* form of love well in his book, *A Theology of Love* (London: T & T Clark, 2010). See also Virginia Burrus and Catherine Keller, eds., *Toward a Theology of Eros: Transfiguring Passion at the Limits of Discipline* (New York: Fordham University Press, 2007). Gonwa, Janna. "Eros, Agape, and Neighbour-Love as Ontological Gift," *Toronto Journal of Theology*, 31:1 (Spring 2015): 84-93.

Philosophical assumptions undergird four doctrines Augustine and other classical theists affirm. According to them, God is timeless, immutable, impassible, and simple. Each doctrine is incompatible with love, however. Affirming them makes it difficult, if not impossible, for Augustine to talk coherently about God and love. He advises silence but then does not follow his own advice.

A robust theology rejects the four doctrines of classical theism outlined in this chapter. It assumes bi-directional analogies between God and creatures. I offered seven analogies of love that point to what God and creatures share in common, but also how they differ: Creator and creatures give and receive in loving relationship; love in the ongoing flow of time; can promote overall well-being; love as experiencers; are agents who love freely; have the needs of love; and are valuable in themselves.

Augustine's views address questions of value. Although I reject much of what he proposes, I accept *eros* as a form of love, and affirm it. I say that *eros* promotes overall well-being *because of* the value it encounters. Both God and creatures can express *eros*, and all that exists is intrinsically valuable.

Eros plays a crucial role in robust theologies of love.

7

Open and Relational, Essential Kenosis, and Amipotence

*A*ugustine calls attention to the role philosophy plays in theologies of love. But the philosophical ideas he embraces, as we have seen, fail to fit the way most biblical writers describe love, both creaturely and divine. Scripture mostly understands love as promoting well-being; Augustine mostly understands it as desire. Augustine's assumptions lead him to say God is unaffected, timeless, unchanging, unresponsive, unable to love us for our own sakes, and concerned primarily, if not exclusively, with Godself.

In response to these inadequacies, I offered seven analogies of love. They better account for similarities and differences between divine and creaturely love as described in scripture and evident in experience. In this chapter, I will offer open and relational theology as a theological framework for the theology of love I find most attractive.

While open and relational theology comes in many forms, I find Christian open and relational theology most appealing. Jesus stands at the center of the theology of love I propose. This focus on Jesus' revelation of divine love helps me address the primary reason most atheists believe a loving God does not exist: the problem of evil. Given how most Christians think about God, it's a problem for them too. If God always loves everyone, why doesn't God prevent pointless pain and unnecessary suffering? My answer says Jesus' kenotic love reveals God as essentially kenotic, and divine kenosis is necessarily self-giving, others-empowering, and, therefore, uncontrolling.

A God of uncontrolling love does not want, cause, or permit genuine evil.

OPEN AND RELATIONAL THEOLOGY

Until the second half of the twentieth century, only a few scholars knew well the ideas at the core of open and relational theology. Those who embraced those ideas identified with labels like personalism,[1] process,[2] feminism,[3] relational,[4] freewill theism,[5] Arminian,[6]

---

[1] Edgar Sheffield Brightman was an open and relational theologian, although to my knowledge he did not use the phrase. Other personalists are also open and relational. On personalism, see Edgar S. Brightman, *Is God Personal?* (New York: Association, 1932); Albert C. Knudson, *The Philosophy of Personalism* (New York: Abingdon, 1927). For contemporary personalist theologies, see Rufus Burrow, Jr., *Personalism: A Critical Introduction* (St. Louis, Mo.: Chalice, 1999); Mark Y. A. Davies and Randall Auxier, *Hartshorne and Brightman on God, Process, and Persons* (Nashville, Tenn.: Vanderbilt University Press, 2001).

[2] Alfred North Whitehead and Charles Hartshorne are generally credited as providing process theology's basic conceptual framework. See Alfred North Whitehead, *Process and Reality: An Essay in Cosmology*, corrected edition, ed. David Ray Griffin and Donald W. Sherburne (New York: Free, 1978; orig. ed., 1929); Charles Hartshorne, *The Divine Relativity: A Social Conception of God* (New Haven, Conn.: Yale University Press, 1948). For introductions to process theology, see Bradley Shavit Artson, *God of Becoming and Relationship* (Jewish Lights, 2016); Joseph A. Bracken, *Christianity and Process Thought* (Philadelphia: Templeton Foundation, 2006); John B. Cobb, Jr. and David Ray Griffin, *Process Theology: An Introductory Exposition* (Louisville, KY: Westminster/John Knox, 1976); Monica Coleman, *Making a Way Out of Now Way: A Womanist Theology* (Philadelphia: Fortress, 2008); Bruce Epperly, *Process Theology* (London: T&T Clark, 2011); Catherine Keller, *On the Mystery* (Minneapolis: Fortress, 2007); Jay McDaniel and Donna Bowman, eds., *Handbook of Process Theology* (St. Louis: Chalice, 2006).

[3] See the work of Rosemary Radford Reuther, Elizabeth Johnson, and Marjorie Hewitt Suchocki. For more recent work, see Monica Coleman, Nancy Howell, and Helene Russell, eds., *Creating Women's Theology* (Eugene, Or.: Pickwick, 2011).

[4] To explore relational theology, see Terence Fretheim, *God So Enters Relationships That* (Minneapolis: Fortress, 2020); Curtis Holtzen, *The God Who Trusts* (Downers Grove, Ill.: IVP Academic, 2019); Karen Baker-Fletcher, *Dancing with God: The Trinity from a Womanist Perspective* (St. Louis, Mo: Chalice, 2006); Brint Montgomery, Thomas Jay Oord, and Karen Winslow, *Introducing Relational Theology* (San Diego: Point Loma University Press, 2008).

[5] See David Basinger, *The Case for Freewill Theism* (Downers Grove, Ill.: IVP, 1996).

[6] Roger Olson argues for the compatibility of Arminianism and open theology in "Is Open Theism a Type of Arminianism?" http://www.patheos.com/blogs/rogereolson/2012/11/is-open-theism-a-type-of-arminianism/

Methodist,[7] or something else. In the 21st century, these ideas began moving into the mainstream. "Open and relational theology" has become the label under which these various ideas, people, and movements reside.

Open and relational theology comes in many forms, with multiple interpretations, emphases, and nuances. There is plenty of diversity and difference. But the two words — "open" and "relational" — comprise the umbrella under which this variety stirs.[8] To explain it, I start with those two words.

"Open" indicates an open future. Open and relational thinkers believe God and creation move through time moment by moment into an undetermined future. Neither creatures nor the Creator predetermine what will occur. Neither Creator nor creatures foreknow with certainty everything that will happen. The future does not exist as a set of actual occurrences; it's a realm of possibilities. While creatures are born into time's flow, God experiences time everlastingly.[9]

Love involves actions, and a consistently acting God loves moment by moment.

"Relational" stands for the idea God and creatures influence others and others influence them. Creatures affect God's experience, and

---

[7] On ties between open and relational theology and Methodist/Wesleyan thought, see Lorenzo Dow McCabe, *Divine Nescience of Future Contingencies a Necessity* (New York: Phillips and Hunt, 1882) and *The Foreknowledge of God* (Cincinnati: Cranston and Stowe, 1887); Bryan P. Stone and Thomas Jay Oord, eds., *Thy Name and Thy Nature is Love: Wesleyan and Process Theologies in Dialogue* (Nashville: Kingswood, 2001); John B. Cobb, Jr. *Grace and Responsibility* (Nashville: Abingdon, 1995); Michael Lodahl, *God of Nature and of Grace: Reading the World in a Wesleyan Way* (Nashville: Abingdon, 2003); Rory Randall, *An Open Theist Renewal Theology* (Grasmere, Id.: SacraSage, 2021).

[8] For an introduction to open and relational theology, see Thomas Jay Oord, *Open and Relational Theology* (Grasmere, Id.: SacraSage, 2021).

[9] See Charles Hartshorne, *The Divine Relativity* (New Haven: Yale University Press, 1948); selections from Gregory E. Ganssle and David M. Woodruff, eds, *God and Time: Essays on the Divine Nature* (New York: Oxford University Press, 2002); R.T. Mullins, *The End of the Timeless God* (Oxford: Oxford University Press, 2016); Nicholas Wolterstorff, "God Everlasting" in *Philosophy and Faith*, David Shatz, ed. (New York: McGraw, 2002), 62-69.

R.T. Mullins does admirable work describing the problems that arise when thinking God is in all ways impassible in *The End of the Timeless God*. See also Schubert M. Ogden, *The Reality of God* (Dallas: Southern Methodist University Press, 1992).

the divine experience changes in response. God and other creatures affect creatures, and their experiences change in response. God's nature is eternally unchanging, but as an experiential agent, God gives and receives in relations with creatures and creation.

Love is inherently relational, and an omni-relational God relates with all others.

Open and relational thinkers emphasize other ideas. Many privilege love as the lens through which to best understand God. Many think God calls humans to love others, themselves, God, and all creation. Open and relational thinkers reject the idea we are entirely determined by God or creation, believing humans have genuine, though limited, freedom.[10] Some speculate other creatures and even the smallest of entities have a measure of agency, self-determination, or self-organization. Many open and relational thinkers believe experience — divine and creaturely — is the fundamental category of reality. To be is to experience.[11]

What scholars commonly label "Open theism" and "Process theism" represent the most influential perspectives in the open and relational family.[12] When comparing the two, Clark Pinnock lists their similarities. His list also applies to many theologies under the open and relational tent. This theology:

- makes the love of God a priority;
- holds to libertarian human freedom;
- is critical of conventional theism;

---

[10] For instance, see Jeffery F. Keuss, *Freedom of the Self: Kenosis, Cultural Identity, and Mission at the Crossroads* (Eugene, Or.: Pickwick, 2010); Christian J. Barrigar, *Freedom All the Way Up* (Victoria, B.C.: Friesen, 2017).

[11] David Ray Griffin coined the word "panexperientialism" to describe the idea that all existing actualities are experiential. See "Some Whiteheadian Comments," in *Mind in Nature: Essays on the Interface of Science and Philosophy*, eds. John B. Cobb, Jr., and David Ray Griffin (Washington, DC: University Press of America, 1977).

[12] Richard Rice first presented the label, "openness of God," and the basic ideas of Open theology in his book, *The Openness of God* (Nashville, Tenn.: Review and Herald, 1980). Rice recounts these events in *The Future of Open Theism: Antecedents and Opportunities* (Downers Grove, Ill.: IVP Academic, 2020). For an accessible introduction to open theism, see Chad Bahl, *God Unbound* (Grasmere, Id.: SacraSage, 2021).

- seeks a more dynamic model of God;
- contends God has real, not merely rational, relationships with the world;
- believes God is affected by what happens in the world;
- says God knows what can be known, which does not amount to exhaustive foreknowledge;
- appreciates the value of philosophy in helping to shape theological convictions.[13]

Open and relational thinkers reject the four doctrines common among classical theists I noted earlier. Rather than construing God as timeless, open and relational theology says God is everlastingly time-full. Rather than God being immutable, God's experience changes, although God's essence does not. Rather than being impassable, the God of open and relational theology is relational/passable. Rather than being simple, God acts, relates, and enjoys as a personal though universal agent with an everlasting series of divine experiences.

Open and relational thinkers have diverse interests. They are attracted to various philosophical approaches, political persuasions, artistic expressions, economic theories, and scientific fields. In addition to Christian thinkers, many Jews, Muslims, theistic Buddhists, Bahai, Spiritual But Not Religious, and Nones embrace open and relational ideas.[14] Most who adopt this perspective, however, are Christians trying to follow Jesus.

---

[13] Clark H. Pinnock, *Most Moved Mover: A Theology of God's Openness* (Grand Rapids, Mich.: Baker, 2001), 142-143. For comparisons between Open theology and Process theology, see Thomas Jay Oord, "Evangelical Theologies," in *Handbook of Process Theology*, Jay McDaniel and Donna Bowman, eds. (St. Louis, Mo.: Chalice, 2006) and Donald Wayne Viney, "The Varieties of Theism and the Openness of God: Charles Hartshorne and Free-Will Theism," in *The Personalist Forum* 14/2 (Fall 1998): 199-238. For essays on the relationship between Wesleyan theology and Process theology, see Bryan P. Stone and Thomas Jay Oord, eds., *Thy Nature and Thy Name is Love.* John Culp was one of the first Wesleyan Evangelicals to consider positively how Process resources may be helpful to Evangelicals ("A Dialogue with the Process Theology of John B. Cobb, Jr." *Wesleyan Theological Journal* 17 [Fall 1980]: 33-44).

[14] Many Mormons embrace open and relational theology. Because some think Latter-Day Saints should be included in the Christian tradition, I did not list Mormons among my non-Christian examples.

To explore a Christian version of open and relational theology, I now turn to Clark H. Pinnock.

CLARK H. PINNOCK'S OPEN AND RELATIONAL THEOLOGY

During his life, Clark Pinnock moved from affirming a classical view of God — like Nygren's and Augustine's — to an open and relational theology. He transitioned, in large part, because he wanted to be faithful to the biblical witness as he understood it.[15] Pinnock gives particular weight to biblical narrative and the language of personal relationships described in scripture. Although he rejects fundamentalism, he considers the Bible his principal authority for theology.

Changing one's theology can be unsettling; deconstruction can cause angst. Pinnock overcame his anxiety as he realized that core ideas of open and relational theology grow out of the biblical witness and support Christian experience. "How can we expect Christians to delight in God or outsiders to seek God," he asks rhetorically, "if we portray God in biblically flawed, rationally suspect, and existentially repugnant ways?" "Rather than worry about *our* discomfort, perhaps we should be concerned about *God's* reputation."[16]

Pinnock led in editing and producing the groundbreaking book *The Openness of God: A Biblical Challenge to the Traditional Understanding of God*.[17] In its introduction, he says the book offers a theology that "is biblically faithful and intellectually consistent, and that reinforces, rather than makes problematic, our relational

---

[15] For book-length expositions of Pinnock's life and theology, see Barry L. Callen, *Clark H. Pinnock: Journey Toward Renewal* (Nappanee, Ind.: Evangel, 2000); Andrew Williams, *Boundless Love: A Companion to Clark H. Pinnock's Theology* (Salem, Or.: Wipf and Stock, 2021).

[16] Pinnock, "Systematic Theology" in *The Openness of God*, 104.

[17] Clark H. Pinnock, et. al., *The Openness of God: A Biblical Challenge to the Traditional Understanding of God* (Downers Grove, Ill.: InterVarsity, 1994). Richard Rice provides the "Biblical Support for a New Perspective," John Sanders addresses "Historical Considerations," Pinnock addresses "Systematic Theology," William Hasker provides "A Philosophical Perspective," and David Basinger suggests "Practical Implications."

experience of God."[18] Pinnock's later monograph, *Most Moved Mover*, offers his own fullest explanation of open and relational theology.[19] I draw primarily from these books for what follows.

Pinnock aims to offer a coherent doctrine of God, in which each divine attribute "should be compatible with one another and with the vision of God as a whole."[20] This vision aims to "combine love and power perfectly."[21] According to Pinnock, God is a self-sufficient, though relational, Trinitarian being who voluntarily created the world out of nothing. Divine love, says Pinnock, includes responsiveness, generosity, sensitivity, openness, and vulnerability.[22]

Unfortunately, says Pinnock, leading voices in the Christian tradition have not portrayed God well. Traditional theologies lose a biblical focus or offer odd interpretations of scripture. The package of divine attributes we find in classical theism tends toward divine immobility, nonrelationality, all-controlling sovereignty, and hyper-transcendence.[23]

A biblical vision presents God as a lover who seeks relationship with free creatures, says Pinnock. And "if choices are real and freedom significant," he says, "future decisions cannot be exhaustively known."[24] "The Bible itself assumes libertarian freedom when it posits personal give-and-take relationships and when it holds people responsible for their actions," argues Pinnock. "On this matter I am moved by the Bible itself."[25]

---

[18] Ibid., 7-8.

[19] Another valuable resource is John Sanders's book, *The God Who Risks: A Theology of Providence* (Downers Grove, Ill.: Intervarsity, 1998).

[20] Pinnock, *Most Moved Mover*, 101.

[21] Ibid. This is a book Pinnock co-edits with John B. Cobb, Jr. exploring similarities and differences between Open theology and Process theology. It is appropriately called, *Searching for an Adequate God* (Grand Rapids, Mich.: Eerdmans, 2000).

[22] Pinnock, "Systematic Theology," in *The Openness of God*, 103.

[23] Pinnock, *Most Moved Mover*, 41.

[24] Pinnock, *The Openness of God*, 123. Abraham Heschel argues similarly. See Shai Held, *Abraham Joshua Heschel: The Call of Transcendence* (Bloomington, Ind.: Indiana University Press, 2013).

[25] Ibid., 115.

Biblical evidence for an open view of divine omniscience comes in many forms.[26] Dozens of biblical passages, for instance, report God saying "perhaps." This uncertainty suggests the future remains open, not completely certain.[27] God makes covenants, asking Israel to choose one course of action over another. Such covenants imply God is uncertain what Israel will do.[28]

Jeremiah, for instance, records God offering two futures for Israel: "If you will indeed obey this word, then through the gates of this house shall enter kings who sit on the throne of David....But if you will not heed these words, I will swear by myself, says the LORD, that this house shall become a desolation" (Jer. 22: 4-5). God's course of action depends, in part, upon Israel's choices. God can't be certain what those choices will be.

God is not timeless, says Pinnock. Divine timelessness implies God is totally actualized, immutable, impassible, and outside of time and sequence. A timeless God is static and aloof, not relational and responsive. We more accurately describe God as temporally everlasting. This means "past, present, and future are real to God," says Pinnock.[29] "The living God is...the God of the Bible," he says, "the one who is genuinely related to the world, whose nature is the power of love, and whose relationship with the world is that of a most moved, not unmoved, Mover."[30]

God interacts in history, facing an unsettled future.

"It is difficult to believe the conventional model of God," says Pinnock, "because of its intellectual contradictions and lack of existential appeal." It says, for example, that "God is timeless yet acts in

---

[26] One of the more accessible books examining biblical evidence for the idea that the future is open is Gregory A. Boyd, *God of the Possible: A Biblical Introduction to the Open View of God* (Grand Rapids, Mich.: Baker, 2001).

[27] Pinnock, "Systematic Theology," in *The Openness of God*, 122.

[28] Christopher Fisher explores biblical passages for and against the openness view in *God is Open: Examining the Open Theism of the Biblical Authors* (2017).

[29] Pinnock, *Most Moved Mover*, 120.

[30] Ibid., 3.

time; God's knowledge is exhaustive, yet freedom is real; God's power is all-controlling, yet things happen contrary to his will; God is unchangeable and yet knows and relates to a changing world." Classical theism, he says, "makes God seem like a metaphysical iceberg."[31]

Open and relational themes appear throughout the biblical witness. We see them, says Pinnock, in "the idea of God taking risks, God's will being thwarted, God being flexible, grace being resistible, God having a temporal dimension, God being impacted by creatures, and God not knowing the entire future as certain."[32] Open and relational theology affirms dynamic and relational philosophies, instead of substantive philosophies of impermanence and unchangeableness. "Excessive Hellenization" has unduly influenced conventional theology, says Pinnock.[33] Relational philosophy better fits the biblical witness.

Open and relational theology corresponds with life better than classical theism. "It is no small point in favor of the openness model," Pinnock argues, "that it is difficult to live life in any other way than the way it describes."[34] It "releases people to live their lives meaningfully," he says. "We are significant in God's eyes…the things we do and say, the decisions and choices we make, and our prayers all help shape the future."[35]

Open and relational theology says our lives matter.

Friendship with God makes sense if open and relational theology is true. Most classical theologies reject friendship with God and reject creaturely freedom vis-à-vis God. Open and relational theology fits our intuition that love is persuasive rather than coercive. It embraces genuine responsibility in discipleship and corresponds with the view that God calls and empowers growth in Christlikeness.[36]

---

[31] Pinnock, *Most Moved Mover*, 118.

[32] Ibid, 64.

[33] Ibid., 101.

[34] Ibid., 23.

[35] Ibid., 23.

[36] See chapter four of *Most Moved Mover* for further explanation of these items.

Take petitionary prayer as an example. "People pray passionately when they see purpose in it, when they think prayer can make a difference and that God may act because of it," says Pinnock. "There would not be much urgency in our praying if we thought God's decrees could not be changed and/or that the future is entirely settled."[37] Most versions of classical theism cannot make sense of this type of prayer, because they say God foreordains and/or foreknows all things. But petitions cannot affect an already settled future or an impassible God.

Above all, Pinnock's open and relational theology considers love God's chief attribute.[38] "God created the world out of love and with the goal of acquiring a people who would, like a bride, freely participate in his love."[39] Or, like a loving parent who possesses "qualities of love and responsiveness, generosity and sensitivity, openness and vulnerability." God experiences the world, responds to what happens, relates to humans, and interacts dynamically with creatures.[40] "God is a serious lover who wants relationships of love most deeply," says Pinnock.[41]

Open and relational theology "is a model of love."[42]

JESUS IN OPEN AND RELATIONAL THEOLOGY

Clark Pinnock offers a version of open and relational theology I find winsome, although my version differs in some respects. His arguments, as I describe them, address God's love, relationships, creating, power, knowledge, and time-fulness. The theology of love I propose also focuses upon Jesus and how he reveals God. In what follows,

---

[37] Ibid., 172.

[38] See also Clark H. Pinnock and Robert C. Brow, *Unbounded Love: A Good News Theology for the 21st Century* (Downers Grove, Ill.: InterVarsity, 1994).

[39] Pinnock, *Most Moved Mover*, 126.

[40] Pinnock, "Systematic Theology," in *The Openness of God*, 103.

[41] Pinnock, *Most Moved Mover*, 140.

[42] Ibid., 179

I will further sketch this out in a way I suspect Pinnock would appreciate.

Jesus is the center of my Christian open and relational theology of love.

Jesus Christ is the focus of Christian faith. "In the beginning was the Word," writes the Apostle John, "and the Word was with God, and the Word was God" (Jn. 1:1). This Word "became flesh" — as Jesus of Nazareth — and "lived among us." His life was glorious, John adds, full of grace and truth (Jn. 1:14).

This witness to Jesus and the witness of other scripture writers reverberate with meaning, complexity, and insight. Christians interpret witnesses to Jesus in diverse ways, leading to various Christologies. Whatever the interpretation, biblical writers stress the central role Jesus plays in revealing who God is and what God wants.[43]

The same writer who tells us the Word was with God and was God says, "God is love" (1 Jn. 4:8,16). God's self-disclosure emerges in various ways, but especially in Jesus. "God's love was revealed among us in this way: God sent his only Son into the world so that we might live through him" (1 Jn. 4:9). In Jesus, the God whose nature is love makes it possible for creatures to know something profound about their Creator.

Matthew, Mark, and Luke also bear witness to God's love revealed in Jesus. We see profound love in the life, words, ministry, death, and resurrection of Jesus. He healed the sick, preached good news, ate with sinners, ministered to the poor, wept over the dead, encouraged the downhearted, and showed compassion.[44] The person

---

[43] For some of the more influential open and relational Christologies, see Gregory Boyd, *Cross Vision* (Fortress, 2018); John B. Cobb, Jr., *Christ in a Pluralistic Age Jesus' Abba* (Fortress, 2016); Tripp Fuller, *Divine Self-Investment: A Constructive Open and Relational Christology* (Grasmere, Id.: SacraSage, 2019); Brad Jersak, *A More Christlike God* (Plain Truth, 2016); Brian Zahnd, *Sinners in the Hands of a Loving God* (London: Waterbrook, 2017).

[44] F. Scott Spencer explores Jesus' emotions in *Passions of the Christ: The Emotional Life of Jesus in the Gospels* (Grand Rapids, Mich.: Baker, 2021). See also Kurt Willems, *Echoing Hope* (London: Waterbrook, 2021).

and work of Christ stands as the fullest revelation of God's loving nature and activity.[45]

In Jesus were light and life and love.

Jesus' suffering death on a cross tells us something significant about God's love, says the Apostle Paul. "God proves his love for us in that while we were still sinners Christ died for us," he writes (Rm. 5:8). As an expression of love, says John, God "sent his son to be the atoning sacrifice for our sins" (1 Jn. 4:10). Christians debate how best to make sense of atonement. But one compelling explanation says Jesus' suffering and death reveals God as One who experiences pain and joy, sorrow and happiness: a God who feels alongside and cares for creatures.[46]

As Emmanuel, God with us, this Nazarene carpenter reveals God's restorative work of love. For "in Christ God was reconciling the world to himself" (2 Cor. 5:19). We can know love because we "know the love of Christ" — although *complete* knowledge "surpasses understanding" (Eph. 3:19). We need the light we find in Jesus (2 Cor. 4:6) to be "taught by God to love one another" (1 Thess. 4:9).

God's love makes creaturely love possible.[47] "We love, because he first loved us," says John (1 Jn. 4:19). Jesus' two love commands offer a framework to make sense of love's forms. "Love the Lord your God with all your heart, and with all your soul, and with all your mind, and with all your strength," says Jesus, and "love your neighbor as yourself" (Mk. 12:29-30). "There is no other commandment greater than these," he adds (Mk. 12:31). These commands appear in the Old Testament; are found in the synoptic gospels; play a central role in

---

[45] On Jesus' revelation of God as love, see Bradley Jersak, *A More Christ-Like God* (Pasadena, Ca.: Plain Truth Ministries, 2016); John Sanders, *Embracing Prodigals* (Eugene, Or.: Cascade, 2020); Keith Ward, *Love is His Meaning: understanding the Teaching of Jesus* (London: SPCK, 2017).

[46] The classic open and relational work on this is Jürgen Moltmann, *The Crucified God* (London: SCM, 1974). See also Anna Case Winters, *God Will Be All in All* (Louisville, Ky.: Westminster John Knox, 2021).

[47] For a strong biblical argument for the centrality of love for Christian ethics, see Paul Victor Furnish, *The Love Command in the New Testament* (Nashville: Abingdon, 1972).

the writing of James, John, and Paul; and exist in noncanonical literature as well.

Our loving like Jesus means living a life of love. "Beloved, let us love one another," says John, "because love is from God; everyone who loves is born of God and knows God. Whoever does not love does not know God, for God is love" (1 Jn. 4:7-8). By following Jesus' example, we can "be merciful, just as your Father is merciful" (Lk. 6:36). Love establishes the kingdom of God.[48]

In the love bonds of Jesus, Christians "abound" in love for each other (1 Thess. 4:10; Phil. 1:9). This love includes "brotherly affection" (Rm. 12:10a) and loving enemies and strangers (Dt. 10:19; Mt. 5:43). The life of love means being renewed in the image of God (Col. 3:10) and participating in the divine nature (2 Pt. 1:4). This instills love as the fruit of the Spirit (Gal. 5:22). The Christian life develops "faith working through love" (Gal. 5:6) so that Christians can "walk in love" (2 Jn. 1:6).

The life of love that Jesus commands overcomes sin, because sin and love stand in opposition. But there is "no condemnation for those who are in Christ Jesus." The loving "law of the Spirit of life in Christ Jesus" sets lovers "free from the law of sin and of death" (Rom. 8:1-2). Our loving God, whom we name with the intimate words, "Abba, Father," makes freedom from sin and a life of love possible (Rom. 8:15). We need not fear a loving God. And nothing "will be able to separate us from the love of God in Christ Jesus our Lord" (Rm. 8:39).[49]

Living a life of love means developing Christian virtues and growing in Christlikeness. Christians mature as they develop Christ-like character: "above all, clothe yourselves with love" (Col. 3:14). God not only intends that we love in each moment, but God desires that we develop into loving persons and form loving communities. Love

---

[48] Paul Furnish connects the kingdom of God with the centrality of love: "God's Kingdom is the heralding of the sovereign power and saving purpose of God's love. The Rule of God is the rule of love. Love is the law of life in the Kingdom" (*The Love Command in the New Testament*, 68).

[49] See Paul R. Sponheim, *Love's Availing Power: Imaging God, Imagining the World* (Minneapolis: Fortress, 2011).

is both personal and corporate. Paul's all-inclusive words express this well: "Let all that you do be done in love" (1 Cor. 16:14).[50]

Empowered by the Spirit, Jesus reveals pluriform love for enemies and friends, sinners and saints, ourselves and God. "God's love has been poured into our hearts through the Holy Spirit," reports Paul (Rom. 5:5). And this Spirit has been poured out on all flesh (Joel 2:28) and on all creation (Acts 17:28). Those with the "Spirit of Christ" have authentic life (Rom. 8:9-11).[51]

Jesus is the center of a Christian theology that makes love central.

JESUS' KENOSIS AND THE REALITY OF EVIL

A Christian open and relational theology that places Jesus at the center helps us address the problem of evil. Jesus reveals God's activity and nature as love, say open and relational theologians, and God does not cause or want evil. An open and relational God does not predestine evils nor foreknow when they will occur. As relational, God suffers with victims. As the Great Physician, God works to heal the wounded and hurting.

Are these ideas enough to solve the problem of evil?

I don't think so. It's important to say God doesn't cause evil and wants love to reign. It's crucial to say God neither foreordains nor foreknows evil; it's not built into God's providential plan from the beginning. But Christians should also try to explain why God doesn't *prevent* genuine evil. And they should explain why God created a universe in which evil could occur, instead of creating one without the possibility for evil. A loving God would prevent preventable evils.

---

[50] On the relationship between God, Jesus, and Christian community, see Marjorie Suchocki, *God-Christ-Church,* rev. ed. (New York: Crossroad, 1993).

[51] For open and relational pneumatologies, see Robert D. Cornwall, *Unfettered Spirit* (Gonzalez, Fl.: Energion, 2021); Clark H. Pinnock, *Flame of Love* (IVP, 1999); See Joshua D. Reichard, "Relational Empowerment: A Process-Relational Theology of the Spirit-filled Life," in *Pneuma: The Journal of the Society for Pentecostal Studies* 36:2 (2014): 1-20; Amos Yong, *Spirit of Love* (Waco, Tex.: Baylor University Press, 2012)

Open and relational thinkers offer various arguments relevant to these issues.[52] In what follows, I offer my own. I say the kenotic (self-giving) love of Jesus reveals divine love itself to be kenotic. In fact, *kenosis* is *essential* to who God is and how God acts. An essentially kenotic God is inherently uncontrolling, which means God *cannot* prevent evil singlehandedly.[53] An essentially kenotic God is blameless.

Let me explain.

Contemporary theologians often build from a passage about Jesus in Philippians.[54] In it, the Apostle Paul offers insights into how Jesus reveals God's nature. Paul begins by urging readers to promote overall well-being; they should care about interests wider than their own. He writes,

> If then there is any encouragement in Christ, any consolation from love, any sharing in the Spirit, any compassion and sympathy, make my joy complete: be of the same mind, having the same love, being in full accord and of one mind. Do nothing from selfish ambition or conceit, but in humility regard others as better than yourselves. Let each of you look not to your own interests, but to the interests of others. (Phil. 2:1-4)

Paul's encouragement in Christ commends love's consolation, compassion, and sympathy. And, if his readers choose love, he will be joy-full. Love shuns self-centeredness and conceit because lovers

---

[52] William Hasker is an open and relational philosopher who offers one of the best theodicies in the openness tradition. See Hasker's works, *Providence, Evil and the Openness of God* (London: Routledge, 2004) and *The Triumph of God over Evil: Theodicy for a World of Suffering* (Downers Grove, Ill.: Intervarsity, 2008). David Ray Griffin offers one of the best process theodicies. See his works, *God, Power, and Evil: A Process Theodicy* (Philadelphia: Westminster, 1976); *Evil Revisited: Responses and Reconsiderations* (Albany, N.Y.: State University of New York Press, 1991.

[53] For explorations on the implications of uncontrolling love, see Chris Baker, et. al., *Uncontrolling Love* (San Diego.: SacraSage, 2017); L. Michaels, *What About Us? Stories of Uncontrolling Love* (Grasmere, Id.: SacraSage, 2019).

[54] One of the better books on *kenosis* by a New Testament scholar is Michael J. Gorman, *Inhabiting the Cruciform God: Kenosis, Justification, and Theosis in Paul's Narrative Soteriology* (Grand Rapids, Mich.: Eerdmans, 2009).

seek humility. They look not merely to their own interests, but also to the interests of others.[55]

Paul connects pursuing the promotion of well-being with the love of Jesus. He recommends readers follow Jesus' example.

> Let the same mind be in you that was in Christ Jesus, who, though he was in the form of God, did not regard equality with God as something to be exploited, but emptied himself, taking the form of a slave, being born in human likeness. And being found in human form, he humbled himself and became obedient to the point of death — even death on a cross. (Phil. 2:5-8)

The phrase translated "emptied himself" comes from the Greek word *kenosis*. Scholars also translate it "gave himself," "self-emptied," "made himself nothing," and more.[56] *Kenosis* occurs in verb form a half dozen times in scripture, and the word allows for a range of acceptable translations.[57] I will use "self-giving."[58]

---

[55] I prefer translations other than NRSV for Philippians 1:4. The NRSV says readers should "look not to your own interests," which seems to dismiss self-love. Other translations, such as the NASB, say, "do not merely look out for your own personal interests, but also for the interests of others." These translations affirm self-love.

[56] "Self-emptying" is a poor translation of *kenosis* in this passage. Rather than the personal language of love, "self-empty" makes Jesus sound like a container whose contents pour out. Biblical scholar Gordon Fee says "self-empties" is at best metaphorical, because "the suggestion that Christ 'emptied himself' *of* something is quite foreign to Paul's own concern." Relational language, rather than container language, is better, especially if we take seriously the references to servanthood, humility, and crucifixion in the passage. See Gordon D. Fee, "The New Testament and Kenosis Christology," in *Exploring Kenotic Christology: The Self-Emptying of God*, C. Stephen Evans, ed. (Vancouver, BC: Regent College Publishing, 2006), 29. On problems with translating *kenosis* as "self-emptying," see *The Uncontrolling Love of God*, ch. 7.

[57] Some distinguish between *kenosis* and *plerosis*. The latter word connotes fullness of giving. The addition of *plerosis* makes sense if *kenosis* is translated, as Jürgen Moltmann does, in terms of God's "withdrawing." But defining *kenosis* as self-giving love, as I do, overcomes the need for *plerosis*. (see Jürgen Moltmann, "God's Kenosis in the Creation and Consummation of the World," in *The Work of Love: Creation as Kenosis*, John Polkinghorne, ed. [Grand Rapids, Mich.: Eerdmans, 2001], 146).

[58] By "self-giving," I do not mean anyone becomes utterly without a self. I agree with many feminist theologians who argue for the fundamental importance of self when loving.

According to Paul, Jesus expressed self-giving love. We see this in Jesus' humility and servanthood. In fact, self-giving led to Jesus' death on a cross. He obeyed the call of love, and this obedience led to his crucifixion.

Some theologians have used this passage to say Jesus set aside divine attributes (e.g., omnipresence, omniscience, and omnipotence) when becoming human. Many claim this in deference to the Chalcedonian creed (451), which says Jesus has two natures "communicated to" one person. Such Christologies parse which divine attributes Jesus supposedly retained in human life and which, because of self-emptying, he deserted.[59]

Kenosis discussions today more often explore how Jesus reveals God's nature.[60] Instead of asking which attributes he divested, they focus on the love Jesus invested.[61] His taking "the form of a slave," "humbling himself," and dying "on a cross" point to servant-like power and sacrificial love.[62] God is not overpowering or aloof, but empowering and present. The cross of Jesus especially reveals God's

---

See Elizabeth Johnson, *She Who Is: The Mystery of God in Feminist Theological Discourse* (New York: Crossroad, 1993) and Margaret A. Farley, *Just Love: A Framework for Chrisitan Sexual Ethics* (New York: Continuum, 2006).

[59] "The phrase 'emptied himself' in 2:7 should not be read as a reference to the divestiture of something (whether divinity itself or some divine attribute)," says Michael Gorman, "or even as self-limitation regarding the use of divine attributes...." *Inhabiting the Cruciform God*, 21. On the historical debate of *kenosis* and Jesus' two natures, see David Brown, *Divine Humanity: Kenosis and the Construction of a Christian Theology* (Waco, TX: Baylor University Press, 2011); Thomas R. Thompson, "Nineteenth-century Kenotic Christology: Waxing, Waning and Weighing of a Quest for a Coherent Orthodoxy," in *Exploring the Kenotic Christology: The Self-Emptying of God*, C. Stephen Evans, ed. (Vancouver, BC: Regent College Publishing, 2006).

[60] Among recent helpful texts on *kenosis*, see C. Stephen Evans, ed. *Exploring Kenotic Christology*; John Polkinghorne, ed., *The Work of Love: Creation as Kenosis* (Grand Rapids, Mich.: Eerdmans, 2001).

[61] Although Jesus re-presents God's character (Heb. 1:3; 1 Jn. 3:16), he did not re-present every divine attribute. Jesus was neither omniscient nor omnipresent, for instance.

[62] See the work of biblical scholars such as James D. G. Dunn, *Christology in the Making: An Inquiry into the Origins of the Doctrine of the Incarnation*, 2ⁿᵈ ed., (London: SCM, 1989), 116; Donald Macleod, *The Person of Christ: Contours of Christian Theology* (Leicester: InterVarsity, 1998), 215; Ralph P. Martin, *Carmen Christi: Philippians 2:5-11 in Recent Interpretation and in the Setting of Early Christian Worship*, rev. ed. (Grand Rapids, Mich.: Eerdmans, 1983), 170.

noncoercion (see also 1 Cor. 1:18-25).[63] God self-gives, and this self-giving creates, saves, and inspires.

Paul concludes this section by saying, "it is God who is at work in you, enabling you both to will and to work for his good pleasure" (Phil. 2:13). God's self-giving enables creatures to want and to do good. God's love inspires us to love. The idea that creatures rely upon God also fits biblical passages that say, "apart from [God] you can do nothing" (Jn 15:5) and Christ who strengthens makes possible everything we do (Phil. 4:13).

Jesus' self-giving love points to and reveals God's self-giving, others-enabling love.

Key questions remain. Is *kenosis* as self-giving, others-enabling love something God does voluntarily or by nature? Does God freely choose whether to self-give and others-empower? Or is self-giving, others-empowering love a necessary aspect of God's essence?

Philippians 2 does not provide a definitive answer to these questions. As a free human, Jesus could choose not to love. For he "in every respect has been tempted as we are, yet without sin" (Heb. 4:15). If Jesus loved necessarily, he could not sin. The temptations he faced would not have been truly tempting.

But what about God? Does God freely *choose* to love? Or *must* God love? Does God choose whether to self-give and others-empower? Or is it God's nature to do so?

Some open and relational theologians say God's self-giving love is voluntary. To them, God freely self-limits, deciding to give freedom and agency to creatures instead of controlling them. Jürgen Moltmann, for example, offers this view. In *kenosis*, God "withdrew his omnipotence in order to concede space for the presence of creation," he says.[64] In his exploration of *kenosis*, John Polkinghorne says, "God does not will the act of a murderer or the destructive force

---

[63] On this, see Gregory Love, *Love, Violence, and the Cross: How the Nonviolent God Saves Us through the Cross of Christ* (Eugene, OR: Cascade, 2010); and Seibert, *The Violence of Scripture*.

[64] Moltmann, "God's Kenosis in the Creation and Consummation of the World," in *The Work of Love*, 146.

of an earthquake but allows both to happen in a world in which divine power is deliberately self-limited to allow causal space for creatures."[65] Clark Pinnock argues similarly, saying "God is not bound to persuasion alone."[66] "Coercive power is available to God, even if he uses it sparingly."[67] And "God has the power to intervene in the world, interrupting (if need be) the normal causal sequences."[68]

These open and relational thinkers champion love. But each believes God freely self-limits. God allows humans and other creatures to act freely. Some also say God allows less-complex creatures to exercise agency, and God chooses not to override creation's processes.[69] God so understood, *could* control, but usually does not. When creating and relating, as Polkinghorne puts it, God "is deliberately self-limited."

Saying God deliberately self-limits presents obstacles to a theology of love. Perhaps the most crucial is the problem of evil. If God can control creatures or creation, God can prevent evil singlehandedly. And yet, genuine evils occur.

A God who loves perfectly would *want* to prevent genuine evil, if doing so were possible. God may not want to prevent every pain, because some may be necessary for creation's flourishing. But a loving God would want to prevent *genuine* evil. Genuine evils make the world worse, not better, than it otherwise might have been.[70] A

---

[65] John Polkinghorne, "Kenotic Creation and Divine Action," in *The Work of Love*, 102. Jeff B. Pool argues similarly in *God's Wounds*.

[66] Pinnock, *Most Moved Mover*, 146.

[67] Ibid., 148.

[68] Pinnock, "Systematic Theology," in *The Openness of God*, 109.

[69] John Polkinghorne defends a version of the free process defense. See *Science and Providence* (Philadelphia: Templeton, 2005). For an overview of the free process defense, see Garry DeWeese, "Natural Evil: A 'Free Process' Defense," in *God and Evil: The Case for God in a World Filled with Pain*, Chad Meister and James K. Dew, Jr., eds. (Downers Grove, Ill.: IVP, 2013), 53-64.

[70] David Ray Griffin defines a genuine evil as an event that, all things considered, makes the world worse than it might have been. See *God, Power, and Evil: A Process Theodicy* (Louisville, KY: Westminster John Knox, 2004). I compare genuine evil to necessary and gratuitous evil in *The Uncontrolling Love of God*, ch. 3.

God who can control by overriding, taking away, or failing to provide freedom and agency to creatures could prevent evil singlehandedly. The God who deliberately self-limits "to allow causal space for creatures," as Polkinghorne puts it, or can "interrupt (if need be) the normal causal sequences," as Clark Pinnock puts it, could prevent evil singlehandedly.

Voluntary self-limitation is, in principle, self-reversible. When the possibility of genuine evil arises, we would expect a voluntarily self-limited God to stop self-limiting to prevent evil. But genuine evils occur. Victims and survivors wonder if a deliberately self-limited God could love them. They suspect God punishes or abandons them. A voluntarily self-limited God permitted their pointless pain. It would seem morally necessary that a loving God who self-limits ought to un-self-limit to prevent unnecessary suffering.[71]

We rightly blame a deliberately self-limited God for failing to stop evil.

ESSENTIAL KENOSIS

I propose an alternative open and relational theology that affirms a view I call "essential kenosis."[72]

Essential kenosis builds from the revelation of God we find in Jesus and sketched out in Philippians 2. Jesus' life of love reveals that God always loves. But essential kenosis claims God is essentially rather than deliberately kenotic. God *must* self-give and others-empower because it's God's nature to do so.

In earlier chapters, I argued God is essentially loving. I said God always loves because love comes logically first in the divine nature.

---

[71] Tyron L. Inbody explores the idea self-limited God should become un-self-limited in *The Transforming God: An Interpretation of Suffering and Evil* (Louisville, Ky.: Westminster John Knox, 1997). Anna Case-Winters argues similarly in *God's Power: Traditional Understandings and Contemporary Challenges* (Louisville, Ky.: Westminster/John Knox, 1990), 204.

[72] I explain essential kenosis in greater detail in *The Uncontrolling Love of God* and in segments of *Uncontrolling Love*, L Michaels, et. al., eds. (Grasmere, Id.: SacraSage, 2018).

God must love.[73] Essential kenosis adds that God's love is necessarily self-giving, others-empowering, and, therefore, uncontrolling. Because God is essentially kenotic and God loves everyone and everything in this way, God *cannot* control anyone or anything.

God can't control others.[74]

Essential kenosis provides the conceptual tools to affirm God's perfect love while explaining why God is not guilty of failing to prevent genuine evil. It agrees with kenotic theologies that say Jesus reveals the self-giving love of God. God provides freedom, agency, and self-organization to creatures — depending on their complexity — and God originates and sustains the natural processes in creation. Essential kenosis says creation depends moment by moment on the Creator's love.

Essential kenosis differs from many theologies when it says God *necessarily* loves creatures and creation. Because love comes first in the divine nature, God must give creatures freedom, agency, and self-organization. These gifts are, to use the Apostle Paul's language, "irrevocable" (Rm. 11:29). God cannot control those to whom these gifts are given. Because God loves *all* creatures — simple and complex — and all creation — animate and inanimate — God *always* gives and *cannot* control.

I call this the uncontrolling love of God.

Essential kenosis does *not* say external forces, agents, or laws limit God. Nothing outside God imposes restrictions. Uncontrolling love derives from the divine nature, from what it means to be deity. This inability to control does not mean God deliberately, freely, or voluntarily self-limits, as if God purposely chooses not to control.

---

[73] This aligns with Jacob Arminius when he says, "God is not freely good; that is, he is not good by the mode of liberty, but by that of natural necessity." See "It is the Summit of Blasphemy to Say that God is Freely Good," in *The Works of James Arminius*, Vol. 2, James Nichols, trans. (Grand Rapids, Mich.: Baker, 1991 [1828]), 33-34. Jürgen Moltmann argues for this in *The Trinity and the Kingdom* (San Francisco: Harper and Row, 1981), 52-56.

[74] I explain this in an accessible way in *God Can't*. I answer common questions I hear from readers of *God Can't* in a follow-up called *Questions and Answers for God Can't* (Grasmere, Id.: SacraSage, 2020).

Because uncontrolling love comes logically first in the divine nature, it is the primary attribute by which we understand who God is. God can't control by definition.

Uncontrolling love characterizes all divine activities. As one whose nature is love for others, God cannot withdraw, override, or fail to provide freedom and agency. God cannot usurp the law-like regularities of creation, because those regularities arise from God's steadfast love in the universe.[75] Because God loves everyone and everything, God empowers all and cannot overpower any.

Genuine evils occur when creatures misuse their God-given freedom or agency. Or when random accidents or chance calamities occur in a universe God cannot control. Sin, evil, and tragedy undermine rather than promote the well-being God wants. Essential kenosis clears God from any credible charge of guilt for failing to prevent evil, because God can't prevent it singlehandedly.

The uncontrolling God of love cannot be rightly blamed for evil.

Some hear that God's love is essentially uncontrolling and wonder if this applies to human love. Would it be loving, for instance, to prevent a toddler from freely stepping in front of an oncoming truck? Would love call us to grab the gun from a depressed person attempting suicide? Should humans constrain others in the name of love?

Rescuing toddlers and preventing suicide are loving actions. But doing so doesn't involve control in the sense of being the only cause at play. Bodily impact — for instance, grabbing others — doesn't control. Others retain some freedom, even though bodily impact limits their choices.

The Creator differs from creatures in this respect. Essential kenosis affirms the traditional Christian belief God is a spirit without a

---

[75] I agree with John Polkinghorne when he says, "the regularities of the mechanical aspects of nature are to be understood theologically as signs of the faithfulness of the Creator." See Thomas Jay Oord, ed. *The Polkinghorne Reader: Science, Faith and the Search for Meaning* (London: SPCK; Philadelphia: Templeton, 2010), 124-25. I explain the relation of God's love to randomness and regularities in *The Uncontrolling Love of God*, chs. 2-3.

localized body. "God is Spirit," as Jesus put it (Jn. 4:24).[76] God cannot exert bodily impact because God is incorporeal.

As the universal Spirit, God does not possess hands to snatch toddlers from oncoming trucks or grab guns from those attempting suicide. God does not have hands, feet, wings, claws, torso, and so on.[77] God does, however, call creatures to use their own hands, feet, and bodies to prevent evil. When creatures cooperate with that call, they become God's metaphorical hands and feet.

Of course, creatures don't always respond well to God's call or attune themselves to receiving it. And sometimes creatures aren't in the right place at the right time to prevent evil. That's inherent in what it means to be localized. Consequently, God is not always able to prevent evil by persuading creatures to use their bodies.[78] God can't prevent evil *singlehandedly*.

Both because God is a bodiless Spirit and divine love does not coerce, God cannot control.

SOLVING THE PROBLEM OF EVIL

An adequate Christian theology of love offers a plausible solution to the problem of evil. Rather than appealing to mystery, it offers answers to the issue most atheists say prevents them from believing God exists.[79] Those answers also help theists make sense of God's love in light of personal, systemic, and nonhuman evils.

---

[76] Admittedly, biblical passages — mostly Old Testament writers — occasionally refer to a divine body or bodily parts. I consider these references metaphors not literal descriptions. I make this interpretation in light of the preponderance of biblical texts that speak of God as a universal spirit.

[77] Theologians sometimes speak of "the body of God." Typically, they mean creation is metaphorically and not literally God's body. See Grace Jantzen, *God's World, God's Body* (Philadelphia: Westminster, 1984) and Sallie McFague, *The Body of God: An Ecological Theology* (Philadelphia: Fortress, 1993). On God as World-Soul, see Matthew David Segall, *Physics of the World-Soul* (Grasmere, Id.: SacraSage, 2021).

[78] I address evil and divine incorporeality in *Questions and Answers for God Can't*, ch. 5.

[79] The main counterargument to why a loving and powerful God does not prevent evil is not really an argument at all. It's an appeal to mystery. Implicitly or explicitly, many say we cannot know whether events we consider evil are actually so. Some say God has an

A loving God does not want, cause, or permit unnecessary suffering. And some suffering is unnecessary.

The problem of evil has multiple dimensions. Rather than just one, many problems surround God's relation to genuine evil. The uncontrolling love view of essential kenosis addresses the most prominent.[80]

The Prevention Dimension

We might ask the question that animates most discussions of evil this way, "Why doesn't God *prevent* genuine evil?"

My answer, explained above, says God cannot prevent evil singlehandedly. God always loves all creatures and all creation, but divine love is inherently uncontrolling, so God cannot prevent evil by fiat. As essentially kenotic, God cannot control creatures or simpler entities that cause genuine evil. And God cannot interrupt the lawlike regularities of the natural world.[81]

Essential kenosis rejects the idea God "won't" or "doesn't" stop evil. Those words suggest God deliberately self-limits. To hurting people, this sounds like God *could* have prevented their unnecessary suffering but freely chose not to do so. Essential kenosis says God is uncontrolling by nature because God's nature is uncontrolling love.

---

immediate reason or future plan that requires pain and suffering. In some mysterious way, God's preventing evil would be worse than God's allowing it. But appeals to mystery cannot provide satisfying answers to questions about God's love in light of evil. The mystery card spoils the deck. One can find sophisticated but unsatisfying appeals to mystery in the skeptical theism literature. For instance, Trent Doughtery and Justin McBrayer, *Skeptical Theism* (Oxford: Oxford University Press, 2014).

[80] I've explained the dimensions to my solution to evil in *God Can't*. See also "An Essential Kenosis Solution to the Problem of Evil," and "Response to Others" in *God and the Problem of Evil: Five Views*, James K. Dew, Jr. and Chad Meister, eds. (Downers Grove, Ill.: InterVarsity, 2017); "Championing Divine Love and Solving the Problem of Evil," in *The Many Facets of Love: Philosophical Explorations*, Thomas Jay Oord, ed. (Cambridge: Cambridge Scholars, 2007).

[81] On divine action and the laws of nature, see Jeffrey Koperski, *Divine Action, Determinism, and the Laws of Nature* (London: Routledge, 2020).

The Empathy Dimension

Some do not ask why God caused or allowed their pain, but instead wonder if God suffers with them. "Does God feel what I feel?"

I join open and relational thinkers who say God suffers with those who suffer. God empathizes. As one affected by all that happens, God feels the pains and joys of all creatures. God is the "fellow-sufferer who understands," as Alfred North Whitehead put it.[82] To address this dimension of the problem of evil, an adequate theology of love says God empathizes with those in pain.[83]

An increasing number of contemporary theologians embrace the idea that God suffers. Some appeal to it as their primary answer to the problem of evil. But I believe "God suffers with us" does not go far enough. Survivors and victims must also be told God could not have singlehandedly prevented their suffering.[84] The God who could prevent evil singlehandedly but allows it in order to suffer alongside victims is not a loving God. Divine empathy, as important as it is, must be supplemented by saying the uncontrolling God of love cannot, acting alone, stop evil.

The Healing Dimension

Other victims ask, "Will God heal me? And will God heal all creation?" This dimension of the problem of evil seeks a therapeutic response and wonders about God's role in recovery and restoration.

---

[82] Alfred North Whitehead, *Process and Reality: An Essay in Cosmology*, Corrected edition by David Ray Griffin and Donald W. Sherburne (New York: Free, 1978 [1929]), 351.

[83] I address divine empathy and the problem of evil in *God Can't*, ch. 2. See also Anna Case-Winters, *God Will Be All in All: Theology Through the Lens of Incarnation* (Louisville, Ky.: Westminster John Knox, 2021); Edward Farley, *Divine Empathy* (Philadelphia: Fortress, 1996); Paul Fiddes, *The Creative Suffering of God* (Oxford: Oxford University Press, 1988); Terryl and Fiona Givens, *The God Who Weeps* (Crawfordsville, Ind.: Ensign Peak, 2012); Paul Joseph Greene, *The End of Divine Truthiness* (Eugene, Or.: Wipf and Stock, 2017);

[84] Many theologians argue the oppressed can find comfort in a passible God. For one example, see James Cone, *God of the Oppressed* (London: SPCK, 1977); Adam Hamilton, *Why? Making Sense of God's Will* (Nashville: Abingdon, 2011). See Roberto Sirvent for a lengthy argument for the cogency of *imitatio dei* and divine passibility (*Embracing Vulnerability: Human and Divine* [Eugene, Or.: Pickwick, 2014]).

My answer says God works to heal all who hurt from injury and injustice. And God wants the well-being of all creation. But an uncontrolling God cannot heal singlehandedly. For healing to occur, God requires creaturely cooperation or the conditions of creation to be aligned. Healing requires the work of the Great Physician and creation's cooperation or conducive conditions.

This is good news to those who do not heal quickly and to those who do not heal at all. Knowing God can't heal singlehandedly means God did not abandon them and is not punishing them. Sometimes those who hurt cooperate with God mentally, but their cells, muscles, organs, or other bodily members simply do not cooperate. Or conditions in their bodies or creation may not be conducive to support divine healing. When our bodies do not cooperate with God, we need not feel guilty. Other factors and actors are thwarting the healing God wants done.

Some healing will not occur until creatures no longer live in their mortal bodies. Some restoration awaits the afterlife.[85] This belief provides additional hope to those suffering today.

The Didactic Dimension

Suffering sometimes brings good. Various soul-making theodicies build from this insight to suggest God causes or allows evil with a greater good in mind. We sometimes learn from suffering.

Essential kenosis rejects the idea God wants evil as part of a plan, to build character, teach us lessons, or turn our attention toward God.[86] Instead, it says God works with those who suffer to bring

---

[85] I address questions of healing in *God Can't*, ch. 3 and *Questions and Answers for God Can't*, ch. 2-3.

[86] Some biblical writers appeal to the didactic dimension of evil. For analyses of their fruitfulness, see James L. Crenshaw, *Defending God: Biblical Responses to the Problem of Evil* (Oxford: Oxford University Press, 2005); Bart D. Ehrman, *God's Problem: How the Bible Fails to Answer Our Most Important Question — Why We Suffer* (New York: HarperCollins, 2008);

good from bad. God tries to squeeze something positive from the evil God didn't want in the first place.

To the question, "Did God cause or allow this for our good?" essential kenosis says, "No." But God works in all circumstances and with all creatures to bring good from bad and wring right from wrong. God does not leave the hurting, but works to transform the situation and those affected by it.[87] An uncontrolling God redeems suffering instead of wanting, causing, or allowing it.[88]

The Synergistic Dimension

When encountering evil, some ask, "Can evil be overcome?" Instead of asking why evil occurs, this dimension of the problem asks about victory over evil.

Because essential kenosis says God always loves but can't prevent evil singlehandedly, it answers by saying God *needs* creatures in the work of overcoming evil with good. An uncontrolling Lover requires the beloved's cooperation.

I call this indispensable love *synergy*, because both Creator and creatures are indispensable for overcoming evil. God can't prevent evil singlehandedly, and creatures can't prevent it without God's help. But with creaturely cooperation, God can stop evil. God's desire that love reign — what Jesus called the kingdom of God or the kingdom of heaven — can be fully realized in this symbiosis of love.[89] For love to win, a loving Creator needs creation's loving responses.

---

[87] On transformation, see Sheri D. Kling, *A Process Spirituality* (London: Rowman and Littlefield, 2020). See also Patricia Farmer, *Beauty and Process Theology: A Journey of Transformation* (Gonzalez, Fl.: Energion, 2020).

[88] I address this question in *God Can't*, ch. 4. The most influential form of the argument that God uses suffering to build our characters is probably John Hick's *Evil and the God of Love* (San Francisco: Harper San Francisco, 1966). One of the best criticisms of this view from an open and relational perspective comes from C. Robert Mesle, *John Hick's Theodicy: A Process Humanist Critique* (London: MacMillan, 1991).

[89] I explain indispensable love synergy in *God Can't*, ch. 5.

The Origination Dimension

The final dimension to the problem of evil asks about evil's origin. We might pose the question this way: "Why would God create the world in such a way that evil might occur?"

This question asks about the manner of God's creating, now and at the beginning of our universe.[90] I will offer my answer in depth in the next chapter. But briefly, I will say God does not create evil, and God did not singlehandedly determine the conditions for it to occur. Rather than creating the universe from nothing, God everlastingly, in love, creates in relation to what God previously created.[91] This answers this otherwise thorny problem.

Essential kenosis answers other questions an adequate theology of love must address. It explains, for instance, why a loving God does not guarantee the fair distribution of goods among creatures. God can't do so singlehandedly. It explains why God doesn't now and didn't in the past provide the crystal-clear, unambiguous, and error-free revelation necessary for full salvation.[92] God can't do so singlehandedly.[93] Essential kenosis provides a framework for explaining

---

[90] Bethany Sollereder addresses animal suffering and God's love in *God, Evolution, and Animal Suffering: Theodicy without a Fall* (New York: Routledge, 2020), as does Christopher Southgate, *The Groaning of Creation* (London: Westminster John Knox, 2008). Ilia Delio addresses love and evolution in *The Unbearable Wholeness of Being* (Maryknoll, NY: Orbis, 2013).

[91] See also Thomas Jay Oord, "Eternal Creation and Essential Love" in *T&T Handbook on Suffering and the Problem of Evil,* Johannes Grossel and Matthias Grebe, eds. (London: T&T Clark, 2022).

[92] On inspiration and uncontrolling love in biblical inspiration, see Gabriel Gordon, *God Speaks: A Participatory Theology of Inspiration* (Glen Oak, Ca.: Quoir, 2021); on inerrancy, see Gregory Boyd, *Inspired Imperfection* (Minneapolis: Fortress, 2020); and essays in Thomas Jay Oord and Richard Thompsons, eds. *Rethinking the Bible* (Grasmere, ID: SacraSage, 2018).

[93] The idea God cannot control creatures overcomes J. L. Schellenberg's worries about divine hiddenness. The uncontrolling God of love *always* communicates but *cannot* do so unambiguously. Instead of voluntarily hiding, which is what classical theists often claim about God, the uncontrolling God of love never voluntarily hides. For Schellenberg's arguments, see *Divine Hiddenness and Human Reason* (Ithaca, NY: Cornell University Press, 2006); *The Hiddenness Argument* (Oxford: Oxford University Press, 2015).

why creaturely action is necessary to address the climate crisis and why God doesn't fix it.[94] God can't do so singlehandedly.

A theology of love oriented around essential kenosis overcomes the main obstacles to affirming God's love in a world of crises, inequity, confusion, and evil.

GOD IS AMIPOTENT

Upon hearing that essential kenosis denies God can control creatures or creation, some may assume this theology considers God inactive. Some may believe it says God watches creation from afar as a form of deism.[95] Some may think an uncontrolling God is weak.[96] As I say above and will show below, these assumptions are misplaced.

God's uncontrolling love is the most powerful force in the universe.

The God of uncontrolling love acts moment by moment and exerts causal influence upon all. God acts first as a cause in every moment of every creature's life. Creatures feel this influence, even when they are not conscious of it. There is no time when, and no location where, God is not present and influencing.

"Almighty" is the word biblical translators often use to describe God's power (e.g., Joel 1:15, Rev. 1:8, and elsewhere). The Psalmist witnesses to the almighty God: "Mightier than the thunder of the great waters, mightier than the breakers of the sea — the Lord on high

---

[94] On this issue, see Philip Clayton and Wm. Andrew Schwartz, *What is Ecological Civilization?* (Anoka, Minn.: Process Century, 2019); Sharon Delgado, *Love in a Time of Climate Change* (Minneapolis: Fortress, 2017); Pope Francis, *On Care for Our Common Home: Laudato Si* (Vatican City: Liberia Editrice Vaticana, 2015); Thomas Jay Oord, "A Loving Civilization: A Political Ecology that Promotes Overall Well-Being," *The Kenarchy Journal* Vol. 2 (2021).

[95] William Lane Craig commits this error in his response to essential kenosis in *God and the Problem of Evil: Five Views*, James K. Dew, Jr. and Chad Meister, eds. (Downers Grove, Ill.: InterVarsity, 2017), 145.

[96] I join John D. Caputo in rejecting the idea God is sovereign or omnipotent as those words are usually understood. But I don't call God "weak." On Caputo's view, see *The Weakness of God: A Theology of the Event* (Bloomington, Ind.: Indiana University Press, 2006). I do like the way he prioritizes love in *What Would Jesus Deconstruct?* (Grand Rapids, Mich.: Baker, 2007).

is mighty" (93:4). The Hebrew word often translated "almighty" is *El Shaddai*. Its meaning is obscure, but most scholars think it identifies a life-giving breast or a mountain haven.[97] It does *not* mean "all-controlling."

If we delineate with care, we can use "almighty" to describe God's uncontrolling power. God is almighty, 1) in the sense of being mightier than any other being, as God has no equals (Is. 40:25). God is almighty, 2) in the sense of exerting might upon all others. God "upholds" creation (Is. 41:10) and we "live in" this power (2 Cor. 13:4). God is almighty, 3) in the sense that God is the source of might or empowerment for all. In God we live and move and have our being (Acts. 17:28).

Even an almighty God cannot do some things, however. A God of love cannot lie (Num. 23:19; Tit. 1:2; Heb. 6:18). God cannot grow tired (Is. 40:28) or be tempted by evil (Jam. 1:13). A loving God cannot give up on or abandon us (Hos. 11:8; Heb. 13:5). And even "if we are faithless," a loving God "remains faithful, for he cannot deny himself" (2 Tim. 2:13).

The Bible says God cannot do some things.

Some may think an uncontrolling God of love is limited.[98] But this is misleading. Would we say a God who exists necessarily and everlastingly is limited, because this God can't stop existing? Would we say a God who is holy and always loves is limited, because this God cannot sin? Would we say that the God who knows all that's knowable is limited, because this God can't be ignorant? I agree with Jacob Arminius when he says we should take care "that things unworthy of [God] not be attributed to his essence, his understanding,

---

[97] On the meaning of *El Shaddai*, see David Biale, "The God with Breasts: El Shaddai in the Bible," *History of Religions* 21 (3): 244; Jay MacLeod, "Almighty Mistake" *Theology* 2005:108 (842):91-99.

[98] For a concise summary of the issues of God's limitations in relation to omnipotence, see Joshua Hoffman and Gary Rosenkrantz, "Omnipotence," in *A Companion to Philosophy of Religion*, Philip L. Quinn and Charles Taliaferro, eds. (Malden, Mass.: Blackwell, 1999), 229-235. See also Alte Ottesen Sovik, *The Problem of Evil and the Power of God* (Unipub AS, 2009).

and his will."[99] God can't do many things, because to do them, God would not be God.

The idea God is unlimited in *all* respects is incoherent. Biblically faithful and rationally coherent theologies must say God cannot do many activities. The God who must do what deity does, and can't do otherwise, is not limited in any coherent sense.[100]

An uncontrolling God of love is not limited in any coherent way.

The God of essential kenosis is not omnipotent, at least not in the way many use the word. Scholars rarely, if ever, think "omnipotence" means "able to do anything imaginable." Nearly every careful theologian says God cannot do what is illogical, for instance.[101] God can't make round squares. Many think God cannot change the past.[102] Others say God cannot contradict God's own nature. God cannot deny Godself, because God must act like God. And those who think creatures are free say omnipotence does not entail God controlling free creatures. The idea of absolute power is preposterous. After making all the necessary qualifications to what we *don't* mean by "omnipotent," I believe few reasons remain to keep the word.[103]

The God of essential kenosis is not impotent, however. An impotent God implies inaction. The uncontrolling God of love always

---

[99] Jacob Arminius, "Twenty-Five Public Disputations," in *Works of James Arminius*, 135.

[100] Arminius offers a list of things God cannot do in "Twenty-Five Public Disputations," *The Works of James Arminius*, 135. Richard Rice explores the problems with saying God is limited in "Does Open Theism Limit God," in *The Future of Open Theism*. See my review of Rice's book, "Open Theism and Divine Limitations" http://thomasjayoord.com/index.php/blog/archives/open-theism-and-the-question-of-divine-limitations (Accessed 12/6/21)

[101] Thomas Aquinas represents the majority of Christian theologians when he says, "whatever involves a contradiction is not within the scope of [God's] omnipotence" (*Summa Theologica*, Volume I, ques. 15 art. 3 [New York: McGraw Hill, 1963], 163-64).

[102] Jonathan Edwards puts it this way: "In explaining the nature of necessity, that in things which are past, their past existence is now necessary" (Jonathan Edwards, *Freedom of the Will*, s.12 [New York: Leavitt & Allen, 1857], 10.). See also Alvin Plantinga, "On Ockham's Way Out," Faith and Philosophy, 3.3 (July 1986): 235-269; Thomas Aquinas, *Summa Theologica*, Volume I, ques. 25 art. 4 (New York: Cosmo, 2007), 139; Roger Olson, "Can God Change the Past?" https://www.patheos.com/blogs/rogereolson/2021/06/can-god-change-the-past-2/ (Accessed 12/6/21)

[103] Charles Hartshorne expresses this well in the title and arguments of his book, *Omnipotence and Other Theological Mistakes* (Albany, NY: SUNY, 1984).

acts in relation to creation. An impotent God might be ineffective. But the goodness, truth, and beauty we witness in our lives and universe reveal the effectiveness of God's powerful love. An impotent God might watch creation from afar. The God of uncontrolling love is immediately present to all creation. The God of essential kenosis is not impotent.

I prefer to call the God of uncontrolling love "amipotent." I coined this word using the Latin prefix for love we find in positive words like "amity," "amigo," "amicable," and "amiable." "Potent" is the Latin root word of "potency" and "potential."[104] God is amipotent in the sense that divine love preconditions and governs divine power. God always exerts power lovingly. Because love comes logically before power in God's nature and this love is essentially uncontrolling, divine amipotence never controls.

God's almighty power is uncontrolling love: amipotence.

CONCLUSION

Open and relational theology provides a fitting framework for a Christian theology of love. It considers love God's primary attribute and overcomes problems inherent in classical doctrines. As relational, God gives and receives with creatures and creation. Because love is relational, a theological framework that affirms a relational God makes sense of divine love.

God moves through time with creatures into an open future. God's love is intentional and timefull. If love is uncontrolling, the God who predestines cannot love moment by moment. For God to know the future exhaustively, it must be settled and closed. But a settled future is incompatible with divine love, because lovers choose among live possibilities when seeking overall well-being. Therefore, a loving God cannot know the future exhaustively.

---

[104] I first use this word in *Open and Relational Theology*, ch. 5. Bradford McCall argues for something similar with "amorepotent." See *The God of Chance & Purpose: Divine Involvement in a Secular Evolutionary World* (Eugene, Or.: Wipf & Stock, 2021).

Clark Pinnock offers a winsome open and relational theology. He prizes scripture and considers love primary. His proposals overcome problems in classical theism. Pinnock recognizes the positive role relational philosophy can play in making sense of God, ourselves, and existence. Those who seek a Christian theology of love should adopt features of his open and relational theology.

The open and relational theology of love I have proposed additionally centers on Jesus. In his life, teachings, and ministry, this man from Nazareth expressed many forms of love. His love was pluriform. Jesus healed, taught, consoled, liberated, calmed, suffered, counseled, and more. His love is the Christian's benchmark.

Jesus' kenosis points to the kenotic love of God. In God, however, kenosis is essential; it is an aspect of God's immutable and eternal nature. As essentially kenotic, divine love is necessarily self-giving, empowering, and, therefore, uncontrolling. A God who expresses uncontrolling love for everyone and everything cannot control anyone or anything.

An uncontrolling God is not culpable for evil. We can solve the primary dimensions of the problem of evil by saying God can't prevent evil singlehandedly, empathizes with the hurting, works to heal, endeavors to bring good from bad, calls creatures to join in overcoming evil, and does not create evil. These proposals answer the primary questions both theists and atheists ask about God's love and evil.

An open and relational theology of love appeals to the power of God's love. It makes little sense to say an uncontrolling God of love is limited. But this God is not omnipotent, at least not in the traditional sense. Nor is God impotent, in the sense of doing nothing or being ineffective.

An uncontrolling yet almighty God of love is amipotent.

8

Essential Hesed and "Alongside of" Love

*T*o construct a Christian open and relational theology of love, I began by focusing on *agape*. In subsequent chapters, I addressed *eros* at length but *philia* sparingly. At this chapter's conclusion, I will address *philia* and define it as "alongside of" love.

I've referred occasionally to Old Testament understandings of love. This chapter addresses this omission with a focus upon the Hebrew words *ahavah* and *hesed,* concepts central to divine love. A relational God expresses emotional *ahavah* and steadfast *hesed* in covenant.

The oft-repeated phase in the Hebrew Bible, "the steadfast love of the Lord endures forever" suggests God's love is everlasting. To say *hesed* is everlasting suggests it is essential to God, which means God always and necessarily loves creation. I call this "essential hesed."[1]

Although we find biblical support for a Hebrew notion of essential hesed, the Christian tradition has constructed obstacles to embracing it. We noted some obstacles when exploring classical theism's doctrine of God and the problem of evil. Since the fourth century, leading theologians have said God created the universe out of nothing. I will argue that if this view is correct, God's steadfast

---

[1] In other contexts, I've called this God's "essential relations" or "strong passibility." See Thomas Jay Oord "Strong Passibility," in *Divine Impassibility: Four Views on God's Emotions and Suffering*, Robert J. Matz and A. Chadwick Thornhill, eds. (Downers Grove, Ill.: Intervarsity, 2019).

love for creation is not everlasting. In addition, a God who created *ex nihilo* can control creatures, and this God should use that power to stop evil.

I believe that to affirm divine love consistently, we should reject *creatio ex nihilo*. God never has and cannot create something from nothing. I propose an alternative view that says God, in love, everlastingly creates out of that which God previously created. This creation account adds a key piece in a coherent theology of love.

God's everlastingly expresses uncontrolling love for creation.

LOVE IN THE OLD TESTAMENT

The writers of what most Christians call the "Old Testament" offer various words translators render "love" or something similar. We might transliterate the two most prominent as *ahavah* and *hesed*.[2]

Ahavah pertains primarily to care, attachment, and affection. This can be fatherly affection for children: for instance, Abraham had *ahavah* for Isaac (Gen. 37:3; 44:20). It can be affection for friends: David had *ahavah* for Jonathan (2 Sam. 1:26). Biblical writers use *ahavah* for love in marriage: Rebecca had *ahavah* for Jacob (Gen. 25:28). *Ahavah* describes a man's romantic feeling for a woman (e.g., Gen. 24:67; Jud. 14:16; 16:15; 1 Sam 1:5; Prov. 5:19; Ecc. 9:9; 2 Chr. 11:21). This word features prominently in Song of Songs.

Biblical writers sometimes use *ahavah* to describe human love for God and others. The *shema* says God should be loved — *ahavah* — with all of one's heart, soul and strength (Deut. 6:4-5; see also 10:12). *Ahavah* is used in Leviticus for the command to love one's neighbor (Lev. 19:18). God also commands *ahavah* for strangers (Deut. 10:19).

---

[2] Words related to or associated with *hesed* and *ahavah* include *hasid, hen, emeth, berit, rahamim, zadik*. The Hebrew word *hadaq* is used rarely in scripture and might be translated as setting one's heart or desiring. For examinations of these and other Hebrew words translated "love," see Felix Asensio, *Misericordia et Veritas, el Hesed y Emet divinos, su influjo religioso-social en la historia de Israel* (Rome: Apud Aedes Universitatis Gregoianae, 1949); Hans Joachim Stoebe, "Di Bedeutung des Wortes Hasad im Alten Testament, "*Vetus Testamentum* (1952): 244-54. See Terence Fretheim's work on love and creation theology in *God and the World in the Old Testament*.

God expresses *ahavah* for people. Divine *ahavah* is the source of deliverance from Egypt (Deut. 4:37). According to Jeremiah, God experiences *ahavah* as everlasting affection for the people (31:3).[3] This affection involves God experiencing changing emotions and altering plans.[4] Jeremiah, Ezekiel, Hosea, Micah, and Song of Songs employ the marriage metaphor to describe God's *ahavah* for Israel.[5] God loves with affection.

Biblical writers more often use *hesed* to describe God's love. Scholars confess that translating *hesed* is difficult.[6] Among the renderings are "continual doing good," "covenantal love," "devotion," "faithfulness," "goodwill," "grace," "love," "loyal helpfulness," "loyal kindness," "mutual reciprocity," "reliable solidarity," "steadfast love," and "sure-love."[7]

---

[3] See Reuven Kimelman, "'We Love the God Who Loved Us First:' The Second Blessing of the Shema Liturgy," in Isaac Kalimi, ed., *Bridging between Sister Religions* (Leiden: Brill, 2016).

[4] For discussions of the suffering and changing God of the Old Testament, see Brevard Childs, *Biblical Theology in Crisis* (Philadelphia: Westminster, 1970), 44-47; Terence E. Fretheim, *The Suffering of God: An Old Testament Perspective* (Philadelphia: Fortress, 1984); Harold Knight, *The Hebrew Prophetic Consciousness* (London: Luterworth, 1947); George A. F. Knight, *Theology as Narration: A Commentary on the Book of Exodus* (Grand Rapids, Mich.: Eerdmans, 1976), 14, 19; Claus Westermann, *Elements of Old Testament Theology*, trans. Douglas W. Stott (Atlanta: John Knox, 1982), 138-49.

[5] Many writers of scripture use the marriage analogy for the God-Israel relationship. See Gordon P. Hugenburger, *Marriage as a Covenant: Biblical Law and Ethics as Developed from Malachi* (Grand Rapids, Mich: Baker, 1998). For a contemporary defense of love in marriage, see Stephen Post, *More Lasting Unions* (Grand Rapids, Mich.: Eerdmans, 2000).

[6] Most scholars credit Nelson Glueck for launching the contemporary discussion of *hesed* (*Das Wort hesed im altteshatuamentlichen Sprachgebruache als meschiliche und gottliche gemeinschaftgemasse Verhaltungswise*, translated by Alfred Gottschalk as *Hesed in the Bible* (Cincinnati: Hebrew Union College Press, 1967 [1927]). See a reprint with Gerald A. Larue's introductory essay on 20ᵗʰ century explorations of *hesed* (Eugene, Or.: Wipf and Stock, 2011). On the difficulty of translating *hesed,* see Daniel Z. Feldman, *Divine Footsteps: Chesed and the Jewish Soul* (New York: Yeshiva University, 2008), 2.

[7] Most translations listed here are in Gerald A. Larue's summary essay on *hesed* scholarship. See "Recent Studies in *Hesed*," in *Hesed in the Bible* (Eugene, Or.: Wipf and Stock, 2011). See also Harold M. Kamsler, "*Hesed* — Mercy or Loyalty?" *Jewish Biblical Quarterly* 27, no. 3 (1999): 183-85. The translation of *hesed* in the Septuagint (LXX) is rendered by various Greek words. On this, see C. H. Dodds, *The Bible and the Greeks* (London: Hoddern and Stoughton, 1954), 55-69.

In addition to God's love, *hesed* describes the love of a father for a son (Gen. 24:29), husband for wife (Gen. 20:13), host for guests (Gen. 19:19), friend for friend (2 Sam. 16:17), and the helper for the one helped (Judg. 1:24). Micah says Israel should *hesed* (6:8), in the sense of making it their priority in life.[8]

To explain *hesed*'s uniqueness, many focus on how biblical writers describe the benefits a person with greater resources provides to one with lesser. An emperor (suzerain) may choose to *hesed* a lesser king (vassal), for instance. This love is a personal "relationship of service," says Jon Levenson, "founded not in conquest and subjugation but in good relations and mutual benefit."[9] *Hesed* does not assume parties are equal, but it does assume reciprocity.

The greater party makes a covenant with the lesser based on *hesed*. This love covenant pertains primarily to deeds and actions. "The deeds are not dependent on emotion," says Levenson, as individuals "are always obligated to serve their Lord."[10] But emotions can play a factor in initiating covenant and in the results (or lack thereof) that covenant brings.

The comparison of an emperor's love for a lesser king is analogous to God's love for Israel and creation. While God expresses *ahavah*, divine *hesed* is often linked with God's covenants.[11] *Hesed* has connotations of mercy and obligation, compassion and commitment.

Scholars customarily say God's covenants differ from contracts. Contracts are arrangements based primarily upon nonpersonal decisions pertaining to external factors. God's covenant, by contrast, derives primarily from God's loving heart. This means, in part, divine covenants are not arbitrary or capricious but include feelings of affection.

---

[8] See Kathleen O'Connor, "Reflections on Kindness as Fierce Tenderness: Micah 6:1-8," *Journal for Preachers* 39:3 (2016).

[9] Jon D. Levenson, *The Love of God: Divine Gift, Human Gratitude, and Mutual Faithfulness in Judaism* (Princeton: Princeton University Press, 2016), 6.

[10] Ibid., 60.

[11] See Norman H. Snaith, *The Distinctive Ideas of the Old Testament* (London: Epworth, 1944), 95.

Most biblical references to *hesed* point to God's initiating. Israel has not earned God's love, but *hesed* is not unilateral either. God commits to creatures, and creatures are expected to commit to God. Creatures can and should love God with *ahavah* and *hesed*.

God's *hesed* aims to bring good. To put it in terms of my love definition, *hesed* acts intentionally, in relational response, to promote well-being. Those faithful to the covenant are promised health, long life, fertility, wealth, sovereignty over their land, and peace within it. Warnings are given to those who break the covenant; breaking covenant brings negative consequences.

Israel often fails to live up to its part of the covenants. Consequently, God cries out, "O that my people would listen to me, that Israel would walk in my ways!" (Ps. 81:13). Jeremiah describes God wailing in emotional stress over the people's unfaithfulness: "O that my head were a spring of water, and my eyes a fountain of tears, so that I might weep day and night for the slain of my poor people!" (Jer. 9:1). "A commitment to loyalty on the part of God," says Walter Brueggemann, "leads to hurt, anguish, and pathos on God's part."[12]

The God of covenant is relational and experiences emotions.

Covenantal love is unconditional in one sense and conditional in another. "It is unconditional," says Levenson, "in that the love comes into, and remains, in force even when nothing has been done to deserve it." But covenant is conditional "in that it involves expectations and stipulations, and it suffers and turns sour if they are not met." "To the extent that the covenant depends on the human partners meeting its conditions," says Levenson, "covenant is exceedingly fragile. To the extent that it depends on God's reliability, it is rock-solid."[13]

The Psalms speak often of God's *hesed*. Although divine love benefits the beloved, the Psalmist sometimes appeals to divine self-interest when urging God to keep covenant.[14] If God doesn't love, the

---

[12] Walter Brueggemann, "Editor's Foreword," in Katherine Doob Sakenfeld, *Faithfulness in Action: Loyalty in Biblical Perspective* (Philadelphia: Fortress, 1985), xii.

[13] Levenson, *The Love of God*, 61-62, 121.

[14] See Bernhard W. Anderson, *Out of the Depths* (Philadelphia: Westminster, 1983).

argument goes, God would be impotent and not trustworthy (e.g., 6:5; 13:6; 40:11; 115:1). God would fall short of divine responsibilities (25:6; 106; 107).

Sometimes, the Psalmist emphasizes God's exclusive *hesed* for his people (e.g., 147:8-10). At other times, God shows *hesed* for all nations and all creation (e.g., 117:1-2).[15] "The earth is full of the steadfast love of the Lord," says the Psalmist (33:5), and "the earth, O Lord, is full of your steadfast love" (119:64). In these instances, God's interests are universal, and *hesed*'s benefit is revealed throughout the cosmos (see Psalm 33, 36, 103, 117, 147).[16] Other biblical writers also affirm God's universal *hesed* (Jonah 4:2; Ruth 1:8; 2 Sam. 15:20).

In earlier chapters, I said the Hebrew word *olam* means God's unending duration rather than timelessness. God experiences everlastingly. We find *olam* often in the Bible in conjunction with *hesed* and sometimes with *ahavah*. God's *hesed* and *ahavah* are everlasting. "Give thanks to the Lord, for he is good," says the Psalmist, "his steadfast love (*hesed*) endures forever (*olam*)" (106:1). "Great is his steadfast love (*hesed*) toward us, and the faithfulness of the Lord endures forever (*olam*)" (117:2).[17] "I have loved you with an everlasting love (*ahavah olam*)," say the Lord, "I have drawn you with unfailing kindness (*hesed*)" (Jer. 31:3).

The phrase, "the steadfast love of the Lord endures forever," appears over and over. It occurs in all twenty-six verses of Psalm 136, for instance, and repeatedly in Psalms 89 and 118. Exodus says the "merciful and gracious" God "abounds in steadfast love and faithfulness" (Ex. 34:6). Nehemiah says that God is "gracious and merciful" and "abounding in steadfast love" (Neh. 9:17). According to

---

[15] Shai Held argues that traditional Jewish thinkers say the mandate to *hesed* extends beyond human beings to all living creatures. See *Judaism is About Love* (unfinished manuscript at the time of this writing).

[16] See Walter Brueggemann, "Psalm 109: Three Times 'Steadfast Love.'" *Word and World* 5, no. 2:144-54; John Goldingay, *Psalms: Vol. 3, Psalms 90-150* (Grand Rapids: Baker Academic, 2008).

[17] See Rolf A. Jacobson, "'The Faithfulness of the Lord Endures Forever': The Theological Witness of the Psalter," in *Soundings in the Theology of Psalms*, Rolf A. Jacobson, ed. (Minneapolis: Fortress, 2011).

Lamentations, the Lord's "mercies never come to an end" (Lam. 3:22). God repeatedly tells Israel his love is steadfast, and God loves Israel with an "everlasting love" (Is. 54:8).[18] The phrase plays a central role in revealing God's faithful love.

God's *hesed* is everlasting; the steadfast love of the Lord endures forever.

ESSENTIAL HESED

In the previous chapter, I asked whether God's *kenosis* is voluntary or essential. Does God freely choose *kenosis*, which means God *may or may not* self-give and others-empower? Or *must* God self-give, others-empower, and therefore, cannot control?

I turn to divine *hesed* with a similar question. Is God's covenantal, loyal, and steadfast love for creation something God can freely break? Or should we take literally the claim that God's steadfast love endures forever? Should we say *hesed* is essential in the divine nature, which means God *cannot* break covenant? Or is it arbitrary?

The Bible doesn't answer these questions straightforwardly. In some passages, God threatens to withdraw *hesed*. In others, God cannot withdraw *hesed* and must keep covenant. The merciful and gracious God "keeps steadfast love for the thousandth generation," but can also be found "visiting the iniquity of the parents upon the children and the children's children, to the third and the fourth generation" (Exod. 34:6-7). The God whom Jeremiah says threatens to remove "steadfast love and mercy" (16:7) is the same whose *hesed* the Psalmist says, "endures forever, and his faithfulness to all generations" (Ps. 100:5). Joshua says God "will not forgive your transgression or your sins" (Josh. 24:19). But Nehemiah says God is "ready to forgive, gracious and merciful, slow to anger and abounding in steadfast love, and did not forsake them" (Neh. 9:17).

---

[18] In addition to those already cited, see 1 Chron. 16:34,41; 2 Chron. 5:13; 7:3,6; 20:21; Exod. 3:11; Ps. 105, and more.

What do we make of this? Is God fickle? Does God have split-personality disorder? Is God conflicted? Must we hope God's in a good mood when we go astray? To put it philosophically, is God's *hesed* contingent or necessary?[19]

In this book's first chapter, I identified strategies biblical scholars use to address divine violence. These strategies can apply to passages that say or imply God might be unfaithful or stop loving. One strategy appeals to the overall biblical witness. This witness, in general, points to a God of dependable love. This approach discounts the minority witness and affirms God's faithful love for all creatures and creation.[20]

A related strategy distinguishes between who God is and what some texts *say* God is. Terence Fretheim recommends this when dealing with biblical passages that portray God as violent or unfaithful. "The God portrayed in the text does not fully correspond to the God who transcends the text, who is a living, dynamic reality that cannot be captured in words on a page."[21] Fretheim claims God is a loving and living reality based on the broad textual witness.[22]

Some Christians appeal to the revelation of faithful love in Jesus as the most accurate account of God's steadfast love. In this strategy, Jesus's faithful love takes priority over biblical passages that portray

---

[19] Some Christians appeal to the social Trinity as a metaphysical foundation for saying God always and essentially loves. Essential hesed does not require this claim, because it says God always and essentially loves creatures and creation. But Christians who embrace the social Trinity should also embrace essential hesed. Doing so allows one to say God everlastingly expresses love among members of the Godhead and everlastingly loves creation. For an argument on the compatibility of the Trinity and the theology I propose, see Thomas Jay Oord, "Analogies of Love Between God and Creatures: A Response to Kevin Vanhoozer," in *Love, Divine and Human: Contemporary Essays in Systematic and Philosophical Theology* (New York: T & T Clark, 2020).

[20] John Wesley assumed problematic biblical passages could be interpreted to affirm God's love. "No scripture can mean that God is not love, or that his mercy is not over all his works." See "Free Grace," *The Bicentennial Edition of the Works of John Wesley*, Vol. 3 (Nashville: Abingdon, 1984–), 556. On Wesley's hermeneutic of love, see Rem B. Edwards, "John Wesley's Non-Literal Literalism and Hermeneutic of Love" *Wesleyan Theological Journal* 51:2 (2016):26-40; Edwards, *John Wesley's Values — And Ours* (Lexington: Emeth, 2013).

[21] Terence Fretheim and Karlfried Froelich, *The Bible as Word of God: In a Postmodern Age* (Eugene, Or.: Wipf and Stock, 2001), 116.

[22] On this, see Eric Seibert, *Disturbing Divine Behavior* (Philadelphia: Fortress, 2009).

God as unfaithful or as threatening to withdraw love. Just as Jesus loved everyone he met, says this argument, God loves all creation.

Another strategy says we find theological development in scripture itself. It admits that writers sometimes misunderstand or misrepresent God. Writers sometimes project upon God their cultural constructs or personal neuroses. Over time, this argument says, the idea that God that loves faithfully rose to prominence, nullifying claims to the contrary. Writers gradually move from seeing God as occasionally unpredictable and vengeful to believing God is faithfully loving. Humans learn, and this learning leads them to believe divine love is steadfast.

Take the story of Hosea and his wife Gomer as an example of this strategy. The point of this book is that Hosea's love for Gomer is analogous to God's love for Israel. Just as Gomer was unfaithful and broke Hosea's heart, Israel has been unfaithful to the Lord. And, metaphorically, God's heart breaks.

In response to unfaithfulness, God threatens punishments and humiliation. But the text also indicates God cannot follow through. "How can I give you up, Ephraim?" the Lord asks rhetorically. "How can I hand you over, O Israel?" (Hos. 11:8). God won't give up because as God says, "my heart recoils within me," and "my compassion grows warm and tender. I will not execute my fierce anger; I will not again destroy Ephraim." The following lines make the key claim in the passage: "for I am God and no mortal, the Holy One in your midst, and I will not come in wrath" (Hos 11:9).

The phrase, "I am God and no mortal," suggests the Creator differs from creatures in a crucial way. Unlike creatures, *hesed* is an essential attribute of God's nature. God *must* remain loyal in love and *cannot* abandon creation. "The expression 'abounding in loyalty,' is used in the Old Testament only of God, never of human beings," says Katherine Doob Sakenfeld.[23] Creatures can fail to love. *Hesed* is necessary for the essentially loving God.[24]

---

[23] Katherine Doob Sakenfeld, Katherine Doob Sakenfeld, *Faithfulness in Action: Loyalty in Biblical Perspective* (Philadelphia: Fortress, 1985), 49.

[24] Karl Barth comes close to affirming essential hesed when he calls *hesed* "an inner mode of being in God Himself." Karl Barth, *Church Dogmatics*, II/1, G. W. Bromiley and T. F. Torrance, eds. (Edinburgh: T & T Clark, 1957), 353.

In fact, Hosea says God takes creatures as an everlasting bride. "I will take you for my wife forever; I will take you for my wife in righteousness and in justice, in steadfast love, and in mercy. I will take you for my wife in faithfulness; and you shall know the LORD" (2:19-20).

Mortals can stop loving; the God of essential hesed cannot.

"What began as *hesed,* granted as a matter of course," says Walther Eichrodt, "has become, as a result of the thoroughgoing questioning of the old conception, a completely new concept of faithfulness and love." *Hesed* tells us something fundamental about who God is. It signifies "the most profound meaning of the relationship between Creator and creature."[25] In this passage and others, says Edmond Jacob, *hesed* "is no longer the bond upholding the covenant, it is the very source of the attitude which impels God to enter into relation with his people."[26] *Hesed,* says Sakenfeld, "is that attribute of God, that attitude and action of God."[27]

Hesed is essential to who God is and how God acts.

If we embrace the idea God's nature is essential hesed, we interpret biblical passages differently. For instance, the Lord says, "I will not remove from him my steadfast love or be false to my faithfulness. I will not violate my covenant or alter the word that went forth from my lips" (Ps. 89:33-34). Essential hesed interprets the phrase "will not" remove steadfast love or be false to faithfulness, and "will not" violate the covenant or alter the word, to mean God *cannot* do so. If God everlastingly loves creation, God will not, because God cannot.

God's *hesed* is *olam* and essential to who God is.

I am not claiming every Old Testament passage confirms God's love as everlastingly *hesed.* Scripture is inconsistent. In advocating essential hesed, I'm making a theological decision to privilege "the

---

[25] Walther Eichrodt, *Theology of the Old Testament*, vol. 1, J. A. Baker, trans. (Philadelphia: Westminster, 1961), 239

[26] Edmond Jacob, *Theology of the Old Testament*, A. W. Heathcote and P. J. Allcock (New York: Harper, 1958), 106. Jacob refers also to Hos. 2:21; Jer. 3:12; Is. 54:7ff.

[27] Sakenfeld, *Faithfulness in Action*, 56.

steadfast love of the Lord endures forever" as telling the truth about who God essentially is and how God always acts. And I'm saying Old Testament statements to the contrary give an inaccurate account of God.

Privileging *hesed* and considering it essential to God is in many ways fruitful. Saying God *necessarily* and *everlastingly* expresses *hesed* for creatures and creation assures creatures of their Creator's steadfast love.

Take the issue of God abandoning, for instance. Essential hesed fits the words of Moses that "it is the Lord your God who goes with you; he will not fail you or forsake you" (Deut. 31:6,8). It fits the Apostle Paul's claim that "neither death, nor life, nor angels, nor rulers, nor things present, nor things to come, nor powers, nor height, nor depth, nor anything else in all creation, will be able to separate us from the love of God" (Rom. 8:38-39).

Essential hesed says we *can't* be separated from God's love. The God of steadfast love will never leave us nor forsake us, because God *cannot* do so. Our disobedience cannot break relationship with God. God cannot abandon.

The forgiveness included in essential hesed is good news. The steadfast love of God *always* forgives those who break the promises of covenant. And because we both harm and are harmed, we both hurt others and are hurt, it's good news that God's essential hesed always pardons perpetrators and empathizes with victims.[28]

Some people worry God does not love them. Theologies that champion God's sovereign freedom *from* creation instead of God's steadfast love *for* creation justify their worry. Theologies that don't embrace essential hesed or something like it say God chooses whether to love the world. God may or may not love others. It depends. The

---

[28] What some call "lament theodicy" is prevalent in the Hebrew Bible. If this is understood to mean humans lament in response to evil, I accept it as crucial for acknowledging that genuine evils occur. Bad things happen that God does not want and cannot prevent single-handedly. But some understand lament as saying God could stop evil singlehandedly but chooses not to promptly or not at all. I reject this understanding of lament theodicy. It does not portray God as steadfastly loving. Tim Reddish addresses these issues in *Does God Always Get What God Wants?* (Eugene, Or.: Cascade, 2018).

God of essential hesed, though, *must* love everyone and everything, and God has always been doing so.

It's difficult to overemphasize the value of knowing God *always* and *necessarily* loves us. Such knowledge proves crucial when we experience self-doubt or self-loathing. It makes all the difference in making sense of suffering too. Because of God's essential hesed, we are assured God always loves us, even when we do not feel lovable.

Essential hesed supports the empathetic dimension of my solution to the problem of evil. As one engaged in give-and-receive reciprocity, the covenantal God of steadfast love suffers with those who suffer. As essentially related to creation, God will not and cannot ignore creatures. Everlasting *hesed* assures us God loves the harmed and hurting in a relationship of suffering love.

God unconditionally loves and accepts us and all creation.

The confidence that comes from essential hesed sustains wholehearted trust in and worship of God. If we are unsure God loves us, we cannot trust God wholeheartedly. A God who loves half-heartedly might betray us. This lack of confidence can prevent us from worshipping God unreservedly and enthusiastically. Essential hesed, by contrast, offers a conceptual basis for affirming God's covenantal love as rock-solid. We can worship without reservation the God whose steadfast love endures forever.

God will not and cannot stop loving us.

CREATIO EX NIHILO

In the previous chapter, I promised to expand on what I called the "Origination Dimension" of the problem of evil. This dimension asks about evil's origin. A coherent theology of love avoids implicitly or explicitly making God the origin of evil. Essential hesed helps by saying God has always been loving creation and by claiming the possibility for good and evil is inherent in creaturely existence.

I've argued that essential hesed says the steadfast love of the Lord endures forever. If we take "forever" seriously, it means God has always loved creatures and creation. In fact, God never exists without creatures and creation to love. Building from this, we should say God never existed alone and God never decided to create the universe from nothing. This means God does not create evil nor does God singlehandedly create the conditions that make evil possible.

The previous paragraph makes crucial claims. Let me address each.

Many Christians point to the Eden story as an explanation of sin's origin. A serpent tempted Adam and Eve to eat forbidden fruit. If God always loves and wants creatures to love, their yielding to temptation meant failing to love. This story rightly points to human choice as the source of sin. But it makes one wonder, why did God create a world in which choosing to sin is even possible?[29]

To answer this question, a theology of love makes sense of God as Creator. Many Christians today and throughout history have claimed God created the universe from absolutely nothing (*creatio ex nihilo*). Many look to the first lines of Genesis when thinking about God's creating. "In the beginning," the Bible begins, "when God created the heavens and the earth, the earth was a formless void and darkness covered the face of the deep, while a wind from God swept over the face of the waters" (1:1-2).

Genesis 1:1 is best interpreted as a temporal clause: "When God *began to create* the heaven and the earth."[30] This is important, because temporal clauses do not suggest an absolute beginning of time. Contrary to what Augustine thinks, the Genesis author does not claim time began when God created our universe.

According to the passage, God confronted opposing forces in the beginning. These forces are *something* rather than absolutely nothing. God established a benevolent and life-sustaining order by

---

[29] Mark Harris explores this question and others related to creation in *The Nature of Creation: Examining the Bible and Science* (Durham: Acumen, 2013).

[30] Jon D. Levenson explains this point in *Creation and the Persistence of Evil: The Jewish Drama of Divine Omnipotence* (Princeton, N.J.: Princeton University Press, 1994; New York: Harper & Row, 1987), 121.

mastering what was already present. God is the victor over foes existing prior to our universe.[31]

The phrase "formless void" in verse two is *tohu wabohu*. Some translators render the phrase "primordial chaos," others call it "amorphous state" or "undifferentiated mass."[32] God transforms this chaos when creating the universe. Divine creating transforms actualities rather than conjuring them from absolutely nothing.

After referring to the Spirit hovering over chaos, Genesis speaks of darkness covering the "face of the deep." This is *tehom*, which also refers to something nondivine already present as God creates. "The *tehom* signifies here the primeval waters," says Brevard Childs.[33]

Genesis does *not* say God created from absolute nothingness.

Old Testament writers use a dozen Hebrew words for "create." Genesis writers typically use *bara* and *asah*. These words refer to God's activity as Creator and to creaturely activity as co-creators. There is no special word in Hebrew that says God created something out of nothing.[34]

A long list of Bible scholars say the "doctrine" of *creatio ex nihilo* is not found in Genesis.[35] The list includes liberal and conserva-

---

[31] Ibid., 3, 17-18.

[32] Levenson prefers "primordial chaos" (Ibid., xx). David Toshio Tsumura and William P. Brown say God created from something like amorphous state or undifferentiated mass). See Tsumura, *The Earth and the Waters in Genesis 1 and 2: A Linguistic Investigation* (Sheffield: JSOT, 1989); and Brown, *The Ethos of the Cosmos: The Genesis of Moral Imagination in the Bible* (Grand Rapids: Eerdmans, 1999). For a theological exploration, see Eric M. Vail, *Creation and Chaos Talk* (Eugene, Or.: Pickwick, 2012).

[33] Brevard S. Childs, *Myth and Reality in the Old Testament*, Studies in Biblical Theology, No. 27 (London: SCM, 1960), 33.

[34] See Terence E. Fretheim, *God and the World in the Old Testament*.

[35] See, for instance, Fretheim, *God and World in the Old Testament*, 5; Rolf P. Knierim, *Task of Old Testament Theology* (Grand Rapids, Mich.: Eerdmans, 1995), 210; Levenson, *Creation and the Persistence of Evil*; Shalom M. Paul, "Creation and Cosmogony: In the Bible," *Encyclopedia Judaica* (Jerusalem: Keter, 1972), 5:1059-63; Mark S. Smith, *The Priestly Vision of Genesis 1* (Philadelphia: Fortress, 2010), 50; Bruce K. Waltke, *Creation and Chaos* (Portland, Or.: Western Conservative Baptist Seminary, 1974); John H. Walton, *The Lost World of Genesis One* (Downers Grove, IL: IVP, 2009), 42; Claus Westermann, *Genesis 1-11*, John J. Scullion, trans. (London: SPCK, 1994), 110; Frances Young, "Creatio Ex Nihilo: A Context for the Emergence of Christian Doctrine of Creation," *Scottish Journal of Theology* 44 (1991): 139-51.

tive voices — both those who reject *creatio ex nihilo* and those who accept it for other nonbiblical reasons. "Properly understood," says Levenson in summary, Genesis 1:1-2:3 "cannot be invoked in support of the developed Jewish, Christian, and Muslim doctrine of *creatio ex nihilo*."[36]

It's hard to overstate this: Genesis just does not say God creates from nothing.[37]

As the creation account unfolds, according to Genesis, we find God sharing power. God asks creation to take part in creative processes. On day two, God grants the firmament the god-like function of separating waters above from waters below. On days three, five, and six, God invites earth and waters to bring forth living creatures.

Later in Genesis, God grants humans a privilege that noncanonical creation stories reserve only for deities: the opportunity to name other creatures. God blesses creatures with the capacity for co-creative fertility. Creatures are asked to multiply and fill the earth. In all this, the Genesis creation story points "to a God who is generous with power," says Richard Middleton. In fact, "Genesis 1:1-2:3 converges on John 3:16," says Middleton, because "in both creation and redemption, 'God so loved the world that he gave....'"[38]

---

[36] Levenson, *Creation and the Persistence of Evil*, 2.

[37] The only biblical verse to mention God creating from nothing is 2 Maccabees 7:28, a passage not recognized in the Protestant canon. God "did not make them out of existing things" the verse says. But the context conflicts with the notion God creates from absolutely nothing. It identifies a mother who carries, nurses, and educates her son. "In the same way," says the writer of 2 Maccabees, "humankind came into existence." In other words, mothers are creators. Of course, we know that to create, mothers require fathers; sperm and egg are needed. This is not creation from nothing. A better analogy says God created the heavens, earth, humans, and all creatures in the divine womb. These gender connotations should lead a contemporary person to wonder what other factors were involved. In short, the natal analogy requires multiple causes, not just one. For a creative and persuasive *tehomic* theology, see Catherine Keller, *The Face of the Deep* (New York: Routledge, 2003); Andre Rabe, *Creative Chaos* (2019).

[38] J. Richard Middleton in "Creation Founded in Love: Breaking Rhetorical Expectations in Genesis 1:1-2:3," in *Sacred Text, Secular Times: The Hebrew Bible in the Modern World*, Leonard Jay Greenspoon and Bryan F. LeBeau, eds. (Omaha, Neb.: Creighton University Press, 2000), 57, 67.

When we look to the New Testament, we find no explicit references to an idea of *creatio ex nihilo*. Second Peter offers the most explicit statement about God's initial creating when it says God created "out of water and by means of water" (2 Pt. 3:5). Other biblical passages speak of God creating out of unseen things (Heb. 11:3), ungrouped people (Rom. 4:17), and creation generally.[39]

Biblical writers always say God creates from or in relation to something. That "something" may be chaos, unseen actualities, water, unformed matter, disparate entities, people groups, and more. God often creates by speaking. But divine words require creaturely responses. God speaks in relation to something already present and something new emerges.

The reasons to reject teachings about creation from nothing are not limited to its absence in the Bible or its failure to support the view that God literally loves creation everlastingly.[40] *Creatio ex nihilo* presents other obstacles to a coherent theology of love.[41] Chief among them is the doctrine's implications for solving the problem of evil.

---

[39] Early Christian and Jewish theologians believed God created the world out of something. Philo, for instance, postulated pre-existent matter alongside God. Justin, Athenagoras, and Clement of Alexandria spoke of God creating the world out of something. Origin of Alexandria and John Scotus argued God has always been creating. "These theologians," says historian Gerhard May, "could hold an acceptance of an unformed matter was entirely reconcilable with biblical monotheism and the power of God." Gerhard May, *Creatio Ex Nihilo: The Doctrine of 'Creation out of Nothing' in Early Thought* Trans. A. S. Worrall (Edinburgh: T & T Clark, 1994), 74.

[40] On some problems with *creatio ex nihilo*, see Sjoerd L. Bonting, *Creation and Double Chaos* (Minneapolis: Fortress, 2005).

[41] I address these problems in other writings. I note seven here. 1. Absolute nothingness cannot be conceived. 2. Creation out of nothing was first proposed by Gnostics who assumed creation is inherently evil. 3. We have no evidence our universe originally came into being from nothing. 4. We have no evidence creatures or creaturely entities can emerge instantaneously from absolute nothingness (*ex nihil, nihil fit*). 5. Creation out of nothing assumes God once acted all alone, but power is a social concept only meaningful in relation to others. 6. A God who can create something from absolutely nothing could guarantee an unambiguous, inerrant revelation. But such revelation does not exist. 7. The power necessary to create from nothing supports the idea God causes or allows unjust empires and the evil-sustaining status quo. On these and others, see Thomas Jay Oord, "Eternal Creation and Essential Love" in *T&T Handbook on Suffering and the Problem of Evil*, Johannes Grossel and Matthias Grebe, eds. (London: T&T Clark, 2022).

A God who created our universe from nothing is singly responsible for the fundamental structures, laws, and possibilities of existence. Those fundamental conditions would include the conditions and possibilities for evil. Victims and survivors rightly wonder why the God who creates *ex nihilo* could not have done a better job. And they wonder why this God doesn't prevent pointless pain now.

It would seem a God who created from nothing should be able, instantaneously, to create obstacles that prevent evil today. Alvin Plantinga advocates this creating-from-nothing-now view: "There is nothing to prevent God from…creating *ex nihilo* a full-grown horse in the middle of Times Square." An *ex-nihilo* creating God can do so, Plantinga adds, "without violating the principle of conservation of energy."[42]

But if God can do what Plantinga claims, one wonders why God doesn't use this ability to prevent evil.[43]

Let me illustrate. Suppose a mentally disturbed individual fires a semi-automatic pistol at customers in a restaurant. The God who can create something out of nothing could create miniature walls to deflect each bullet. In this *ex-nihilo* creating, God would not violate the assailant's free will. If creating these walls violates the laws of nature — laws this God allegedly decided by fiat — such violation would be justified, because it saves lives. It follows that an *ex-nihilo* creating God would be culpable for failing to prevent genuine evil.

Once we consider ways that the God able to create *ex nihilo* might prevent evils, the problem of evil becomes overwhelming. God must be asleep on the job! Of course, we might imagine reasons God would allow suffering that is not genuinely evil. But it is impossible for me — and I suspect, for most people — to believe that a loving God capable of creating obstacles out of nothing allows *all*

---

[42] Alvin Plantinga, *Where the Conflict Really Lies: Science, Religion, and Naturalism* (Oxford: Oxford University Press, 2011), 78-79.

[43] David Ray Griffin has argued this point in many publications, including "Creation out of Nothing, Creation out of Chaos, and the Problem of Evil," in *Encountering Evil*, Stephen T. Davis, ed. 2nd ed. (Louisville, Ky.: Westminster John Knox, 2001); *Evil Revisited: Responses and Reconsiderations* (Albany, NY: SUNY, 1991).

the suffering we witness because it makes the world better. To believe this would be to believe God permitted every rape, holocaust, genocide, murder, and torture, and to believe our world is better for it. The way we live our lives suggests we don't really believe this.[44]

Because evils occur, we should *not* believe God can create something from nothing.

To overcome these problems, we need a creation theory that instead says God *never* has and *cannot* create something from nothing. This means the possibilities for good and evil are inherent in the creaturely order. God doesn't choose whether evil will be possible; the possibility is baked into what it means to be creaturely. To put it positively, this alternative doctrine of creation says God everlastingly and necessarily creates, loves, and invites creatures to love in response. They may or may not respond well to divine invitations.[45]

GOD EVERLASTINGLY LOVES AND CREATES OUT OF CREATION

It's important to say the steadfast love of the Lord endures forever and God necessarily loves creation. The idea of essential hesed does so. Rejecting the idea that God did, or could, create something from nothing is important too. The God who creates *ex nihilo* would be singly responsible for the conditions of creation, including the possibility evil will occur. This God can also prevent evil by creating obstacles from nothing now, but rarely, if ever, does.

We must reject *creatio ex nihilo*, in part, to portray God as perfectly loving.

---

[44] A variation of this is what Philip Clayton and Steven Knapp call the "not even once" view. It says a loving God creates *ex nihilo* but cannot control after the first moment. See Philip Clayton and Steven Knapp, *The Predicament of Belief* (Oxford: Oxford University Press, 2011), 66. For my response, see Oord, "Eternal Creation and Essential Love" in *T&T Handbook on Suffering and the Problem of Evil.*

[45] I lay out these ideas in "God Always Creates Out of Creation in Love," in *Theology of Creation: Creatio ex Nihilo and Its New Rivals*, Thomas Jay Oord, ed. New York: Routledge, 2014. See also Mary-Jane Rubenstein, *Worlds Without End* (New York: Columbia University Press, 2014).

A robust theology of love should offer an alternative view of God's creating. I call my alternative "God always creates out of creation in love." In Latin, we might render this view as *creatio ex creatione sempiternalis in amore*. It proposes a theory for how God created at the start of our universe (*creatio originalis*) and how God creates today (*creatio continua*). It also offers a reason God would create at all.[46]

God's creating is *always* in relation to creaturely somethings or someones. Saying this fits nicely with essential hesed, because the steadfast and creative love of the Lord endures forever. A God always in relation to creation always creates and loves creatures of various simplicities and complexities.

To explain how God, in love, everlastingly creates in relation to creation, I briefly address the motive, materials, method, and mode of God's creating.

Motive

God everlastingly loves creatures. Steadfast love for creation is a necessary attribute of God, which I call essential hesed. Consequently, love is God's motive for creating. God always wants the best possible, given the circumstances, and God always acts to promote overall well-being. The motive for both God's creating at the start of our universe and ongoing creating derives from God's everlasting love for

---

[46] A few scholars have sketched out what it might mean to say God's creating is somehow out of or in love. See, for instance, Paul Fiddes, "Creation Out of Love," in *The Work of Love*, John Polkinghorne, ed. (Grand Rapids, Mich.: Eerdmans, 2001); Michael Lodahl, *Creatio Ex Amore!* in *Theologies of Creation: Creatio Ex Nihilo and its New Rivals*, Thomas Jay Oord, ed. (New York: Routledge, 2014); J. Richard Middleton, *The Liberating Image* (Grand Rapids, Mich.: Brazos, 2005); Jurgen Moltmann, "God's Kenosis in the Creation and Consummation of the World," in *The Work of Love: Creation as Kenosis*, John Polkinghorne, ed. (Grand Rapids, MI: Eerdmans, 2001); James H. Olthuis, "Creatio Ex Amore," in *Transforming Philosophy and Religion*, Norman Wirzba and Bruce Ellis Benson, eds. (Bloomington, Ind.: University of Indiana Press, 2008); Thomas Jay Oord, "God Always Creates out of Creation in Love: Creatio ex Creatione a Natura Amoris," in *Theologies of Creation: Creatio Ex Nihilo and its New Rivals*, Thomas Jay Oord, ed. (New York: Routledge, 2014); Jordan Wessling, *Love Divine* (Oxford: Oxford University Press, 2020).

creaturely others.[47] To the question, "Why did and does God create?" I answer, "Love compels God to create."

Materials

God always creates out of, or in relation to, that which God previously created. By "always," I mean moment by moment, everlastingly. Even at the Big Bang of our universe, God created in relation to what God had created the moment before. The implication is that because divine creating is everlasting, there have always been creatures and creation out of or in relation to which God creates. God always creates out of what God earlier created, never from absolute nothingness.

Method

God always creates alongside creaturely others. While God is always a necessary cause in the coming to be of every creation or creature, God never acts as a sufficient cause.[48] God's creating in relation to others is persuasive not coercive, empowering but not overpowering, wooing and not by fiat. To put it another way, the Creator always creates in relation to or from co-creators.[49] This fits the biblical witness to God's creating activity, because according to the sacred text, God always creates in relation to something.[50]

---

[47] Genesis 1 "depicts God's founding exercise of creative power in such a way that we might appropriately describe it as an act of love," says Middleton in "Creation Founded in Love: Breaking Rhetorical Expectations in Genesis 1:1-2:3," 57.

[48] Levenson laments the common tendency among theologians to say God created in sovereign solitariness. "When it comes to creation, there remains a strange but potent tendency to resort to static affirmations of God's total power" (*Creation and the Persistence of Evil*, 2).

[49] Philip Hefner has done extensive work arguing for the cogency of the label "created co-creators." See *The Human Factor* (Philadelphia: Augsburg Fortress, 2000).

[50] I agree with Terry Fretheim when he says, "God works creatively with already existing realities to bring about newness." And "while God is certainly the initiator and primary actor in creation, God certainly involves both the human and the nonhuman in the continuing process of creation." See *God and the World in the Old Testament*, 5, 48.

Mode

God necessarily creates in one sense and contingently creates in another. "Creating creaturely others" is a necessary attribute of God. God was creating universes before ours, and God will create universes after.[51] As ever Creator, God necessarily creates. Because the future is open and God moves through time, however, God contingently chooses how to create, given what's possible. Although God must create and that act of creating is always loving, *how* and *what* God creates depends on how God freely acts in relation to creaturely conditions and possibilities. The how and what of God's creating are contingent.

God's creating, relating, and loving are everlastingly and essentially uncontrolling.

ANALOGIES AND OBJECTIONS

New theories are easily misunderstood. I suspect many will jump to the wrong conclusions when first considering mine. One can interpret in several ways the idea God, in love, everlastingly creates from or alongside what God previously created. Let me clarify my meaning for the phrase.

Some may assume, for instance, this theory says our universe exists everlastingly. That interpretation would deny the Big Bang, which is widely embraced by contemporary scientists. Fortunately, saying God, in love, always creates from that which God previously created can align with the Big Bang. It does not require believing our universe is everlasting.

---

[51] The claim that God creates an infinite number of universes simultaneously — an infinite multiverse — has numerous metaphysical problems. But because I don't claim an infinite number of universes exist, those problems do not apply to my theory that God creates an everlasting succession of universes. One problem with "infinite" is that the word has no positive meaning; it simply means "not finite." Additionally, my theory says God could not create an infinite number of universes, because God cannot create in unloving ways. The limited number of universes that will *actually* exist — although they be endless — will always be characterized by the action of a loving Creator.

There are good reasons to affirm our universe had a beginning roughly 13.8 billion years ago. But science offers no empirical evidence for or against what existed prior to that. *Creatio ex creatione sempiternalis in amore* speculates that a previous universe existed. At the beginning of ours, God created in relation to or out of a chaotic universe God had previously created. This chaos would be diffuse, although not entirely formless, as the previous universe would have "died" in increasing entropy. In its last moments, it may have been entirely composed of quarks, subatomic particles, or the most basic entities of existence in radical disorder. So we could say that God sometimes creates from "scratch," but never creates *ex nihilo*.

According to my view, no single universe exists everlastingly. Our universe is not eternal. But a *succession* of elements, entities, creatures, or universes is everlasting. The everlastingly creative God creates each thing in ongoing succession. But every creature and universe is itself temporary; all have a beginning.

No analogy can explain perfectly what I'm proposing, but let me offer something approximate. I spend time with and photograph wild horses in Idaho. Sometimes, a stallion can sire generations in a single herd. He impregnates mares, the fillies of those mares, the fillies of those fillies, and so on.

Imagine a stallion who lived a million years. Suppose it's this stallion's nature to bear offspring, and he always relates to at least one mare, but often to many during their lifetimes. Suppose the lifespan of a typical mare is 25 years. The stallion in this analogy goes through a succession of sexual relationships with mares who bear offspring. Those offspring bear more offspring. And so on. But no single mare lives a million years alongside the stallion.

We can apply this to God and creation. An everlasting God who by nature always creates and loves creatures will always have others with whom to create and love. But no creaturely other — whether a single entity or universe — is everlasting. Each comes and goes. God necessarily creates out of what God previously created and yet no single universe exists necessarily. Because God always creates in relation to what God previously created, there will always be creaturely others.

To say God everlastingly loves and creates might lead some to worry creaturely entities once existed before God. According to this worry, God "stumbled upon" or "found" preexisting materials from which God fashioned a universe. These materials would predate God.

My alternative creation theory denies any creaturely materials predate God. God always creates in each moment out of that which God created in the previous. This means no universe, world, creature, or "thing" predates God's creating, because God created them all. God doesn't create out of "stuff" God never encountered before and never "stumbles upon" something God did not create.

The stallion analogy helps us understand this too, but we'll have to expand it. We speculated this stallion lives a million years and, by nature, relates with and procreates alongside mares. These mares came from his previous procreation with their mothers. The stallion co-creates in relation to what he previously created. In our analogy, he does not "stumble upon" or "find" a mare he had not previously co-created.

Our hypothetical stallion came into existence, of course. He comes from a mare. And he will eventually die. In God's case, procreating in relation with creation had no beginning and will have no end. God exists, loves, and creates everlastingly. But just as the stallion relies upon co-creating mares, God relies upon the contributions of creaturely others.

This analogy works just as well if we speculate God is a mare instead of a stallion. God can be the mare who lives a million years but mates with a succession of stallions who each live for 25 years. In fact, the analogy may work even better — if we think of the gestation of the prenatal colts as like the God whose existence is a womb in which creation arises through divine care. But the mare analogy has the same limitations as the stallion analogy. Mares do not exist everlastingly. Only God is an everlasting creator; creaturely co-creators come and go.

To say God everlastingly creates and loves in relation to creation means God *needs* creatures. I noted this in an earlier chapter when I gave the seven analogies of love. But let's clarify that the Creator "needs" creation in some respects and not others. To say God, in love, always creates out of that which God previously created does not imply God's existence depends upon creatures. God exists necessarily, and nothing can end that.

Yet although God exists necessarily, God needs creatures. God needs them because relational love is never solitary. God depends on others with whom God lovingly gives and receives. Because "the steadfast love of the Lord endures forever," God needs creatures to love.

God also needs creatures in the creative process. This dependence is not about *whether* God creates. God necessarily creates, and God's motive to create comes from love. But the *results* of God's creating depend upon creaturely forces, factors, and choices. God's co-creating depends upon the existence of created co-creators.

There is no logical contradiction in saying that, to exist, God does not need creation, *and yet* God needs creation in each moment. So long as there are always creaturely others whom God creates and loves, God can both necessarily exist and necessarily create through dependent relations. Besides, the notion that God necessarily creates *guarantees* God will always have others to love and with whom to co-create.

Creatio ex creatione sempiternalis in amore overcomes other worries. It denies an eternal dualism of good and evil beings, for instance, and denies a dualism of eternally good and evil matter. Creation is intrinsically good. It also denies the pantheistic notion that God creates out of Godself. Instead, God always creates out of creation. My theory denies that God simply rearranges what already exists. It says, instead, that God creates something new each moment. My theory denies that creation is an illusion or entirely constructed of ideas; it also denies that a lesser god created the universe under the supervision of a greater one. So it cannot be objected to on those grounds.

Some scholars accept *creatio ex nihilo* because they say it clearly distinguishes God from creatures who cannot create something from nothing. They think doctrines that say God cannot create from nothing "shrink" the Creator to creaturely status.

My view retains distinctions between Creator and creature. For instance, my theory says God is the only creative agent who necessarily and everlastingly exists. No single creature or universe exists everlastingly. In my creation view, God is the only creative agent whose nature is love and therefore necessarily creates in love. The creative activity of creatures is not necessarily loving. In my view of creation, God exerts the most creative power on others. Creaturely creating is limited to affecting only some others. In my creation doctrine, God's creative vision includes all possibilities, while creaturely visions are limited.

My creation proposal affirms divine transcendence in a way typical Christian creation theories do not. Saying, as I do, that God *necessarily* creates means God is *essentially* a Creator. Typical Christian views say God may or may not create, which means creating isn't essential to God's nature. In that sense, my view portrays God as transcendent in ways other creation theologies cannot.

Finally, some may worry that saying God necessarily and everlastingly creates and loves undermines divine freedom. To say God necessarily does something means God is not free to do otherwise.[52] This might lead some to worry my theory denies God's freedom.

My view says God is free in some respects when creating, but not free in others. It's God's nature to love and create; God *must* love and *must* create. God is not free to do otherwise. But God is free to choose *how* to create, given creaturely conditions. God freely creates

---

[52] My creation theory differs from Platonic divine emanation theories. Those theories assume, for instance, that God is timeless. My view says God experiences time moment by moment, and the future is open. My theory says that although God must create, God freely chooses how and what to create, given various constraints. Emanationist theories typically don't affirm freedom in God's creating. And my view says that because God everlastingly creates in relation to what God previously created, and creatures are not divine, it overcomes the worry that emanationist views are versions of pantheism. My view aligns with panentheist views, and a version I call theocosmocentrism.

in relation to what is possible in ways that would also be loving. God freely chooses in relation to the past and a yet to be determined future.[53]

The God who everlastingly and necessarily creates is actually the Creator in a stronger sense than the God of classical theism, whose creating is wholly voluntary. The God who, because of essential hesed, always creates out of creation through love is *essentially* a Creator. A God who chooses whether to create is not essentially creative.

One who always, in love, creates out of creation is Ever Creator.[54]

PHILIA AS "ALONGSIDE OF" LOVE

In earlier chapters, I worked through various issues when defining *agape* and *eros* as forms of love. Much of that work required evaluating some theological claims and philosophical assumptions about love, many of which confuse or fail to fit love in our lived experience. The theologies I criticized also fail to align well with love described in Christian scripture.

In this chapter and the previous, I offered open and relational theology as a better framework to construct a Christian theology of love. God so described is relational, giving and receiving with creatures and creation. God moves through time and loves timefully, analogously to creaturely love.

Open and relational theology also helps us understand the final of the three major Greek words of love: *philia*. While *eros* and *agape* are relational expressions of love, *philia* relies on relations in a

---

[53] Open and relational theology's view that the future is open overcomes William L. Rowe's worry that a perfectly loving God cannot be free when creating. The God who cannot foreknow with certainty freely chooses among possible choices when creating. See Rowe's argument in *Can God Be Free?* (Oxford: Oxford University Press, 2004).

[54] *Ever Creator* is the title of my book in progress that explains the creation theory I outline here.

sustained way.[55] To return to my definition of love, we might define *philia* as acting intentionally, in relational response to God and others, to promote overall well-being by seeking cooperative friendship.

Philia co-labors, in relationship, for good.

Open and relational theology provides conceptual grounds to understand how we can be friends with God and others. Despite its presence in the biblical text, classical theologies rarely affirm *philia* between God and creatures. They cannot affirm this *philia* consistently, because they assume God is impassible, in all ways timeless, with no need of creation's help, and wholly unlike creatures. So defined, God cannot be a Friend to the world — at least not in any way we understand friendship.

I add *philia* to this chapter, which was primarily devoted to *hesed* and other loves in the Old Testament, because both Testaments witness to the meaning of *philia*. "The friendship of the Lord is for those who fear him," says the Psalmist, "and he makes his covenant known to them" (Ps. 25:14). Moses and Abraham are examples of people whom God loved as friends (Ex. 33:12; 2 Chr. 20:7; Is. 41:8; Jas. 2:23). Enoch, Noah, and Adam metaphorically walked alongside God (Gen. 5:22, 24; 6:9). Job fondly remembers a time "when the friendship of God was upon my tent" (Job 29:4).[56]

New Testament writers speak approvingly of *philia*. God expresses *philia* for Jesus and for disciples (Jn. 5:20; 16:27). Jesus expresses *philia* for sinners (Mt. 11:19; Lk. 7:34). Peter admonishes readers to *philia* (1 Pt. 3:8; 2 Pt. 1:7). Hebrews commands *philia* toward strangers (Heb. 13:1, 2). Paul says Christian leaders should *philia* what is good (Tit. 1:8) and he names it as one mark of the true Christian (Rom. 12:10; 12:13). According to Paul, we can express *philia* for God (2 Tim. 3:4), and God expresses *philia* for humans (Tit. 3:4).

---

[55] For how theologians have understood friendship, see Liz Carmichael, *Friendship: Interpreting Christian Love* (London: T & T Clark, 2004); Mary E. Hunt, *Fierce Tenderness: A Feminist Theology of Friendship* (New York: Crossroad, 1994); Gilbert C. Meilander, *Friendship* (Notre Dame: University of Notre Dame Press, 1981).

[56] On friendship with God, see Jacqueline E. Lapsley, "Friends with God? Moses and the Possibility of Covenantal Friendship," *Interpretation* 58:2 (2004).

Philia says God befriends creatures, and they can be friends with God and others.

Philia is a form of love that acts "alongside of" those with whom we relate as friends and co-workers. Like *agape* and *eros*, creaturely expressions of *philia* require God's preceding and empowering action. God initiates loving relationships, provides the possibilities for *philia*, and empowers creatures to choose these possibilities. God is both the exemplar of *philia* and the source of creaturely *philia*. We express friendship love when we cooperate alongside God and others to promote overall well-being.[57]

The God of essential hesed is one who consistently expresses and seeks *philia*. This God is essentially a Friend to creatures and creation. God's *philia* necessarily promotes overall well-being by seeking deeper degrees of cooperation. God loves with *philia* and seeks collaboration.[58]

We can trust God to love steadfastly as our everlasting Friend.

CONCLUSION

Scripture uses various words to describe love. In this chapter, we looked at Old Testament references, focusing specially on *ahavah* and *hesed*. These loves, when expressed by God, do good, involve affection, express covenant, and involve loyal helpfulness.

The idea of essential hesed affirms that the steadfast love of the Lord *literally* endures forever. It builds upon biblical claims that God *cannot* remove love or abandon. We can trust the God of essential hesed to be faithful.

If essential hesed is true, there must always be creatures to love. I argued this means we should reject the theory of *creatio ex nihilo*. The doctrine has no explicit biblical support, however, and it betrays

---

[57] For various proposals for what it means to cooperate with God, see Timothy Reddish, Bonnie Rambob, Fran Stedman, and Thomas Jay Oord, eds. *Partnering with God: Exploring Collaboration in Open and Relational Theology* (SacraSage, 2021).

[58] For the biblical justification of the idea creatures can work with or alongside God, see 1: Cor 3:9; 2 Cor 5:20; 6:1; 2 Tim. 2:3-4, 12; Eph. 6:11-12, Rev. 5:10, 20:6, 22:5.

the common biblical claim that creatures co-create alongside their Creator. Rejecting creation from nothing helps us make sense of God's love in relation to evil, because a God who created from nothing in the past and could create from nothing in the present would be responsible for the possibility of evil and yet does not create obstacles to prevent it.

I have proposed an alternative creation doctrine which I call *creatio ex creatione sempiternalis in amore*: God everlastingly, in love, creates out of or in relation to that which God previously created. Adopting this view answers questions about God's creating and evil's source. It better fits the common biblical refrain that the steadfast love of the Lord endures forever.

A discussion of the Hebrew word *hesed* fits well with an exploration of the Greek word *philia. Philia* is one form of love among others that promotes well-being in relations of friendship and collaboration. I say God always expresses *philia,* but creatures can express it too. I call *philia* "alongside of" love, because it emphasizes the relational dynamics at play in collaboration for good.

A Theology of Pluriform Love

THE PRIMACY AND MEANING OF LOVE

A theology of pluriform love makes sense of God, scripture, and our existence. The arguments I've been making support this claim. Perhaps a summary can bring this into focus.

Few theologians consider love their orienting concern. Despite its prominence in the Bible, love has often not functioned as theology's prominent theme. The reasons for this vary. Some scholars seem worried that popular ideas about love are so deeply ingrained that promoting a proper view of love is impossible. Others hold to views of God's predestining, self-centeredness, damnation, and absolute independence that make their love proposals implausible. An idea of divine sovereignty — understood as God controlling or capable of control — conceptually precedes love in many Christian theologies.

Although scripture talks often about love, points to its many forms, and makes a myriad of love claims, biblical writers never define love. At least not concisely or well. This lack of clarity leads to confusion. To make matters worse, the same scriptures that say God *is* love sometimes portray God as unloving. Some passages say God wants violence, revenge, and genocide; others say God may withdraw the love that is supposedly steadfast.

The biblical witness to love is powerful, but not entirely consistent.

I offer a definition of love I think fits the dominant biblical witness. This definition aligns with love as we know it in personal experience and is consonant with contemporary science. In my definition, to love is to act intentionally, in relational response to God and others, to promote overall well-being. This definition applies both to creaturely love and God's love.

Love acts. This action involves deliberation, motives, and freedom, although in varying degrees. Love is relational. Lovers influence others and are influenced by others. God is the relational source of all love, and creatures can love because God first loves them moment by moment. While love often, if not always, includes emotions and desires, it is more than either. Love seeks overall well-being, which means acting for the common good. Love promotes flourishing.

I argue an adequate definition of love proves crucial for constructing an adequate theology of love. Without a good definition, confusion reigns. Without clarity about love's meaning, we cannot identify well the forms of love in scripture and love we express in everyday life.

A clear definition of love proves crucial for understanding central claims of love in the Christian tradition. Statements such as "God loves the world," "love one another," or "love God and neighbor as yourself" require some idea of what "love" means. We also need a definition to make sense of what it means to love enemies, strangers, ourselves, and all creation. Without knowing what love is, we would have no reason to be happy God loves us, and no idea what it means to love like Jesus.

Although love takes various forms, I show each shares the goal of promoting well-being. This means, for instance, that God's love for creation is action that seeks to promote creation's well-being. Loving one another, neighbors, enemies, ourselves, strangers, and all creation means acting to promote overall well-being.

Love's meaning is uniform, but its expressions are pluriform.

IN SPITE OF OBSTACLES AND DIFFICULTIES

Among Christians, *agape* is the best known biblical word for love. It's the word New Testament writers use most when speaking of love, human and divine. But *agape* has several meanings in scripture, and it takes many forms. Despite this variety, New Testament writers overwhelmingly use *agape* to describe positive or beneficial action. Love has good motives and aims to promote well-being.

According to scripture writers, love builds up and is generous. It spurs us to humility, patience, and peace. Love nourishes and cherishes; it is kind and forgiving. Love opposes idolatry. It shares with those in need, practices hospitality, feeds the hungry, and gives drink to the thirsty. Love rejoices with those who rejoice and mourns with those who mourn. It blesses instead of curses and tries to live in harmony with others. Loving people will associate with those in low position. Love encourages, helps, and consistently seeks well-being.

We can express love through many practices, according to scripture. We can show love at meals, with kisses, and by warm greetings. Love washes dirty feet and shares with others. It cares for brothers and sisters, the hurting and harmed, for strangers and enemies. Marriage partners should love one another, according to scripture; parents should love children and children should love parents. Love characterizes exemplary leaders and healthy communities. It motivates us to seek healing and to be healing agents for others. Love casts out evil spirits and helps the mentally unstable. Love liberates the oppressed.

Listing every form love takes would be impossible. Writers of scripture could not include every form in their time, and we could not list every form today. Besides those mentioned, we could add others. We can see that love engages in activism, for instance, in the sense of trying to change social patterns and overcome practices that harm. Love encourages artistic expression in many forms. Love tries to protect the vulnerable; it lives in harmony with creation. Love expands our vision of the good life and prompts us to learn how life works. It encourages practical wisdom and self-realization that promotes overall flourishing. And so much more.

To identify *agape* with a general form of love, I suggest it does good in response to enemies, harm, or foreigners. *Agape* does not turn the stranger away but takes the risk of welcome. It does not take revenge; it overcomes evil with good. *Agape* turns the other cheek and responds to curses with blessings. *Agape* promotes, extends, or attempts to establish *shalom* in response to that which promotes sin, evil, and the demonic.

Agape is "in spite of" love, because it seeks good in spite of obstacles and difficulties.

DIVINE AND CREATURELY ACTION

Our exploration of Anders Nygren's theology made clear that theologies of love make claims about who God is, how God acts, and the God-creation relationship. Nygren's theology, however, fails to fit well the biblical witness to love. It also fails to fit our deep intuitions and experiences of love. This is particularly apparent in how Nygren describes divine and creaturely action.

Nygren's failures come partly from his approach to scripture. In his quest to identify *agape* as distinctively Christian, he disregards much of the Old Testament's witness to love. He does not embrace New and Old Testament passages that speak of God's desires and needs. Instead, he considers God absolutely independent and thinks creatures are without intrinsic value. Consequently, Nygren does not embrace biblical statements that say God wants relational friendship with creatures and finds them valuable.

Nygren thinks God controls creatures. In his view, they have no independent power alongside God and make no free choices regarding love. As he sees it, humans are predestined. They are passive tubes through which God loves rather than partners with whom God gives and receives. But if love requires free actions in relation to others, Nygren's theology fails to account for love.

Despite his theology's problems, Nygren affirms that God's nature is love. I say we make best sense of this by saying love is an essential attribute of the divine nature. Love comes logically first in God, which means God must love and we should understand God's other attributes in light of love.

Divine love is unconditional, in the sense that God loves by nature. It is conditional, however, in the sense that divine love takes various forms, depending on the situation and the recipients. God necessarily loves, but freely chooses what forms divine love takes. I call this God's "essence-experience binate," because God's essence of love is unchanging, but God's loving experience changes.

God initiates loving relationship with everyone, all the time. Rather than electing some and predestining others to damnation, God lovingly offers everyone opportunities to love. Creatures can love in any moment because God first loves them.

A theology of pluriform love assumes God is the source of the love creatures express. But being love's source is not the same as being the *only* one capable of love. Nor is it the same as forcing creatures to love. Instead, divine love empowers and inspires through persuasion, and creatures can freely choose whether to love in response.

God loves by nature; creatures choose whether to love.

FOR OUR SAKE AND GOD'S

Any Christian theology of love should address the thought of Augustine, because his ideas have most affected the development of Christian theology. Augustine considers love primarily as desire, however, not primarily as promoting well-being. Because only God can satisfy our desires, he says, only God deserves our love. We should enjoy and use creatures as means to enjoying the Creator rather than treating them as ends in themselves.

I point out that most Christians overlook or fail to realize the problems that arise when defining love as desire instead of as promoting well-being. There is nothing wrong with desires, of course, and we should prioritize them. But a pluriform theology of love affirms both divine and creaturely desires, and it says love's primary aim is promoting well-being.

One problem with thinking of love as desire emerges when Augustine interprets Jesus' love commands. For Augustine, loving our neighbor as ourselves means loving God *through* our neighbors rather than loving neighbors as ends in themselves. Augustine thinks humans should orient themselves to the unchangeable and perfectly good, which is God, rather than toward what is changeable and not perfectly good. This means, he says, we should not love neighbors or ourselves for our sakes; we must love them for God's sake.

The pluriform theology of love I propose says Jesus' two love commands call us to promote the well-being of neighbors, ourselves, and God. We enjoy and help them for their own sakes, not merely as means to something else. When we love, we can enhance the well-being of God, others, ourselves, and creation.

Problems with Augustine's theology deepen when he explains God's love for the world. God does not love creatures, he says, in the sense of enjoying them. Creatures have nothing valuable to enjoy that God doesn't already have. So God uses creatures, Augustine says, although this is not use as we understand it. He thinks God has no needs, so creatures have nothing God needs to use. When we understand love as desire and conceive of God as only desiring the ultimate good, God cannot love creation in the sense of enjoying, using, or desiring it. God only loves Godself. After looking carefully at Augustine's theology in *Teaching Christianity*, I say Christians should reject his views of love, creaturely and divine.

A pluriform theology of love should adopt *eros*, however, as a particular form of love. Rather than defining *eros* as desire, we might think of it as a form of love that promotes well-being when appreciating what is valuable, worthwhile, or beautiful. *Eros* not only "thinks on" true, honorable, pleasing, and excellent things, it "keeps on doing these things" (Phil. 4:8, 9). Understood this way, God and creatures can express *eros*.

Eros is "because of" love, because it promotes well-being when appreciating values.

ANALOGIES OF LOVE

At the root of Augustine's problems are 1) his view that love is desire rather than action to promote well-being and 2) his doctrine of God. Both problems have strong ties to philosophical ideas common in Augustine's day and that still influence Christian theologians now. Many call the tradition Augustine exemplifies "classical theism." Among other claims, classical theists say God is timeless, immutable, impassible, and simple.

The theology of pluriform love I propose rejects classical theism. Instead of saying God is timeless, it says God experiences the flow of time everlastingly. This makes better sense of God's love as particular divine actions expressed moment by moment. A theology of pluriform love says God's essence is unchanging, but God's experience changes moment by moment. God always loves, because it's God's nature to do so, but God's love influences creatures and creatures influence God in response. God is relational rather than impassible. A theology of pluriform love says God is unified rather than simple in the sense that God's actions, attributes, and existence are identical.

Classical theism's assumptions make it difficult, if not impossible, to talk about God as loving. It considers divine love entirely different from creaturely love. Because of this radical dissimilarity, classical theism cannot support analogies between God and creation. The classical God shares no likeness with creatures, has no relations with self or others, and does not act in any way creatures know as acting. The classical God has no emotions in relation to creation and needs no one.

Classical theism's claims about divine love often, if not always, end up in appeals to absolute mystery. While we will never understand love fully, appeals to absolute mystery are not supported by biblical claims about God's love. Saying "God loves the world," "God is love," or that we should imitate God's love makes absolutely no sense if God's love is absolutely mysterious.

God's love cannot be altogether different in kind from our love.

I suggest seven analogies that point to similarities and differences between the love God and creatures express. These analogies align with themes in scripture and provide language to talk coherently about love. I suggest both Creator and creatures give and receive in loving relationship, but only God does so perfectly, and only God relates to all others. Both Creator and creatures love in the ongoing flow of time, but only God loves everlastingly. Both Creator and creatures love by promoting overall well-being, but only God promotes well-being directly to everything in the universe. Both creatures and Creator love as experiencers, but only God feels the emotional tones of every creature. Both Creator and creatures love freely, but creatures can choose not to love. God necessarily loves. Both creatures and Creator have needs, but to exist, God does not rely upon creatures, whereas creatures rely upon God for their existence. Both Creator and creatures are valuable in themselves, but God is supremely valuable.

These analogies of similarity and difference provide grounds to say God transcends creation in some ways but is immanent in others. If God were altogether transcendent, claims about divine love would be meaningless. If God were altogether immanent, claims about divine love would not differ from claims about creaturely love. To make sense of love in scripture and our experience, an adequate theology points to differences, but also similarities between Creator and creatures.

THE PROMISE OF OPEN AND RELATIONAL THEOLOGY

Open and relational theology offers a helpful framework for a theology of pluriform love. Although diverse, this theological movement embraces the idea that God gives and receives in relation to creatures and creation. So conceived, God moves through time like creatures do, experiencing moment by moment. Open and relational theologians typically embrace creaturely freedom, the intrinsic value of creation, experience as fundamental, love as central to God's nature, and love as the aim for creatures.

Clark Pinnock offers a winsome version of Christian open and relational theology. His views not only align with the broad biblical witness, but also account for relational themes present in human experience. God inspires free creatures to love, says Pinnock. Rather than being immobile and impassible, the God Pinnock describes engages in mutually influencing relationships with creation. I believe that those constructing a Christian theology of love should adopt most of Pinnock's views.

But besides embracing open and relational views about God and creation like Pinnock's, my theology of pluriform love focuses especially upon Jesus. Jesus reveals divine love in powerful ways. In his life, teachings, ministry, death, and resurrection, Jesus enacts the way of love. He healed the sick, preached good news, was a friend to sinners, ministered to the poor, wept over the dead, encouraged the downhearted, partied with celebrants, and showed compassion. His death highlights God's suffering and that God wants to save all. Jesus' resurrection provides hope of continuing life and love after bodily death.

Christians would be wise to follow Jesus' example. This not only means loving in communities of common cause, but it also means loving strangers, enemies, themselves, all creation, and God. Jesus' life inaugurated new ways of existing and new communities of followers. In him are light and life and love.

Jesus Christ is the center of a Christian theology that makes love central.

Jesus' kenotic love provides a solution to the problem of evil. His love was not overpowering or coercive; it was self-giving and others-empowering. Jesus was humble, servant-like, self-sacrificial, and looked not only to himself but also to the common good. He embodied *kenosis*.

Jesus' revelation of love suggests God is essentially kenotic. I argue that rather than being deliberately self-limiting, God essentially self-gives and others-empowers. I call this "essential kenosis." It claims that because God loves everyone and everything, God cannot control anyone or anything. Divine love is uncontrolling.

ESSENTIAL KENOSIS AND EVIL

Most Christian theologies fail to address well the primary reason many people do not think God loves perfectly or does not exist at all. That reason: the evil we experience personally and witness every day in the world. People rightly wonder why a powerful and loving God doesn't prevent pointless pain and unnecessary suffering.

The usual answers given to the problem of evil fail. They may contain a kernel of truth, but they do not answer well our central questions. I believe it's impossible to portray a God of perfect love if we also say God could prevent genuine evil but fails to do so. A God who wants, causes, or even permits pointless pain is not a God who loves everyone and everything all the time. Skeptics rightly reject theologies of love that do not solve the problem of evil.

Traditional views of divine power are the root of most failures to account for evil. But we can solve the prominent dimensions of the problem of evil if we embrace essential kenosis. This view says God necessarily self-gives to and others-empowers everyone and everything, which means God cannot control anyone or anything. The God who cannot control cannot prevent evil singlehandedly.

Rethinking God's power as uncontrolling allows a theology of pluriform love to say that God is not culpable for causing or allowing evil. This uncontrolling God suffers with those who suffer, however, and works to heal creatures and creation. God does not abandon the harmed and hurting, but works with them to squeeze something good from bad. God calls creatures to join in the work of overcoming evil with good through indispensable love synergy.

The God of uncontrolling, pluriform love opposes evil.

Classical theism's grip on Christian theology is so strong that claiming God's love is uncontrolling will strike many as unorthodox. To many Christians, a God who cannot control must be limited. But biblical writers and leading theologians say there are many things God cannot do. Essential kenosis adds that divine love is uncontrolling. But this does not mean God is limited in any coherent way, any more than other types of limitation we already accept.

Christian theologies that make love a priority require new conceptions of divine power. These concepts should fit the primary witness of scripture and Jesus' witness to kenotic love. Both witnesses suggest God is neither omnipotent *nor* impotent. I recommend saying God is "amipotent:" divine power is the power of love. As One mightier than any other, exerting might upon all others, and the source of might for all others, God's almighty influence is uncontrolling love.

ESSENTIAL HESED AND UNFAITHFULNESS

The Old Testament's witness to love is powerful. Although scholars translate several Hebrew words as love or something similar, *ahavah* and *hesed* are the most prominent. *Ahavah* usually describes the care, attachment, and affection lovers show to others. According to biblical writers, God expresses *ahavah* for creatures and creation. This biblical witness aligns with open and relational theology's view that God is relational, has desires, and experiences emotions.

Biblical scholars translate *hesed* in various ways, including "covenantal love," "loyal faithfulness," and "steadfast love." According to scripture, God expresses *hesed* by helping, being generous, and doing good. Those faithful in covenant enjoy health, meaningful life, and well-being. The covenantal love of *hesed* fits the open and relational vision, because it assumes God is influenced and does not know with certainty what creatures will do in response to covenant.

"The steadfast love of the Lord endures forever" is a recurring theme in the Old Testament. God's everlasting love provides well-being. God makes covenants with particular persons, Israel, other nations, and all creation. Because divine *hesed* is everlasting and universal, we can count on God's faithful goodness.

We have good reasons to say *hesed* is essential to God. Divine *hesed* is unconditional, in the sense that God loves, and creatures did not earn this love. This corresponds with the idea God is essentially loving. How God chooses to express *hesed* varies, however. This is another way to affirm God's essence-experience binate.

Creatures are not always faithful. But God is no creature; God cannot be unfaithful. I call this "essential hesed." It says God is necessarily faithful, which means God cannot leave us, cannot forsake us, always suffers with us, always empathizes, always accepts, and is essentially *for* creation.

Essential hesed says the covenantal God faithfully loves.

A pluriform theology of love offers hope and security to people who feel hopeless and abandoned. The always present, always caring, and faithful Friend can be counted on to do good and never desert us. The God of essential *hesed* is everlastingly faithful to everyone and all creation.

It's difficult to worship a God who loves half-heartedly. We can't worship a God whose love makes no sense. A being like this would be neither perfect nor praiseworthy. But the God of essential hesed and essential kenosis loves uncontrollingly, wholeheartedly, and faithfully. We can trust a God who is in no sense culpable and always seeks well-being.

It makes sense to connect love and worship if our actions can enhance God's well-being. We can desire God, in the sense of wanting God's direction and appreciating God's glory, and we can love God, in the sense of blessing God in praise and adoration. Our praise and worship enhance our well-being and God's; creation and Creator benefit.

We can worship without reservation the God of uncontrolling love.

GOD, IN LOVE, EVERLASTINGLY CREATES IN RELATION TO CREATION

If God steadfastly loves creation forever, there must *always* be creation to love. We should reject the idea God once existed alone and reject the idea God creates from absolutely nothing. As we have seen, the Bible does not explicitly endorse those ideas. Rejecting them allows us to say God never used controlling power and cannot create from nothing to prevent genuine evil.

The doctrine of *creatio ex nihilo* directly and indirectly renders God culpable for evil. The God who created our universe from nothing would be responsible for the possibilities of evil. This God could instantaneously create from nothing obstacles to evil in the present, but doesn't do so, leading to moral incoherence.

Creatio ex nihilo also implies God is essentially solitary and not essentially related to creation. A God not essentially related to creatures does not essentially love them; that God is independent by nature. If we want to say love for creation is God's nature and the steadfast love of the Lord endures forever, we need an alternative creation doctrine.

In the name of love, we should reject *creatio ex nihilo*.

I propose a new creation theory that says God, in love, everlastingly creates out of or in relation to creation. We might render it in Latin as *creatio ex creatione sempiternalis in amore*. God's motive for creating is love, and God uses materials God previously created. God always creates alongside creatures, who are created co-creators. And God never controls when creating, because divine love is necessarily uncontrolling. A theology of pluriform love places love as the center of its doctrine of creation.

New theories are often misunderstood. To clarify, my theory does not say our universe is eternal. It had a beginning, likely as a Big Bang, but another universe preceded it. Nor does my theory say creaturely "stuff" predates God. God creates all creatures and creations. *Creatio ex creatione sempiternalis in amore* does not make God's existence dependent upon creation. God exists necessarily and necessarily creates alongside others. My theory denies an eternal dualism between good and evil and denies God creates out of Godself. It does not say God simply rearranges what already exists; God always creates something new.

We might call the God who always, in love, creates out of what God previously created the "Ever Creator." Creating is an aspect of God's essential nature. But an open and relational God freely chooses *how* and *what* to create, given creaturely conditions and God's own nature of love. Unlike the God of classical theism, creating is what the God of essential hesed always does, because it's God's nature to be Creator.

ALONGSIDE OF LOVE

An open and relational theology of pluriform love emphasizes themes of collaboration, cooperation, and mutuality. Love's aims require both Creator and creatures. The reign of love is not possible by divine fiat, nor is it possible through creaturely effort alone. Love requires co-operating and co-laboring.

The relational dimensions of *hesed* fit nicely with *philia*, a Greek word New Testament writers sometimes use to describe both divine and creaturely love. As a form of love, I say that *philia* acts intentionally, in relational response to God and others, to promote overall well-being through cooperation and friendship. It co-labors in seeking good. *Philia* is companion love.

I call *philia* the "alongside of" form of love. This alongside of dimension, over time, leads to the qualities we identify with friendship. Creatures can enjoy friendship love with their Creator and other creatures, which means God's experience and the experience of creatures can be enhanced. The God of essential *hesed* consistently expresses and seeks *philia* as creation's everlasting Friend.

God's inability to control creation and the reality of an open future mean that for love to win, God relies upon creatures. This reliance means creatures and creaturely choices *really* matter. Classical theologies assume the end has already been determined or God can determine it unilaterally. In such scenarios, our lives and choices don't ultimately count. But a theology of pluriform love says God can't control, and it provides a foundation to affirm ultimate significance for creaturely lives and actions.

What we do makes a difference to God and to the future.

PLURIFORM LOVE

Most Christian theologies restrict divine love. According to many, God only expresses *agape*. According to others, God only expresses *eros*. Some theologies may say God expresses *hesed* but cannot affirm divine *ahavah*. Other theologians mix and match loves, depending on their philosophical and theological assumptions.

The theology I propose says God expresses *agape, eros, philia, kenosis, ahavah, hesed*, and more. Divine love is pluriform. The biblical witness, the history of creation, and our lives bear witness to God at work in wild and wonderful ways. Our imitating God requires that we express pluriform love. The diversity of love forms to which God calls fills a lifetime of enjoying and sharing abundant life.

To illustrate visually how I understand the definition of love as uniform but its expressions as pluriform, I offer the figure below. Note that some forms mentioned are quite broad, while others are fairly specific.

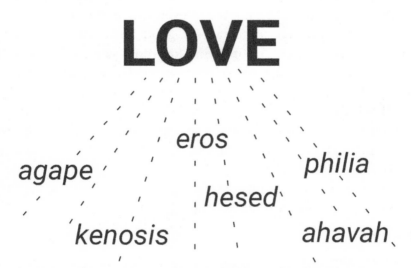

LOVE

eros

agape   *philia*

hesed

kenosis   *ahavah*

enemy love	stranger love	self-love	friendship love
self-sacrificial love	compassion	sex/romance love	family love
protective love	activist love	artistic love	hospitality love
forgiving love	love of nature	playful love	love of community
healing love	liberative love	caregiving love	partying love
suffering love	philanthropic love	self-improving love	love of nation

There are millions more forms of love than I list. And many forms mix with others. For instance, I can both love my daughter appreciating her value and love her by expressing my disappointment that she made an unhealthy decision. I can act for my nation's well-being in collaboration with others while actively opposing policies the majority seem to adopt. And so on. God's love is mixed too. God both loves by appreciating the value of creatures while loving in anger when they abuse one another.

Rather than one-dimensional, God's love is pluriform.

God loves creation in at least three primary ways. First, God acts for creation's good, even when creatures harm themselves and others. God loves even when we are unfaithful to God and sin. God's love takes the form of acting for good in spite of the negative that creatures have done. As a forgiving lover, God expresses *agape.*

Second, God acts for creation's good when encountering its intrinsic value. This form of divine love does good because of the beauty, worth, and importance of creation. The world God created and creates is good. As an artistic lover, God expresses *eros.*

Third, God loves by coming alongside creatures in the work of promoting well-being. God empowers and seeks collaboration from creation for the common good. As a loving friend, God expresses *philia.*

Each broad form of divine love takes various expressions. But in each, God seeks to promote well-being.

RELENTLESS LOVE

If the steadfast love of the Lord endures forever, it does not end when we die. God loves us in the afterlife too. Divine love is relentless.[1]

In the opening chapters, I said an adequate theology of love denies that a loving God sends anyone to hell. A loving person would not condemn another to eternal conscious torment. Divine love,

---

[1] I explain my view of the afterlife and relentless love in several books. See, for instance, *Questions and Answers for God Can't,* ch. 8.

as the Apostle Paul puts it, "always hopes" and "never ends" (1 Cor. 13:7,8), even after we leave these mortal coils.

A loving God doesn't suddenly take up coercion in the afterlife, of course, or force everyone to experience heavenly bliss. God's love remains uncontrolling in the afterlife too. God continues to invite every creature capable of responding to enjoy the well-being love provides. God is the everlasting beckoner.

Creatures who cooperate with God's invitation flourish. They enjoy the natural positive consequences that come from embracing God's gift of well-being. But creatures now and in the afterlife can choose not to cooperate. When they do, they suffer the natural negative consequences that come from choosing something other than well-being. As the Apostle John puts it, we pass "from death to life because we love one another." But John adds that "whoever does not love abides in death" (1 Jn. 3:14). I take "death" here to point to negative natural consequences and "life" to positive ones.

A loving God doesn't punish, and God always forgives. But creatures who choose something other than love choose something other than well-being. They hurt themselves and others.

The God of relentless love never gives up. Ever. While creatures can say "No" to God now and in the afterlife, God everlastingly invites all to live lives of love. Because of relentless love, we have grounds to hope all will eventually say "Yes." Everlasting persuasive love makes it possible for everyone to experience everlasting bliss.

Relentless love reminds us that love for creation isn't a temporary experiment on God's part. Love for creation is God's heart, nature, or essence. And because of divine amipotence, we can imagine the Apostle Paul's vision — that all creation be redeemed (Rom. 8:20-22) — becoming a reality.

CONCLUSION

I began this book by saying it's not hard to argue love stands at the center of the biblical witness. Consequently, I argued, love should be the center of Christian theology. In the chapters that followed, I've pointed to obstacles that prevent Christians from embracing love. I've provided a theology that makes scripture's witness to love central and that takes seriously our own experiences of love.

"...and the greatest of these is love," says Paul to conclude his love hymn (1 Cor. 13:13b). By defining love, exploring influential theologians, and identifying love's forms, I offer a Christian theology of pluriform love.

Immediately after saying, "the greatest of these is love," Paul tells his readers to "pursue love" (1 Cor. 14:1a). A conceptual framework for making sense of love, in general, and for understanding God's love, in particular, helps us acknowledge love's preeminence and pursue love with joy.

Thanks to God's pluriform love, we can receive and express pluriform love.

About the Author

*T*homas Jay Oord, Ph.D., is a theologian, philosopher, and scholar of multi-disciplinary studies. Oord directs the Center for Open and Relational Theology and doctoral students at Northwind Theological Seminary. He is an award-winning and best-selling author who has written or edited more than twenty-five books. A gifted speaker, Oord lectures at universities, conferences, churches, seminaries, and institutions. A world-renown theologian of love, Oord also is known for his research in science and religion, open and relational theology, the problem of suffering, and the implications of freedom for transformational relationships.

For more information, see Dr. Oord's website: thomasjayoord.com

For more on the doctoral program Dr. Oord directs, see northwindseminary.org/center-for-open-relational-theology

For more on the Center for Open and Relational Theology, see c4ort.com

Acknowledgments

Many people have influenced me in the writing of this book. I especially thank those who worked with the manuscript and made suggestions. Those people include Rebecca Adams, Charles Bakker, Gloria Coffin, Alan Crews, John Culp, John Dally, Brian Felushko, Paul Greene, Dan Haley, Shai Held, Curtis Holtzen, E. R. Kelley, Matthew Lee, Jason Lepojarvi, Bob Luhn, Alexa Oord, Cheryl Oord, Stephen Post, Johan Tredoux, and Mathew Voth. I thank my friends at the Starbucks on 12th Avenue in Nampa, Idaho, where I wrote most of this book.

I thank my Northwind Theological Seminary doctoral students in open and relational theology for our conversations exploring the various ideas in this book. Working with them is a great joy!

I dedicate this book to my mother, Louise Liner Oord Kelley.

Bibliography

Adams, Robert Merrihew. *Finite and Infinite Goods: A Framework for Ethics.* Oxford: Oxford University Press, 1999.

Anderson, Bernhard W. *Out of the Depths.* Philadelphia: Westminster, 1983.

Anselm. *Proslogium.* Translated by Sidney Norton Deane. La Salle, IL, 1951.

Aquinas, Thomas. *Summa Contra Gentiles.* Anton C. Pegis, trans. Notre Dame, IN: University of Notre Dame Press, 1981.

———. *Summa Theologica.* Translated by Fathers of the English Dominican Province. London: Burns, Oates, and Washbourne, 1936.

Arendt, Hannah. *Love and St. Augustine.* Chicago: University of Chicago Press, 1998.

Arminius, Jacob. "Twenty-Five Public Disputations." In *The Works of James Arminius.* Vol. 2. Translated by James Nichols. Grand Rapids, MI: Baker, 1991.

———. "It is the Summit of Blasphemy to Say that God is Freely Good." In *The Works of James Arminius.* Vol. 2. Translated by James Nichols. Grand Rapids, MI: Baker, 1991.

Armstrong, A. H. "Platonic *Eros* and Christian *Agape.*" *Downside Review* 79 (Spring 1961): 106-120.

Armstrong, John. *Conditions of Love: The Philosophy of Intimacy.* New York: W.W. Norton, 2002.

Artson, Bradley Shavit. *God of Becoming and Relationship: The Dynamic Nature of Process Theology.* Woodstock, VT: Jewish Lights, 2016.

Asensio, Felix. *Misericordia et Veritas, el Hesed y Emet divinos, su influjo religioso-social en la historia de Israel.* Rome: Apud Aedes Universitatis Gregoianae, 1949.

Augustine of Hippo. "To Simplician — One of Various Questions." In *Augustine: Earlier Writings.* Translated by John H. S. Burleigh. Philadelphia: Westminster, 1953.

———. *City of God*. Translated by Henry Bettenson. London: Penguin Books, 2004.

———. *Commentaries on the Psalms*. Edited by John E. Rotell and translated by Maria Boulding. New York: New City, 2000.

———. *Eighty-Three Different Questions*. Translated by David L. Mosher. Washington, DC: Catholic University of America Press, 1982.

———. *Teaching Christianity: De Doctrina Christiana*. Edited by John E. Rotelle, O.S.A, translated by Edmund Hill, O.P. Hyde Park, NY: New City, 1996.

Avis, Paul. *Eros and the Sacred*. Harrisburg, PA: Morehouse, 1989.

Bahl, Chad. *God Unbound*. Grasmere, ID: SacraSage, 2021.

Baker-Fletcher, Karen. *Dancing with God: The Trinity from a Womanist Perspective*. St. Louis, MO: Chalice, 2006.

Baker, Chris, Gloria Coffin, Craig Drurey, Graden Kirksey, Lisa Michaels, and Donna Fiser Ward, eds. *Uncontrolling Love: Essays Exploring the Love of God*. San Diego: SacraSage, 2017.

Barrigar, Christian J. *Freedom All the Way Up*. Victoria, BC: Friesen, 2017.

Barth, Karl. *Church Dogmatics*. Vol. 2, *The Doctrine of God Part One*. Edited by G. W. Bromiley and T. F. Torrance. Edinburgh: T & T Clark, 1957.

Basinger, David. *The Case for Freewill Theism*. Downers Grove, IL: InterVarsity, 1996.

Bauckham, Richard. *Jesus and the God of Israel: God Crucified and Other Studies on the New Testament's Christology of Divine Identity*. Grand Rapids, MI: Eerdmans, 2008.

Biale, David. "The God with Breasts: El Shaddai in the Bible." *History of Religions* 21, no. 3 (Feb. 1982): 244.

Bonhoeffer, Dietrich. *The Cost of Discipleship*. New York: Macmillan, 1949.

Bonting, Sjoerd L. *Creation and Double Chaos*. Minneapolis: Fortress, 2005.

Boyd, Craig A. *A Shared Morality: A Narrative Defense of Natural Law Ethics*. Grand Rapids, MI: Brazos, 2007.

———. *Visions of Agape: Problems and Possibilities in Human and Divine Love*. Burlington, VT: Ashgate, 2008.

Boyd, Gregory A. *Cross Vision: How the Crucifixion of Jesus Makes Sense of Old Testament Violence*. Philadelphia: Fortress, 2018.

———. *God of the Possible: A Biblical Introduction to the Open View of God*. Grand Rapids, MI: Baker, 2001.

———. *Inspired Imperfection*. Minneapolis: Fortress, 2020.

———. *Is God to Blame?* Downers Grove, IL: InterVarsity, 2003.

Bracken, Joseph A. *Christianity and Process Thought*. Philadelphia: Templeton Foundation, 2006.

Brady, Bernard V. *Christian Love: How Christians Through the Ages Have Understood Love*. Washington, DC.: Georgetown University Press, 2003.

Bray, Gerald. *God is Love: A Biblical and Systematic Theology*. Wheaton, IL: Crossway, 2012.

Brightman, Edgar S. *Is God Personal?* New York: Association, 1932.

Brock, Rita Nakashima. *Journeys By Heart: A Christology of Erotic Power*. New York: Crossroads, 1995.

Brown, David. *Divine Humanity: Kenosis and the Construction of a Christian Theology*. Waco, TX: Baylor University Press, 2011.

Brown, F., S. R. Driver, and C. A. Briggs. *A Hebrew and English Lexicon*. London: Oxford University Press, 1906.

Brown, William P. *The Ethos of the Cosmos: The Genesis of Moral Imagination in the Bible*. Grand Rapids: Eerdmans, 1999.

Brueggemann, Walter. "Psalm 109: Three Times 'Steadfast Love.'" *Word and World* 5, no. 2 (Spring 1985): 144-54.

———. Foreword to *Faithfulness in Action: Loyalty in Biblical Perspective*, by Katherine Doob Sakenfeld. Philadelphia: Fortress, 1985.

———. *Theology of the Old Testament: Testimony, Dispute, Advocacy*. Minneapolis: Fortress, 1997.

Brummer, Vincent. *The Model of Love*. Cambridge: Cambridge University Press, 1993.

Burklo, Jim. *Tenderly Calling*. Haworth, NJ: St. Johann, 2021.

Burnaby, John. *Amor Dei: A Study of the Religion of St. Augustine*. London: Canterbury Press, 1938. Reprint, Eugene, OR: Wipf and Stock, 2007.

Burridge, Richard A. *Imitating Jesus: An Inclusive Approach to New Testament Ethics*. Grand Rapids, MI. Eerdmans, 2007.

Burrow, Jr., Rufus. *Personalism: A Critical Introduction*. St. Louis, MO: Chalice, 1999.

Burrus, Virginia, and Catherine Keller, eds. *Toward a Theology of Eros: Transfiguring Passion at the Limits of Discipline*. New York: Fordham University Press, 2007.

Butler, Roy F. *The Meaning of Agapao and Phileo in the Greek New Testament*. Lawrence, KS: Coronado, 1977.

Byas, Jared. *Love Matters More*. Grand Rapids, MI: Zondervan, 2020.

Callen, Barry L. *Clark H. Pinnock: Journey Toward Renewal*. Nappanee, IN: Evangel, 2000.

———. *God as Loving Grace: The Biblically Revealed Nature and Work of God*. Nappanee IN: Evangel, 1996.

Caputo, John D. *The Weakness of God: A Theology of the Event*. Bloomington, IN: Indiana University Press, 2006.

———. *What Would Jesus Deconstruct?* Grand Rapids, MI: Baker, 2007.

Carmichael, Liz. *Friendship: Interpreting Christian Love.* London: T & T Clark, 2004.

Case-Winters, Anna. *God Will Be All in All: Theology Through the Lens of Incarnation.* Louisville: Westminster/John Knox, 2021.

———. *God's Power: Traditional Understandings and Contemporary Challenges.* Louisville: Westminster/John Knox, 1990.

Chan, Michael J., and Brent A. Strawn, eds. *What Kind of God? Collected Essays of Terence E. Fretheim.* Winona Lake, IN: Eisenbrauns, 2015.

Charnock, Stephen. Collected works in *God Without Passions: A Reader,* edited by Samuel Renihan. Palmdale, CA: Reformed Baptist Academic, 2015.

Chartier, Gary. *The Analogy of Love: Divine and Human Love at the Center of Christian Theology.* Charlottesville, VA: Imprint Academic, 2007.

———. *Loving Creation: The Task of the Moral Life.* Minneapolis: Fortress, 2022.

Childs, Brevard S. *Biblical Theology in Crisis.* Philadelphia: Westminster, 1970.

———. *Studies in Biblical Theology.* Vol. 27, *Myth and Reality in the Old Testament.* London: SCM, 1960.

Clark, Jason. *Prone to Love.* Shippensburg, PA: Destiny Image, 2014.

Clarke, Randolph. "Alternatives for Libertarians." In *The Oxford Handbook of Free Will,* edited by Robert Kane. 2nd ed. Oxford: Oxford University Press, 2011.

Clayton, Philip, and Arthur Peacocke, eds. *In Whom We Live and Move and Have our Being: Panentheistic Reflections on God's Presence in a Scientific World.* Grand Rapids, MI: Eerdmans, 2004.

———and Steven Knapp. *The Predicament of Belief.* Oxford: Oxford University Press, 2011.

——— and Wm. Andrew Schwartz. *What is Ecological Civilization?* Anoka, MN: Process Century, 2019.

Cobb, Jr. John B. "Human Responsibility and the Primacy of Grace." In *Thy Nature and Thy Name is Love,* edited by Bryan P. Stone and Thomas Jay Oord. Nashville: Abingdon, 2001.

——— and David Ray Griffin. *Process Theology: An Introductory Exposition.* Louisville: Westminster/John Knox, 1976.

———. *Christ in a Pluralistic Age Jesus' Abba.* Fortress, 2016.

———. *God and the World.* Philadelphia: Westminster, 1969.

———. *Grace and Responsibility: A Wesleyan Theology for Today.* Nashville: Abingdon, 1995.

———. *Salvation.* Anoka, MN: Process Century, 2020.

Coleman, Monica, Nancy Howell, and Helene Russell, eds. *Creating Women's Theology.* Eugene, OR: Pickwick, 2011.

———. *Making a Way Out of Now Way: A Womanist Theology.* Philadelphia: Fortress, 2008.

Collins, Kenneth J. *The Theology of John Wesley: Holy Love and the Shape of Grace*. Nashville: Abingdon, 2007.

Cone, James. *God of the Oppressed*. London: SPCK, 1977.

Cornwall, Robert D. *Unfettered Spirit*. Gonzalez, FL: Energion, 2021.

Craig, William Lane. *God and the Problem of Evil: Five Views*, edited by James K. Dew, Jr. and Chad Meister. Downers Grove, IL: InterVarsity, 2017.

Crenshaw, James L. *Defending God: Biblical Reponses to the Problem of Evil*. Oxford: Oxford University Press, 2005.

Cullmann, Oscar. *Christ and Time*. Translated by F. V. Filson. London: SCM, 195. Rev. ed. 1962.

Culp, John. "A Dialogue with the Process Theology of John B. Cobb, Jr." *Wesleyan Theological Journal* 17 (Fall 1980): 33-44.

Cupitt, Don. *The New Christian Ethics*. London: SCM, 1988.

D'Arcy, Martin C. "'These Things Called Love,' A review of C. S. Lewis's The Four Loves." *The New York Times* (New York), July 31, 1960.

———. *The Mind and Heart of Love, Lion and Unicorn: A Study in Eros and Agape*. Cleveland: World, 1964.

Davies, Mark Y. A., and Randall Auxier. *Hartshorne and Brightman on God, Process, and Persons*. Nashville: Vanderbilt University Press, 2001.

Davis, Andrew M. *Mind, Value, and Cosmos*. Lanham, MD: Lexington, 2020.

Delgado, Sharon. *Love in a Time of Climate Change*. Minneapolis: Fortress, 2017.

Delio, Ilia. *The Unbearable Wholeness of Being*. Maryknoll, NY: Orbis, 2013.

DeWeese, Garry. "Natural Evil: A 'Free Process' Defense." In *God and Evil: The Case for God in a World Filled with Pain*, Chad Meister and James K. Dew, Jr., eds. Downers Grove, IL: InterVarsity, 2013.

Dodds, C. H. *The Bible and the Greeks*. London: Hoddern and Stoughton, 1954.

Dolezal, James E. *All That Is in God: Evangelical Theology and the Challenge of Classical Christian Theism*. Grand Rapids, MI: Reformation Heritage, 2017.

———. *God without Parts: Divine Simplicity and the Metaphysics of God's Absoluteness*. Eugene, OR: Pickwick, 2011.

Dougherty, Trent, and Justin McBrayer. *Skeptical Theism*. Oxford: Oxford University Press, 2014.

Drobner, Hubertus R. "Christian Philosophy." In *The Oxford Handbook of Early Christian Studies*, Susan Ashbrook Harvey and David C. Hunter, eds. Oxford: Oxford University Press, 2008.

Dunn, James D. G. *Christology in the Making: An Inquiry into the Origins of the Doctrine of the Incarnation*. 2nd ed. London: SCM, 1989.

———, *The Theology of Paul the Apostle*. Grand Rapids, MI: Eerdmans, 1998.

Dunning, H. Ray. *Grace, Faith, and Holiness: A Wesleyan Systematic Theology*. Kansas City, MO: Beacon Hill, 1988.

Edwards, Jonathan. *Freedom of the Will*. New York: Leavitt & Allen, 1857.

Edwards, Rem B. "John Wesley's Non-Literal Literalism and Hermeneutic of Love." *Wesleyan Theological Journal* 51, no. 2 (2016): 26-40.

———. *An Axiological Process Ethics*. Claremont, CA: Process Century, 2014.

———. *John Wesley's Values — And Ours*. Lexington: Emeth, 2013.

Ehrman, Bart D. *God's Problem: How the Bible Fails to Answer Our most Important Question — Why We Suffer*. New York: HarperCollins, 2008.

Eichrodt, Walther. *Theology of the Old Testament*. Vol. 1. Translated by J. A. Baker. Philadelphia: Westminster, 1961.

Epperly, Bruce. *Process Theology*. London: T&T Clark, 2011.

Erickson, Millard J. *Christian Theology*. 2nd ed. Grand Rapids, MI: Baker, 1998.

Evans, C. Stephen, ed. *Exploring Kenotic Christology: The Self-emptying God*. Oxford: Oxford University Press, 2006.

Farley, Edward. *Divine Empathy*. Philadelphia: Fortress, 1996.

Farley, Margaret A. *Just Love: A Framework for Chrisitan Sexual Ethics*. New York: Continuum, 2006.

Farmer, Patricia. *Beauty and Process Theology: A Journey of Transformation*. Gonzalez, Fl.: Energion, 2020.

Fee, Gordon D. "The New Testament and Kenosis Christology." In *Exploring Kenotic Christology: The Self-Emptying of God*, C. Stephen Evans, ed. Vancouver, BC: Regent College Publishing, 2006.

Fehr, Beverley, et. al. *The Science of Compassionate Love*. London: Blackwell, 2009.

Feldman, Daniel Z. *Divine Footsteps: Chesed and the Jewish Soul*. New York: Yeshiva University, 2008.

Fergusson, David. *Faith and Its Critics: A Conversation*. Oxford: Oxford University Press, 2009.

Fiddes, Paul. "Creation Out of Love." In *The Work of Love*, edited by John Polkinghorne. Grand Rapids, MI: Eerdmans, 2001.

———. *The Creative Suffering of God*. Oxford: Oxford University Press, 1988.

Fishburn, Janet. *Confronting the Idolatry of Family*. Nashville: Abingdon, 1991.

Fisher, Christopher. *God is Open: Examining the Open Theism of the Biblical Authors*. Self-published, CreateSpace, 2017.

Fisher, Helen. *Anatomy of Love: A Natural History of Mating, Marriage, and Why We Stray*. New York: Fawcett, 1992.

Fleischer, Matthew Curtis. *The Old Testament Case for Nonviolence*. Oklahoma City, OK: Epic Octavius, 2017.

Flescher, Andrew Michael. *Heroes, Saints, and Ordinary Morality*. Washington, DC: Georgetown University Press, 2003.

Forrest, Peter. *Developmental Theism: From Pure Will to Unbounded Love*. Oxford: Oxford University Press, 2007.

Foster, Jonathan. *Reconstructionist*. Glen Oak, CA: Quoir, 2021.

Francis. *Laudato si': On Care for Our Common Home*. Vatican City: Vatican Press, 2015.

Frankena, William K. *Ethics*. Pearson Education, 1988.

Fredrickson, Barbara L. *Love 2.0: Creating Happiness and Health In Moments of Connection*. New York: Plume, 2013.

Fretheim, Terence E. *God and the World in the Old Testament: A Relational Theology of Creation*. Nashville: Abingdon, 2005.

———. *God So Enters Relationships That*. Minneapolis: Fortress, 2020.

———. *The Suffering of God: An Old Testament Perspective*. Philadelphia: Fortress, 1984.

——— and Karlfried Froelich. *The Bible as Word of God: In a Postmodern Age*. Eugene, OR: Wipf and Stock, 2001.

Fromm, Erich. *The Art of Loving*. New York: Harper, 1956,

Fuller, Tripp. *Divine Self-Investment: A Constructive Open and Relational Christology*. Grasmere, ID: SacraSage, 2019.

Furnish, Paul Victor. *The Love Command in the New Testament*. Nashville: Abingdon, 1972.

Gale, Herbert M. *The Use of Analogy in the Letters of Paul*. Philadelphia: Westminster, 1965.

Ganssle, Gregory E., and David M. Woodruff, eds. *God and Time: Essays on the Divine Nature*. New York: Oxford University Press, 2002.

Gavrilyuk, Paul. *The Suffering of the Impassible God: The Dialectics of Patristic Thought*. Oxford: Oxford University Press, 2004.

Gilson, Etienne. *The Christian Philosophy of St. Thomas Aquinas*. Notre Dame: University of Notre Dame Press, 1956.

Givens, Terryl, and Fiona Givens. *The God Who Weeps*. Crawfordsville, IN: Ensign Peak, 2012.

Glueck, Nelson. *Hesed in the Bible*. Translated by Alfred Gottschalk. Cincinnati: Hebrew Union College Press, 1967. Reprint, Eugene, OR: Wipf and Stock, 2011.

Goldingay, John. *Old Testament Theology*. Vol. 1, *Israel's Gospel*. Downers Grove, IL: InterVarsity, 2003.

———. *Psalms*, Vol. 3, *Psalms 90-150*. Grand Rapids: Baker Academic, 2008.

Gonwa, Janna. "Eros, Agape, and Neighbour-Love as Ontological Gift," *Toronto Journal of Theology*, 31:1 (Spring 2015): 84-93.

Gordon, Gabriel. *God Speaks: A Participatory Theology of Inspiration*. Glen Oak, CA: Quoir, 2021.

Gorman, Michael J. *Inhabiting the Cruciform God: Kenosis, Justification, and Theosis in Paul's Narrative Soteriology*. Grand Rapids, MI: Eerdmans, 2009.

Grant, Colin. *Altruism and Christian Ethics*. Cambridge: Cambridge University Press, 2001.

Greenberg, Yudit, ed. *The Encyclopedia of Love in World Religions*, 2 Vols. Santa Barbara: ABC-CLIO, 2008.

Greene, Paul Joseph. *The End of Divine Truthiness*. Eugene, OR: Wipf and Stock, 2017.

Greenway, William. *Agape Ethics: Moral Realism and Love for All Life*. Eugene, Or.: Cascade, 2016.

Griffin, David Ray. "Creation out of Nothing, Creation out of Chaos, and the Problem of Evil." In *Encountering Evil*, Stephen T. Davis, ed. 2nd ed. Louisville: Westminster John Knox, 2001.

———. "Some Whiteheadian Comments." In *Mind in Nature: Essays on the Interface of Science and Philosophy*, edited by John B. Cobb, Jr., and David Ray Griffin. Washington, DC: University Press of America, 1977.

———. *Evil Revisited: Responses and Reconsiderations*. Albany, NY: SUNY Press, 1991.

———. *God, Power, and Evil: A Process Theodicy*. Louisville: Westminster John Knox, 2004.

———. *Reenchantment without Supernaturalism: A Process Philosophy of Religion*. Ithaca, NY: Cornell University Press, 2001.

———. *Unsnarling the World-Knot: Consciousness, Freedom, and the Mind-Body Problem*. Berkeley: University of California Press, 1998.

Gutierrez, Gustavo. *The God of Life*. Maryknoll, NY: Orbis, 1996.

Hallett, Garth L. *Priorities and Christian Ethics*. Cambridge: Cambridge University Press, 1998.

Hamilton, Adam. *Why? Making Sense of God's Will*. Nashville: Abingdon, 2011.

Harnack, Adolf. *History of Dogma*. Neil Buchanan, trans. London: Williams and Norgate, 1897.

Harris, Mark. *The Nature of Creation: Examining the Bible and Science*. Durham: Acumen, 2013.

Hartshorne, Charles. "The Dipolar Conception of Deity." *Review of Metaphysics* 21, no. 2 (1967): 273-89.

———. *Man's Vision of God and the Logic of Theism*. Chicago and New York: Willett, Clark, and Co., 1941.

———. *Omnipotence and Other Theological Mistakes*. Albany, NY: SUNY Press, 1984.

———. *The Divine Relativity: A Social Conception of God*. New Haven: Yale University Press, 1948.

———. *The Logic of Perfection*. LaSalle, IL: Open Court, 1962.

———. *Wisdom as Moderation: A Philosophy of the Middle Way*. Albany, NY: SUNY Press, 1987.

Hasker, William. *God, Time, and Knowledge*. Ithaca, NY: Cornell University Press, 1989.

———. *Providence, Evil and the Openness of God*. London: Routledge, 2004.

———. *The Triumph of God over Evil: Theodicy for a World of Suffering*. Downers Grove, IL: InterVarsity, 2008.

Hays, Richard. *The Moral Vision of the New Testament: A Contemporary Introduction to New Testament Ethics*. San Francisco: Harper and Row, 1996.

Hefner, Philip. *The Human Factor*. Philadelphia: Augsburg Fortress, 2000.

Held, Daniel K. *Love's Resurrection*. Springfield, OH: Higher Ground, 2013.

Held, Shai. *Judaism is About Love*. Forthcoming.

———. *Abraham Joshua Heschel: The Call of Transcendence*. Bloomington, IN: Indiana University Press, 2013.

Hendrick, Susan, and Clyde Hendrick. "Love." In *Handbook of Positive Psychology*, edited by C. R. Snyder and Shane J. Lopez. Oxford: Oxford University Press, 2002.

Henry, Carl F. H. *God, Revelation, and Authority*. Vol. 5, *God who Stands and Stays, Part One*. Waco, TX: Word, 1982.

Heschel, Abraham. *The Prophets*. New York: Harper and Row, 1962.

Hick, John. *Evil and the God of Love*. San Francisco: Harper San Francisco, 1966.

Hoffman, Joshua, and Gary Rosenkrantz. "Omnipotence." In *A Companion to Philosophy of Religion*, edited by Philip L. Quinn and Charles Taliaferro. Malden, MA: Blackwell, 1999.

Holland Jr., Richard. *God, Time, and the Incarnation*. Eugene, OR: Wipf and Stock, 2012.

Holtzen, Wm. Curtis. *The God Who Trusts*. Downers Grove, IL: IVP Academic, 2019.

hooks, bell. *All About Love: New Visions*. New York: HarperCollins, 2001.

Hugenburger, Gordon P. *Marriage as a Covenant: Biblical Law and Ethics as Developed from Malachi*. Grand Rapids, MI: Baker, 1998.

Hunt, Mary E. *Fierce Tenderness: A Feminist Theology of Friendship*. New York: Crossroad, 1994.

Inbody, Tyron L. *The Transforming God: An Interpretation of Suffering and Evil*. Louisville: Westminster John Knox, 1997.

Jackson, Timothy. *Love Disconsoled: Meditations on Christian Charity*. Cambridge: Cambridge University Press, 1999.

———. *The Priority of Love: Christian Charity and Social Justice*. Princeton: Princeton University Press, 2003.

Jacob, Edmond. *Theology of the Old Testament*. Translated by A. W. Heathcote and P. J. Allcock. New York: Harper, 1958.

Jacobs, Alan. *A Theology of Reading: A Hermeneutics of Love*. New York: Routledge, 2018.

Jacobson, Rolf A. "'The Faithfulness of the Lord Endures Forever': The Theological Witness of the Psalter." In *Soundings in the Theology of Psalms*, edited by Rolf A. Jacobson. Minneapolis: Fortress, 2011.

Jamner, Margaret Schneider, and Daniel Stokols, eds. *Promoting Human Well-Being: New Frontiers for Research, Practice, and Policy*. Berkeley, CA: University of California Press, 2000.

Jantzen, Grace. *God's World, God's Body*. Philadelphia: Westminster, 1984.

Jeanrond, Werner. *A Theology of Love*. London: T & T Clark, 2010.

Jersak, Bradley. *A More Christlike God: A More Beautiful Gospel*. Pasadena, CA: Plain Truth, 2016.

Johnson, Elizabeth. *She Who Is: The Mystery of God in Feminist Theological Discourse*. New York: Crossroad, 1993.

Jüngel, Eberhard. "La ignification de l'analogie pour la theologie." In *Analogie et dialectique*, edited by J. L. Marion. Switzerland: Labor et Fides, 1982.

———. *God as the Mystery of the World: On the Foundation of the Theology of the Crucified One in the Dispute between Theism and Atheism*. Translated by Darrell L. Gruder. Grand Rapids, MI: Eerdmans, 1983.

Kaminsky, Joel S. *Yet I Loved Jacob: Reclaiming the Biblical Concept of Election*. Nashville: Abingdon, 2007.

Kamsler, Harold M. "Hesed — Mercy or Loyalty?" *Jewish Biblical Quarterly* 27:3 (1999): 183-85.

Kane, Robert. *The Significance of Free Will*. Oxford: Oxford University Press, 1998.

Karris, Mark Gregory. *Divine Echoes: Reconciling Prayer with the Uncontrolling Love of God*. Orange, CA: Quoir, 2018.

Kegley, Charles W., ed. *The Philosophy and Theology of Anders Nygren*. Carbondale, IL: Southern Illinois University Press, 1970.

Kelle, Brad E., and Stephanie Smith Matthews, eds. *Encountering the God of Love: Portraits from the Old Testament*. Kansas City, MO: Foundery, 2021.

Keller, Catherine. *From a Broken Web*. Boston: Beacon, 1986.

———. *On the Mystery*. Minneapolis: Fortress, 2007.

———. *The Face of the Deep*. New York: Routledge, 2003.

Keuss, Jeffery F. *Freedom of the Self: Kenosis, Cultural Identity, and Mission at the Crossroads*. Eugene, OR: Pickwick, 2010.

Kimelman, Reuven. "'We Love the God Who Loved Us First:' The Second Blessing of the Shema Liturgy." In *Bridging between Sister Religions*, edited by Isaac Kalimi. Leiden: Brill, 2016.

Kitamori, Kazoh. *Theology of the Pain of God*. Richmond: John Knox, 1965.

Kling, Sheri D. *A Process Spirituality*. London: Rowman and Littlefield, 2020.

Knierim, Rolf P. *Task of Old Testament Theology*. Grand Rapids, MI: Eerdmans, 1995.

Knight, George A. F. *Theology as Narration: A Commentary on the Book of Exodus.* Grand Rapids, MI: Eerdmans, 1976.

Knight, Harold. *The Hebrew Prophetic Consciousness.* London: Luterworth, 1947.

Knudson, Albert C. *The Philosophy of Personalism.* New York: Abingdon, 1927.

Koester, Helmut. *Introduction to the New Testament.* Vol. 1, *History, Culture, and Religion of the Hellenistic Age.* 2nd ed. Berlin: Walter de Gruyter, 1995.

Koperski, Jeffrey. *Divine Action, Determinism, and the Laws of Nature.* London: Routledge, 2020.

Ladd, Eldon G. *A Theology of the New Testament.* Grand Rapids, MI: Eerdmans, 1974.

Lapsley, Jacqueline E. "Friends with God? Moses and the Possibility of Covenantal Friendship." *Interpretation* 58:2. 2004.

Lee, Jung Young. *God Suffers for Us.* Netherlands: Martinus Nijhoff, 1974.

Lee, Matthew T., and Amos Yong, eds. *The Science and Theology of Godly Love.* DeKalb, IL: Northern Illinois University Press, 2012.

——— Laura D. Kubazansky, and Tyler J. VanderWeele. *Measuring Well-Being: Interdisciplinary Perspectives from the Social Sciences and Humanities.* Oxford: Oxford University Press, 2021.

Leidenhag, Joanna. *Minding Creation: Theological Panpsychism and the Doctrine of Creation.* London: T & T Clark, 2021.

Lepojarvi, Jason. *God Is Love but Love Is Not God: Studies on C.S. Lewis's Theology of Love.* PhD thesis, University of Helsinki, 2015.

Levenson, Jon D. *Creation and the Persistence of Evil: The Jewish Drama of Divine Omnipotence.* Princeton, NJ: Princeton University Press, 1994.

——— *The Love of God: Divine Gift, Human Gratitude, and Mutual Faithfulness in Judaism.* Princeton: Princeton University Press, 2016.

Lewis, C.S. *The Four Loves.* Glasgow: Collins, 1981.

Lewis, Jacqui. *Fierce Love.* London: Harmony, 2021.

Lightbown, Andrew, and Nick Fane. *ReDiscovering Charity.* Buckingham: University of Buckingham Press, 2009.

Lindberg, Carter. *Love: A Brief History Through Christianity.* Oxford: Blackwell, 2008.

Lodahl, Michael. "Creatio Ex Amore!" In *Theologies of Creation: Creatio Ex Nihilo and its New Rivals,* edited by Thomas Jay Oord. New York: Routledge, 2014.

———. *God of Nature and of Grace: Reading the World in a Wesleyan Way.* Nashville: Abingdon, 2003.

Love, Gregory. *Love, Violence, and the Cross: How the Nonviolent God Saves Us through the Cross of Christ.* Eugene, OR: Cascade, 2010.

MacIntyre, Alasdair. *After Virtue*. 2nd ed. Notre Dame: University of Notre Dame Press, 1984.

Macleod, Donald. *The Person of Christ: Contours of Christian Theology*. Leicester: InterVarsity, 1998.

MacLeod, Jay. "Almighty Mistake." *Theology* 108, no. 842 (2005): 91-99.

Macquarrie, John. *Principles of Christian Theology*. 2nd ed. New York: Scribner's, 1977.

Maddox, Randy L. *Responsible Grace: John Wesley's Practical Theology*. Nashville: Abingdon, 1994.

Markham, Ian. *Do Morals Matter?* London: Blackwell, 2007.

Martin, Mike W. *Love's Virtues*. Lawrence, KS: University Press of Kansas, 1996.

Martin, Ralph P. *Carmen Christi: Philippians 2:5-11 in Recent Interpretation and in the Setting of Early Christian Worship*. Rev. ed. Grand Rapids, MI: Eerdmans, 1983.

Mascall, E. L. *Existence and Analogy: A Sequel to "He Who Is."* London: Longmans, Green, and Co., 1949.

May, Gerhard. *Creatio Ex Nihilo: The Doctrine of 'Creation out of Nothing' in Early Thought*. Translated by A. S. Worrall. Edinburgh: T & T Clark, 1994.

McCabe, Lorenzo Dow. *Divine Nescience of Future Contingencies a Necessity*. New York: Phillips and Hunt, 1882.

———. *The Foreknowledge of God*. Cincinnati: Cranston and Stowe, 1887.

McCall, Bradford. *The God of Chance & Purpose: Divine Involvement in a Secular Evolutionary World*. Eugene, OR: Wipf & Stock, 2021.

McCann, H. J. *Creation and the Sovereignty of God*. Bloomington: Indiana University Press, 2012.

McDaniel, Jay, and Donna Bowman, eds. *Handbook of Process Theology*. St. Louis: Chalice, 2006.

McFague, Sallie. *The Body of God: An Ecological Theology*. Philadelphia: Fortress, 1993.

McKnight, Scot. *The Jesus Creed: Loving God, Loving Others*. Brewster, MA: Paraclete, 2007.

McLaren, Brian. *A New Kind of Christianity*. New York: Harper One, 2010.

Meilander, Gilbert C. *Friendship*. Notre Dame: University of Notre Dame Press, 1981.

Mesle, C. Robert. *John Hick's Theodicy: A Process Humanist Critique*. London: MacMillan, 1991.

Michaels, L. *What About Us? Stories of Uncontrolling Love*. Grasmere, ID: SacraSage, 2019.

Michelson, Marty Alan. *The Greatest Commandment: The LORD's Invitation to Love*. Oklahoma City, OK: Dust Jacket, 2012.

Middleton, J. Richard. "Creation Founded in Love: Breaking Rhetorical Expectations in Genesis 1:1-2:3." In *Sacred Text, Secular Times: The Hebrew Bible in the Modern World*, edited by Leonard Jay Greenspoon and Bryan F. LeBeau. Omaha, NE: Creighton University Press, 2000.

———. *The Liberating Image: The Imago Dei in Genesis 1*. Grand Rapids, MI: Brazos, 2005.

Milgrom, Jacob. *Leviticus 17-22: A New Translation with Introduction and Commentary*. New York: Doubleday, 2000.

Mitchell, Roger Haydon, and Julie Tomlin Arran, eds. *Discovering Kenarchy: Contemporary Resources*. Eugene, OR: Cascade, 2014.

Moberly, R. W. L. *Old Testament Theology: Reading the Hebrew Bible as Christian Scripture*. Grand Rapids, MI: Baker Academic, 2013.

Moffatt, James. *Love in the New Testament*. London: Hodder and Stoughton, 1929.

Moltmann, Jürgen. "God's Kenosis in the Creation and Consummation of the World." In *The Work of Love: Creation as Kenosis*, John Polkinghorne, ed. Grand Rapids, MI: Eerdmans, 2001.

———. *The Crucified God*. London: SCM, 1974.

———. *The Trinity and the Kingdom*. San Francisco: Harper and Row, 1981.

Montgomery, Brint, Thomas Jay Oord, and Karen Winslow, eds. *Relational Theology: A Contemporary Introduction*. San Diego: Point Loma University Press, 2008.

Mooney, Edward F. "Love, This Lenient Interpreter: On the Complexity of a Life." In *Transforming Philosophy and Religion*, edited by Norman Wirzba and Bruce Ellis Benson. Bloomington, IN: University of Indiana Press, 2008.

Mullins, Ryan T. "Classical Theism." In *T & T Clark Handbook of Analytic Theology*, edited by James M. Arcadi and James T. Turner, Jr. London: Bloomsbury, 2021.

———. *The End of the Timeless God*. Oxford: Oxford University Press, 2016.

Newlands, George M. *Theology of the Love of God*. Atlanta: John Knox, 1980.

Nygren, Anders. *Agape and Eros*. Translated by Philip S. Watson. New York: Harper and Row, 1969.

O'Connor, Kathleen. "Reflections on Kindness as Fierce Tenderness: Micah 6:1-8." *Journal for Preachers* 39, no. 3 (2016).

———. *Persons and Causes: The Metaphysics of Free Will*. Oxford: Oxford University Press, 2000.

———. "Agent-Causal Theories of Freedom." In *The Oxford Handbook of Free Will*, edited by Robert Kane. Oxford: Oxford University Press, 2011.

O'Donovan, Oliver. *The Problem of Self-Love in St. Augustine*. Eugene, OR: Wipf and Stock, 1980.

Ogden, Schubert M. *The Reality of God*. Dallas: Southern Methodist University Press, 1992.

Oliner, Pearl M. *Toward a Caring Society: Ideas in Action*. Westport, CT: Praeger, 1995.

Olson, Roger. "Can God Change the Past?" *My Evangelical Arminian Theological Musings* (blog). Patheos, June 8, 2021. https://www.patheos.com/blogs/rogereolson/2021/06/can-god-change-the-past-2/.

———. "Is Open Theism a Type of Arminianism?" *My Evangelical Arminian Theological Musings* (blog). Patheos, November 10, 2021. http://www.patheos.com/blogs/rogereolson/2012/11/is-open-theism-a-type-of-arminianism/.

Olthuis, James H. "Creatio Ex Amore." In *Transforming Philosophy and Religion*, edited by Norman Wirzba and Bruce Ellis Benson. Bloomington, IN: University of Indiana Press, 2008.

Oord, Thomas Jay, and Michael Lodahl. *Relational Holiness: Responding to the Call of Love*. Kansas City, MO: Beacon Hill Press of Kansas City, 2005.

——— and Richard Thompson, eds. *Rethinking the Bible*. Grasmere, ID: SacraSage, 2018.

——— and Wm. Andrew Schwartz. "Panentheism and Panexperientialism for Open and Relational Theology." In *Panentheism and Panpsychism: Philosophy of Religion Meets Philosophy of Mind*, edited by Godehard Brüntrup, et. al. Paderborn, Ger.: Mentis Verlag/Brill, 2020.

——— ed. *The Polkinghorne Reader: Science, Faith and the Search for Meaning*. London: SPCK, 2010.

———. "A Loving Civilization: A Political Ecology that Promotes Overall Well-Being." *The Kenarchy Journal* 2 (2021).

———. "A Postmodern Wesleyan Philosophy and David Ray Griffin's Postmodern Vision." *Wesleyan Theological Journal* 35, no. 1 (2000): 216-244.

———. "An Essential Kenosis Solution to the Problem of Evil." "Response to Others." In *God and the Problem of Evil: Five Views*, edited by James K. Dew, Jr. and Chad Meister. Downers Grove, IL: InterVarsity, 2017.

———. "Analogies of Love Between God and Creatures: A Response to Kevin Vanhoozer." In *Love, Divine and Human: Contemporary Essays in Systematic and Philosophical Theology*. New York: T & T Clark, 2020.

———. "Eternal Creation and Essential Love." In *T&T Handbook on Suffering and the Problem of Evil*, edited by Johannes Grossel and Matthias Grebe. London: T&T Clark, 2022.

———. "Genuine but Limited Freedom for Creatures and for a God of Love." In *What's with Free Will? Ethics and Religion After Neuroscience*, edited by Philip Clayton and James W. Walters. Eugene, OR: Pickwick, 2020.

———. "God Always Creates out of Creation in Love: Creatio ex Creatione a Natura Amoris." In *Theologies of Creation: Creatio Ex Nihilo and its New Rivals*, edited by Thomas Jay Oord. New York: Routledge, 2014.

———. "Strong Passibility." "My Response." In *Divine Impassibility: Four Views on God's Emotions and Suffering*, edited by Robert J. Matz and A. Chadwick Thornhill. Downers Grove, IL: InterVarsity, 2019.

———. *Defining Love: Philosophical, Scientific, and Theological Investigations*. Grand Rapids, MI: Brazos, 2010.

———. *God Can't: How to Believe in God and Love after Tragedy, Abuse, and Other Evils*. Grasmere, ID: SacraSage, 2019.

———. *Open and Relational Theology: An Introduction to Life-Changing Ideas*. Grasmere, ID: SacraSage, 2021.

———. *Questions and Answers for God Can't*. Grasmere, ID: SacraSage, 2020.

———. *The Altruism Reader: Selections of Writings on Love, Religion, and Science*. Philadelphia: Templeton, 2012.

———. *The Science of Love: The Wisdom of Well-Being*. Philadelphia: Templeton, 2005.

———. *The Uncontrolling Love of God: An Open and Relational Account of Providence*. Grand Rapids, MI: InterVarsity, 2015.

Osborne, Catherine. *Eros Unveiled: Plato and the God of Love*. Oxford: Clarendon, 1994.

Outka, Gene. *Agape: An Ethical Analysis*. New Haven: Yale University Press, 1972.

Padilla, Elaine. *Divine Enjoyment: A Theology of Passion and Exuberance*. New York: Fordham University Press, 2015.

Paul, Shalom M. "Creation and Cosmogony: In the Bible." In *Encyclopedia Judaica*. Edited by Cecil Roth, 5:1059-63. Jerusalem: Keter, 1972.

Pinnock, Clark H. and Robert C. Brow. *Unbounded Love: A Good News Theology for the 21st Century*. Downers Grove, IL: InterVarsity, 1994.

———. *Flame of Love*. Downers Grove, IL: InterVarsity, 1999.

———. *Most Moved Mover: A Theology of God's Openness*. Grand Rapids, MI: Baker, 2001.

——— and John B. Cobb, Jr. *Searching for an Adequate God*. Grand Rapids, MI: Eerdmans, 2000.

———, et. al., *The Openness of God: A Biblical Challenge to the Traditional Understanding of God*. Downers Grove, IL: InterVarsity, 1994.

Placher, William. *Narratives of a Vulnerable God: Christ, Theology, and Scripture*. Louisville: Westminster John Knox, 1994.

Plantinga, Alvin. "On Ockham's Way Out." *Faith and Philosophy* 3, no. 3 (July 1986): 235-269.

———. *Where the Conflict Really Lies: Science, Religion, and Naturalism*. Oxford: Oxford University Press, 2011.

Polk, David P. *God of Empowering Love*. Anoka, MN: Process Century, 2016.

Polkinghorne, John, ed. *The Work of Love: Creation as Kenosis*. Grand Rapids, MI: Eerdmans, 2001.

———. *Science and Providence*. Philadelphia: Templeton, 2005.

Pool, Jeff B. *God's Wounds: Hermeneutic of the Christian Symbol of Divine Suffering*. Eugene, OR: Pickwick, 2009.

Pope, Stephen J. *The Evolution and Ordering of Love*. Washington, DC: Georgetown University Press, 1994.

Post, Stephen, et. al. *Altruism and Altruistic Love*. Oxford: Oxford University Press, 2001.

———. *More Lasting Unions*. Grand Rapids, MI: Eerdmans, 2000.

———. *Unlimited Love: Altruism, Compassion and Service*. Philadelphia: Templeton, 2003.

———. *Research on Altruism and Love: An Annotated Bibliography of Major Studies in Psychology, Sociology, Evolutionary Biology, and Theology*. Stephen G. Post, et. al., eds. Philadelphia: Templeton Press, 2003.

Powell, Samuel M. *The Impassioned Life: Reason and Emotion in the Christian Tradition*. Minneapolis: Fortress, 2016.

Pregeant, Russell. *Knowing Truth, Doing Good*. Minneapolis: Fortress, 2008.

Queen, Chuck. *A Faith Worth Living*. Eugene, OR: Wipf and Stock, 2011.

Rabe, Andre. *Creative Chaos: The Surprising Mystery of Time, Self, and Meaning*. Andre Rabe Publishing, 2019.

Ramm, Bernard. *Protestant Biblical Revelation*. 3rd ed. Grand Rapids, MI: Baker, 1980.

Ramsey, Paul. *Basic Christian Ethics*. Chicago: University of Chicago Press, 1950.

Randall, Rory. *An Open Theist Renewal Theology*. Grasmere, ID: SacraSage, 2021.

Reddish, Timothy, Bonnie Rambob, Fran Stedman, and Thomas Jay Oord, eds. *Partnering with God: Exploring Collaboration in Open and Relational Theology*. SacraSage, 2021.

———. *Does God Always Get What God Wants?* Eugene, OR: Cascade, 2018.

Reichard, Joshua D. "Relational Empowerment: A Process-Relational Theology of the Spirit-filled Life." In *Pneuma: The Journal of the Society for Pentecostal Studies* 36, no. 2 (2014): 1-20.

Rice, Richard. *The Future of Open Theism: Antecedents and Opportunities*. Downers Grove, IL: IVP Academic, 2020.

———. *The Openness of God*. Nashville: Review and Herald, 1980.

Rogers, K. A. *Perfect Being Theology*. Edinburgh: Edinburgh University Press, 2000.

Rolnick, Philip A. *Analogical Possibilities: How Words Refer to God*. AAR Academy Series no. 81. Atlanta: Scholars, 1993.

Rowe, William L. *Can God Be Free?* Oxford: Oxford University Press, 2004.

Rubenstein, Mary-Jane. *Worlds Without End.* New York: Columbia University Press, 2014.

Runehov, Anne L.C. *The Human Being, the World, and God.* Switzerland: Springer, 2016.

Ruud, Niq. *Only Love.* Glen Oak, CA: Quoir, 2021.

Saarinen, Risto. *God and the Gift.* Collegeville, MN: Liturgical, 2005.

Sakenfeld, Katherine Doob. *Faithfulness in Action: Loyalty in Biblical Perspective.* Philadelphia: Fortress, 1985.

Sanders, John. *Embracing Prodigals.* Eugene, OR: Cascade, 2020.

———. *The God Who Risks: A Theology of Divine Providence.* Downers Grove, IL: IVP Academic, 2007.

Schellenberg, J. L. *Divine Hiddenness and Human Reason.* Ithaca, NY: Cornell University Press, 2006.

———. *The Hiddenness Argument.* Oxford: Oxford University Press, 2015.

Schmid, Manuel. *God in Motion: A Critical Exploration of the Open Theism Debate.* Waco, TX: Baylor University Press, 2021.

Schmidt, Brent J. *Relational Grace.* Provo, UT: BYU Press, 2015.

Schoonhoven, C.R. *International Standard Bible Encyclopedia,* s.v. "Eternity." 2 vols. Edited by G. W. Bromiley. Grand Rapids, MI: Eerdmans, 1982.

Scrutton, Anastasia Philippa. *Thinking Through Feeling: God, Emotion and Passibility.* New York: Continuum, 2011.

Segall, Matthew David. *Physics of the World-Soul.* Grasmere, ID: SacraSage, 2021.

Seibert, Eric A. *Disturbing Divine Behavior,* Philadelphia: Fortress, 2009.

———. *The Violence of Scripture: Overcoming the Old Testament's Troubling Legacy.* Philadelphia: Fortress, 2012.

Singer, Irving. *The Nature of Love.* Vol. 1, *Plato to Luther.* 2nd ed. Chicago: University of Chicago Press, 1987.

Sirvent, Roberto. *Embracing Vulnerability: Human and Divine.* Eugene, OR: Pickwick, 2014.

Small, Meredith F. *What's Love God to Do with it? The Evolution of Human Mating.* New York: Anchor, 1995.

Smith, James K. A. *Desiring the Kingdom: Worship, Worldview, and Cultural Formation.* Grand Rapids, MI: Baker, 2009.

———. *You are What You Love: The Spiritual Power of Habit.* Grand Rapids, MI: Brazos, 2016.

Smith, Mark S. *The Priestly Vision of Genesis 1.* Philadelphia: Fortress, 2010.

Snaith, Norman H. *The Distinctive Ideas of the Old Testament.* London: Epworth, 1944.

Soble, Alan. *Agape, Eros, and Philia: Readings in the Philosophy of Love*. New York: Paragon, 1989.

Sollereder, Bethany. *God, Evolution, and Animal Suffering: Theodicy without a Fall*. New York: Routledge, 2020.

Southgate, Christopher. *The Groaning of Creation*. London: Westminster John Knox, 2008.

Sovik, Atle Ottesen. *The Problem of Evil and the Power of God*. Netherlands: Brill, 2011.

Spencer, F. Scott. *Passions of the Christ: The Emotional Life of Jesus in the Gospels*. Grand Rapids, MI: Baker, 2021.

Spicq, Ceslaus. *Agape in the New Testament*. 3 vols. Translated by Sisters Marie Aquinas McNamara and Mary Honoria Richter. St. Louis, MO: Herder, 1966. Reprint, Eugene, OR: Wipf and Stock, 2006.

Spohn, William C. *Go and Do Likewise: Jesus and Ethics*. New York: Continuum, 2000.

Sponheim, Paul R. *Love's Availing Power: Imaging God, Imagining the World*. Minneapolis: Fortress, 2011.

Stoebe, Hans Joachim. "Di Bedeutung des Wortes Hasad im Alten Testament." *Vetus Testamentum* (1952): 244-54.

Stone, Bryan P. and Thomas Jay Oord, eds. *Thy Name and Thy Nature is Love: Wesleyan and Process Theologies in Dialogue*. Nashville: Kingswood, 2001.

Strawn, Brent A., ed. *The Bible and the Pursuit of Happiness*. Oxford: Oxford University Press, 2012.

Suchocki, Marjorie. *God-Christ-Church*. Rev. ed. New York: Crossroad, 1993.

Tallman, Bruce, *God's Ecstatic Love* (Apocryphile Press, 2021).

Taylor, Mark Lloyd. *God is Love: A Study in the Theology of Karl Rahner*. AAR Academy Series no. 50. Atlanta: Scholars, 1986.

TeSelle, Eugene. *Augustine the Theologian*. Eugene, OR: Wipf and Stock, 2002.

Thompson, Thomas R. "Nineteenth-century Kenotic Christology." In *Exploring the Kenotic Christology: The Self-Emptying of God*, C. Stephen Evans, ed. Vancouver, BC: Regent College Publishing, 2006.

Tillich, Paul. *Love, Power, and Justice: Ontological Analyses and Ethical Applications*. Oxford: Oxford University Press, 1960.

———. *Systematic Theology*. Vol. 1, *Reason and Revelation, Being and God*. Chicago: University of Chicago Press, 1951.

Timpe, Kevin. *Free Will: Sourcehood and its Alternatives*. 2nd ed. New York: Bloomsbury, 2013.

Torrance, Alan. "Does God Suffer? Incarnation and Impassibility." In *Christ in Our Place: The Humanity of God in Christ for the Reconciliation of the World*, Trevor A. Hart, ed. Eugene, OR: Wipf and Stock, 1989.

Tredoux, Johan. *Mildred Bangs Wynkoop: Her Life and Thought*. Kansas City, MO: Foundery, 2017.

Truesdale, Al, *God Reconsidered: The Promise and Peril of Process Theology*. Kansas City, MO: Beacon Hill, 2010.

Tsumura, David Toshio. *The Earth and the Waters in Genesis 1 and 2: A Linguistic Investigation*. Sheffield: JSOT, 1989.

Vacek, Edward Collins. *Love, Human and Divine: The Heart of Christian Ethics*. Washington, DC: Georgetown University Press, 1994.

Vail, Eric M. *Creation and Chaos Talk*. Eugene, OR: Pickwick, 2012.

Vanhoozer, Kevin J. "Introduction: The Love of God — Its Place, Meaning, and Function in Systematic Theology." In *Nothing Greater, Nothing Better, Theological Essays on the Love of God*, Kevin J. Vanhoozer, ed. Grand Rapids, MI: Eerdmans, 2001.

Viney, Donald Wayne. "Hartshorne's Dipolar Theism and the Mystery of God." *Philosophia* 35 (Dec. 2007): 341-350.

———. "The Varieties of Theism and the Openness of God: Charles Hartshorne and Free-Will Theism." *The Personalist Forum* 14, no. 2 (Fall 1998): 199-238.

Waltke, Bruce K. *Creation and Chaos*. Portland, OR: Western Conservative Baptist Seminary, 1974.

Walton, John H. *The Lost World of Genesis One*. Downers Grove, IL: InterVarsity, 2009.

Ward, Keith. *Love is His Meaning: Understanding the Teaching of Jesus*. London: SPCK, 2017.

———. *Morality, Autonomy, and God*. London: One World, 2013.

———. *The Christian Idea of God: A Philosophical Foundation for Faith*. Cambridge: Cambridge University Press, 2017.

Watson, Francis. *Agape, Eros, Gender: Towards a Pauline Sexual Ethic*. Cambridge: Cambridge University Press, 2000.

Wesley, John. "Free Grace." *The Bicentennial Edition of the Works of John Wesley*. Vol. 3. Nashville: Abingdon, 1984.

———. "The General Spread of the Gospel," Sermon 63. *The Works of John Wesley*. Vol. 2. Nashville: Abingdon, 1985.

Wessling, Jordan. *Love Divine: A Systematic Account of God's Love for Humanity*. Oxford: Oxford University Press, 2020.

West, Cornel. *The American Evasion of Philosophy*. Madison, WI: University of Wisconsin Press, 1989.

Westermann, Claus. *Elements of Old Testament Theology*. Douglas W. Stott, trans. Atlanta: John Knox, 1982.

———. *Genesis 1-11*. John J. Scullion, trans. London: SPCK, 1994.

Whitehead, Alfred North. *Process and Reality: An Essay in Cosmology.* Corrected and edited by David Ray Griffin and Donald W. Sherburne. New York: Free, 1979.

Willems, Kurt. *Echoing Hope.* London: Waterbrook, 2021.

Williams, Andrew. *Boundless Love: A Companion to Clark H. Pinnock's Theology.* Salem, OR: Wipf and Stock, 2021.

Williams, Daniel Day. *The Spirit and the Forms of Love.* New York: Harper and Row, 1968.

Williams, T. "Introduction to Classical Theism." In *Models of God and Alternative Ultimate Realities*, J. Dillerand and A. Kasher, eds. New York: Springer, 2013.

Wilson, Kenneth. *Augustine's Conversion from Traditional Free Choice to "Non-free Free Will."* Tübingen: Mohr Siebeck, 2018.

Wirzba, Norman. "The Primacy of Love." In *Transforming Philosophy and Religion*, edited by Norman Wirzba and Bruce Ellis Benson. Bloomington, IN: University of Indiana Press, 2008.

———. *The Way of Love: Recovering the Heart of Christianity.* New York: Harper One, 2016.

Wischmeyer, Oda. *Love as Agape: The Early Christian Concept and Modern Discourse.* Translated by Wayne Coppins. Waco, TX: Baylor University Press, 2021.

Wispe, L. G. "The Distinction between Sympathy and Empathy." *Journal of Personality and Social Psychology* 50 (1986).

Wolterstorff, Nicholas. "God Everlasting." In *God and the Good*, edited by Clifton J. Orlebeke and Lewis B. Smedes. Grand Rapids, MI: Eerdmans, 1975.

———. "Suffering Love." In *Philosophy and the Christian Faith*, edited by Thomas V. Morris. Notre Dame: University of Notre Dame Press, 1990.

———. *Justice in Love.* Grand Rapids, MI: William B. Eerdmans, 2011.

Woodley, Randy. *Shalom and the Community of Creation: An Indigenous Vision.* Grand Rapids, MI: Eerdmans, 2012.

Wynkoop, Mildred Bangs. *A Theology of Love: The Dynamic of Wesleyanism.* Kansas City, MO: Beacon Hill, 1972.

Yong, Amos. *Spirit of Love.* Waco, TX: Baylor University Press, 2012.

Young, Frances. "Creatio Ex Nihilo: A Context for the Emergence of Christian Doctrine of Creation." *Scottish Journal of Theology* 44 (1991): 139-51.

Zahnd, Brian. *Sinners in the Hands of a Loving God.* London: Waterbrook, 2017.

Index

TO READ MORE
Thomas Jay Oord...

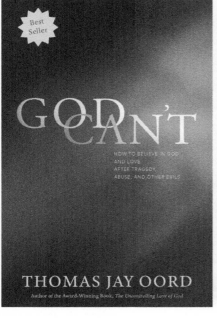

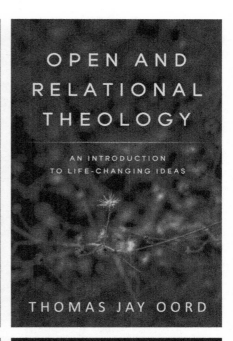

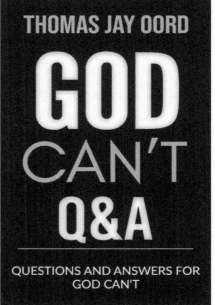

TO READ MORE
Thomas Jay Oord...

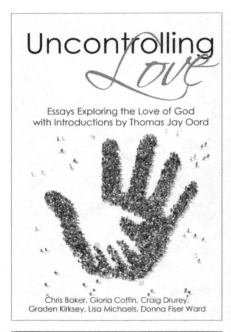

Uncontrolling *Love*

Essays Exploring the Love of God
with Introductions by Thomas Jay Oord

Chris Baker, Gloria Coffin, Craig Drurey,
Graden Kirksey, Lisa Michaels, Donna Fiser Ward

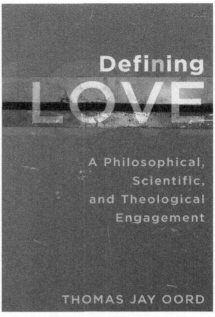

Defining **LOVE**

A Philosophical,
Scientific,
and Theological
Engagement

THOMAS JAY OORD

OPEN AND
RELATIONAL
LEADERSHIP

Leading with Love

Roland Hearn, Sheri D. Kling, & Thomas Jay Oord,
EDITORS

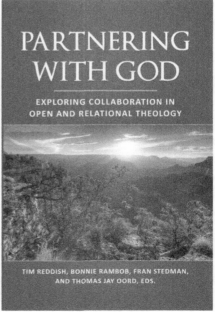

PARTNERING
WITH GOD

EXPLORING COLLABORATION IN
OPEN AND RELATIONAL THEOLOGY

TIM REDDISH, BONNIE RAMBOB, FRAN STEDMAN,
AND THOMAS JAY OORD, EDS.